THE
KNOWLEDGE-
VALUE REVOLUTION

SOME OF TAICHI SAKAIYA'S OTHER, UNTRANSLATED BOOKS

Yūdan! [Oil Cut-off!]
Dankai no sedai [A Generation of Clods]
Ōinaru kuwadate [The Grand Plan]
Gunka no kōzu [Anatomy of Groupism]
Nihonjin e no keikoku [A Warning to the Japanese
    People]
Tōge kara Nihon ga mieru [Japan Seen from the
    Peak]
Rekishi kara no hassō [Concepts from History]
Jidai shikō no zahyōjiku [Touchstones for
    Thinking About the Future]
Toyotomi Hidenaga [The Life of Hidenaga]

THE

KNOW

VALUE

TRANSLATED

LEDGE-
REVOLUTION

or a
History of the Future

TAICHI SAKAIYA

TRANSLATED BY
George Fields and William Marsh

Kodansha International
Tokyo • New York • London

Originally published in 1985 in Japanese
by PHP Kenkyūjo, Kyoto, Japan as *Chika kakumei*.

Distributed in the United States by Kodansha America, Inc.,
114 Fifth Avenue, New York, New York, 10011.
Published by Kodansha International Ltd., 17–14, Otowa 1-chome,
Bunkyo-ku, Tokyo 112 and Kodansha America, Inc.

Printed in the United States of America

First edition, 1991

91   92   93   94   7   6   5   4   3   2   1

Library of Congress Cataloging-in-Publication Data
Sakaiya, Taichi, 1935–
    [Chika kakumei. English]
    The knowledge-value revolution, or, a history of the future /
Taichi Sakaiya ; translated by George Fields and William Marsh. —
1st ed.
        p.   cm.
    Translation of: Chika kakumei.
    Includes bibliographical references and index.
    ISBN 0-87011-942-7 (U.S.)
    ISBN 4-7700-1442-2 (in Japan)
    1. Social prediction.   2. Technology and civilization.
3. Professions.   4. Information society.   I. Title.   II. Title:
History of the future.
HN60.S2613   1991
303.49—dc20   91-15253
                                                            CIP

The text of this book was set in Caslon No. 540
Composed by Folio Graphics Company, Inc.
New York, New York

The jacket was printed by
Toppan Printing Company (America), Inc.
Clark, New Jersey

Printed and bound by
Arcata Graphics
Fairfield, Pennsylvania

Contents

WHAT CHANGES ARE OCCURRING NOW? . . . 210

4 THE ESSENCE OF THE KNOWLEDGE-VALUE SOCIETY . . . 245

FROM OBJECTIVE TO SUBJECTIVE, FROM SYMBIOTIC TO INDEPENDENT . . . 252

A BIRD'S-EYE VIEW OF THE KNOWLEDGE-VALUE SOCIETY . . . 267

Translators' Note

Often the challenge a book poses is that of grasping language rooted in a past that no longer exists or never did exist for the reader. The unique challenge posed by Mr. Sakaiya's book is that of grasping through language a future that does not yet exist. As author, he is the first to acknowledge that such an effort necessarily invites awkward uncertainties rather than assured eloquence, but he argues that we must embrace the risk if we hope to move beyond the comforting certitudes of the foreknown.

As translators, we must echo Mr. Sakaiya's plea, and assure our particular readers (as he assures his original audience) that while we have done all we can to ease their task, challenges do remain. This brief note is an attempt to minimize difficulties by identifying them.

At present, Westerners writing on society are typically specialists. They consciously limit themselves to making only statements or conclusions that they feel can be "objectively verified" by citing evidence and engaging in a rational discourse modelled on the scientific method. Few aspire to become what F. Scott Fitzgerald describes as "that most limited of specialists, the 'well-rounded man,' " for, as he notes, "Life is much more successfully looked at from a single window, after all."

It follows that for today's successful Western specialist, precision and specificity are the only virtues when it comes to language; words without clearcut meanings can contaminate an enterprise for which the sterility of the laboratory represents an ideal.

Taichi Sakaiya, on the other hand, writes in an East Asian historical tradition in which the ongoing generic continuity of human experience is assumed. His readers expect him, as an outstanding example of a "well-rounded man," to draw upon his vast reading and experience to make broad and sweeping statements that synthesize and interrelate multiple facets of reality. His language is deliberately one of multidimensional referentiality, and our challenge as translators has been to find English that can mean as many complementary things in as many different situations.

The character *chi* which makes up the "knowledge" component in the compound phrase *chika* (knowledge-value) coined by Sakaiya for the book's title provides an excellent example of the linguistic cross-pollination that can occur in languages where the roots of words remain visible. The same character *chi* is equally visible as a component in *chijin* ("known-person," that is, acquaintance), *chinō* ("knowing-ability," that is, intellect), *chishi* ("wisdom tooth"), *chie* ("knowledge-blessings," that is, wisdom), or *chishiki* ("knowledge-processed," that is, intelligence). To deploy a language in which such linkages between words leap out at the reader fosters an awareness of the linkages between things, and Sakaiya makes the most of it.

For the reader of *The Knowledge-Value Revolution*, to search for the single, strictly literal meaning of a phrase like "knowledge-value" is to miss the point. There is no single, strictly literal meaning for *chi*: in the context of this book it can mean everything from "knowledge" and "wisdom" to "intelligence" and "sophistication," and *chika* (knowledge-value) can refer to the perceived value of any of those variants of *chi*. Readers will also be glad to know that the context almost always provides pointers as to which meaning is being stressed; neither Mr. Sakaiya nor his translators are trying to lead them down the primrose path to nebulosity or vagueness. We only ask that the reader remember that as the context shifts, meanings can shift as well.

Central to Mr. Sakaiya's work is the idea that human survival is due to the "empathetic impulse" which makes the species sense what is plentiful or scarce in an environment and behave accordingly. This instinctive awareness of where his "enlightened self-interest" lies may not seem at first glance like the definitive attribute of man, but Mr. Sakaiya must be given room to build his case. We only wish to point out here that a single Japanese phrase, *ningen no jōchi* (literally, the "felt knowledge" or "informing instinct" of man), has been translated as "the empathetic impulse" or "enlightened self-interest" interchangeably throughout the text. It is our hope and belief that the context will inform and clarify the intended meaning in every instance.

It is ironic that the phrase which mutates according to context more than any other—and is thus hardest of all to follow—should be one which can be translated literally: *shakai no shukan* has exactly the same meaning as "social subjectivity" does in English. It is Sakaiya's sweeping use of this abstraction to describe such disparate phenomena as medieval religion and contemporary fashion that obliges the non–Japanese reader to open his heart and mind to a logic of association that is "common sense" to those who grew up reading and writing in Japanese. If the present translation makes it possible for readers in English to discern the logic of such usage, the translators will have accomplished their task.

Finally, let it be noted that this book was first written for Japanese readers in 1985. Mr. Sakaiya has added new material

and pruned passages which address specifically Japanese concerns, but the book rightfully remains the product of its original context. As a "well-rounded man" speculating on the future of mankind, he was empowered by his audience to make
bold and sweeping statements about human history and to
take for granted that Asian history would be familiar to his
readers. The absence of footnotes is not surprising, given the
emphasis on speculation, but we should hardly be surprised if
some readers find themselves frustrated by it. (The Editor's
Notes listed at the back for further reading may help to alleviate such frustration.) For ourselves as translators, a bewildering task has been to emulate that grasp of Asian history which
Mr. Sakaiya assumes to be a given when addressing his Japanese audience. The historical Chinese names, dates, and periods cited here follow the system used by Arthur Cotterell in
China: A Cultural History (New York: Mentor, 1989). We apol-
ogize in advance for any inconsistencies.

—William Marsh
April 1991

Introduction
to the English Language Edition

Two major political events that occurred recently—the collapse of the Communist system in Eastern Europe and Iraq's invasion of Kuwait—may be read as indications that in the 1990s the knowledge-value revolution described in this book will move into high gear. The former event illustrates all too clearly that the materialism on which socialist ideology was based, which views objectivity in absolute terms, was incapable of effectively responding to the changes confronted by societies in the real world; while the latter event will expedite the knowledge-value revolution to the extent that it is dealing yet another powerful blow to the notion that cultures based on high resource consumption can hope to maintain their current habits.

My purpose in writing this book was to talk about the gigantic transformation contemporary society is undergoing and to give a clear sense of the essence of the new society that will emerge from it. What is being offered here, then, is not an interpretation of current issues, or a list of concrete suggestions regarding political policy, or a collection of hints and advice for business managers; it is not that sort of book. Rather, it is an effort to predict, by looking at how the major transition we are going through at present fits into the larger pattern of human history, what sort of future social paradigm we are in fact moving toward.

Many who have researched the topic are suggesting that we have passed a major turning point in world history over the period of the last twenty years. The behavior of the economy and society, particularly since the 1980s began, presents numerous instances that defy explanation in terms of the experience and knowledge we have so far gathered. There are, of course, many odd examples of this we could cite from the recent short-term patterns of the financial markets and prices; but more fundamental trends involving the directions in which technological progress seems to be moving, or the types of jobs people want, likewise seem so atypical as to appear inscrutable. Against such a backdrop, the statement that the world is likely to undergo some major changes over the decade to come hardly seems outrageous.

However, it is not enough simply to predict that there will be change. Those who must live with the actuality of what society becomes are naturally most anxious to know what sort of world will emerge in the wake of these changes.

The greater the scale on which a transformation occurs, the more important—and difficult—it becomes to predict what sort of reality will be created in its wake. It is that much more difficult if the change is likely to affect the very essence of the society itself. When what is at issue is merely quantitative change that does not affect the paradigm of the society— changes in the rate of economic growth or technological development, say, such as those Japan experienced during its period of breathtaking economic growth in the 1960s—it is possible to hazard guesses as to their outcome that, if they are not precisely on target, still come reasonably close.

But when the predictions involve an emerging society whose very essence will diverge radically from that which has existed up to now, attempting to construe what shape the new paradigm will take becomes a somewhat more daunting task.

Yet if one painstakingly observes man's long history and the progression of global movements over time, it is possible to hazard a reasonably accurate guess as to what lies in store. The present volume represents an outspoken attempt to make such an informed prediction. That is why readers should expect to find many allusions to the histories of Europe, China, Japan, and other civilizations, stretching far back in time, as they read this book.

When the first edition appeared in Japan at the end of 1985, it created quite an uproar. Korean and Chinese editions appeared the following year. The events of the intervening five years seem to suggest that my predictions were anything but farfetched. In particular, the abrupt collapse of the various socialist governments that began in the fall of 1989 seems to bear out the validity of my theory that industrial society as such would decline and that a knowledge-value society would emerge to take its place. I also see the assertion of their ethnic identities by groups in the Eastern bloc and Europe, a phenomenon that has become a movement in itself, as supporting my thesis, which postulates a deepening emphasis on subjective values.

The invasion of Kuwait by Iraq in August 1990 has in turn brought on a shift in the world economy that will propel us even more rapidly into the knowledge-value revolution during the 1990s. I say this in the belief that the impact of watching the oil supply, which was stable during the second half of the 1980s, suddenly plunge into a period of turbulent uncertainty with the arrival of the new decade is going to reinforce the serious doubts people have started to entertain about an industrial civilization based on heavy resource consumption. The positive impact of such doubts will be a shift in demand that will favor the consumption of "knowledge-value" rather than resources.

To incorporate a response to these recent developments, I have written a special chapter, Chapter 6, to this English edition. Chapter 5 has also been altered for this edition, particularly in the sections dealing in detail with Japanese history, which I have abridged somewhat to make room for the supplementary comments on recent events.

As the reader may know, a quite substantial share of the books and articles that appear in English are translated into Japanese; this is particularly true of anything of great topical interest or notoriety. However, only a tiny portion of what is published in Japanese ever finds its way on to American bookshelves. The United States as a culture possesses a tremendous capacity for dispatching information throughout the world, but there are only a few routes that news traveling in the direction from Asia to America can take.

These conditions, with information tending to flow only in one direction, make it especially difficult to translate a text from Japanese into English, and in the case of the current text, the translators' difficulties are compounded by the fact that much of the context involves either facets of Eastern history most English-speaking readers will not be familiar with, or radical new concepts that the emerging knowledge-value society will introduce, but that are difficult to express from the present perspective. For persisting in the effort to create this edition in spite of such difficulties, I want to express my heartfelt thanks to the translators, George Fields and William Marsh, and to Paul De Angelis and Minato Asakawa of Kodansha International.

September 1990

1

What Sort of New Society?

The Next Stage of the Known, or
a Completely New Paradigm?

Many thoughtful people have suggested that the decade ahead is one in which Japan and the entire world will undergo a major transformation. What the interested parties disagree on is whether this process of change, already well under way, will take us but one step farther in the direction of an advanced technological society, or will instead result in an entirely new definition of the purpose of technology and industrial organizations. In other words, is what we see going on around us today only the continuation of the process that began with the industrial revolution, or will it lead to an unprecedented transformation of the world as we know it?

Those who see it as no more than a variation on a theme tend to hail from academic departments charged with scientific research, or companies and government agencies dealing with the nuts and bolts of commercial enterprise, while those who perceive the changes to come as all-embracing are more likely to be economists or sociologists with a research orientation. Examples of books by this second group, thinkers who see a new society ahead, are Daniel Bell's *The Coming of Post-Industrial Society: A Venture in Social Forecasting* and Alvin Toffler's *The Third Wave*.

Since the advocates of either school of thought are deeply concerned with rapid change, the development and diffusion of new technology, and the resulting structural transforma-

3

tion, they make many of the same points. This makes it tempting for some observers to lump them together or downplay the differences. There are even scholars and critics among us who suggest that the postindustrial society will simply evolve out of the advanced technological society.

But the real truth of the matter is that on the most fundamental level, these two points of view sharply oppose each other. Those who say they see an advanced industrial society on the horizon speak of the present in terms of "the progress so far" and view the current society as having passed the halfway point in a process that, as progress on the technological and industrial fronts continues, leads only to further degrees of advancement.

The other side doesn't see it that way. The thinkers who foresee a postindustrial society or the birth of a new society believe that the society we have experienced thus far will give way to a social structure quite unlike the one we now take for granted. So if the phase we have passed through so far is referred to as the "industrial society" and the first group of thinkers is inclined to label the next phase (which to them is merely one of progressive development) as an "advanced industrial society," their counterparts in the second group foresee the death of industrial society as such, to be followed by a new phase. Indeed, they say that to usher in this new phase, the industrial society that has so far been advancing by degrees must now in fact retreat to make way for the initial stage of what will follow.

But what are the concrete differences between the future societies these two groups foresee? Until we get clear answers to that question, our discussion cannot progress beyond semantics.

Each of the several basic forms human society has assumed up to now has had its own unique social frameworks and paradigms; when certain definitive changes in these occur, a new form of society is born. We are referring to such forms when we make distinctions between ancient, medieval, and modern societies. What distinguishes those futurologists who foresee merely an "advanced technological society" in the offing from those who herald the arrival of a "new society" is that the former perceive only an upgrading in technology, industrial structure, and personal life-styles, while the latter believe that the main framework and social paradigm of industrial society will be replaced by forms as radically different from what we have known as medieval society was different from modern.

There are, of course, many distinctions to be made among the specific ideas and viewpoints being pushed by the futurologists who belong to one or the other of these two main groups. The members of the "advanced technological society" contingent point to different examples or stress different aspects to make their case, as do their peers among those who foresee some form of "new society." Few if any of the scholars and critics in the field would identify themselves as a member of either the "advanced technological society" group or the "new society" group; the distinction is mine, and where I see a basis for noting affinities among them is precisely where the parties so grouped would see a basis for making clear distinctions.

As for those who argue that the society of the future will evolve more or less on the outlines of industrial society as it has been up until now, their predictions have a tendency to seem realistic because they are based on what we already know. However, most of these evolutionists seem to concentrate too heavily on isolated elements at the expense of the big picture, seizing upon changes in one area such as technology, or industrial structure, or the family or politics, and mistaking this single facet for the whole. They fail to realize just how heterogeneous the world at large is; their visions cannot accommodate a macrocosmic perspective whose overall historical pattern may run counter to the behavior they perceive. Too committed to the specialized fields from which they survey reality, they are not likely to detect changes in the framework of society as a whole. It is hardly surprising that many of those who espouse such a point of view should be experts from academia or the government bureaucracy who deliberately restrict their frame of reference to certain areas.

By comparison, the cosmic perspective and soaring imaginations of those who foresee a vastly different future society can seem compelling, but since the future they foresee lies beyond the range of our experience or current system of knowledge, the ideas involved can be difficult to grasp and off-putting. Moreover, the theories so far put forward have offered very little in the way of concrete details about the form the "new society" will take; instead, their authors tend to spend much of their energy on elucidating the structure and social norms of the industrial society we now inhabit; they don't do enough to suggest what the concepts and norms of the new society will be. Daniel Bell's *Post-Industrial Society* is an example. Its title tells us that the industrial society will end, but the text itself follows the title in resorting to an essentially negative characterization of what the future will be: The future will not be the past.

Similarly, Alvin Toffler's *The Third Wave* goes so far as to suggest that developments in communications and computer technology will create new possibilities and modes of work that will lead to changes on the scale of those wrought by the agricultural and industrial revolutions—but there Toffler stops. And so we hear the present age lamented as one rife with premonitions of change but no bona fide sense of what the future will bring. Our frustration leads us to demean our own era with labels like "The Age of Uncertainty" or "The Age of Opacity."

Those who foresee an advanced technological society also

fail to make much of a case. They are telling us that the advanced technological society will merely continue along the path blazed by the industrial revolution, but they fail to prove how industrial society as it is now constituted will be able to absorb major technological and industrial developments without changing its fundamental norms and structure. They haven't bothered to do their homework.

It is probably frustration and despair at our inability to get a clear sense of the future that has helped make the study of long-term waves something of a fad. Researchers such as those of France's Annales School and their peers at the Braudel Center at the State University of New York, Binghamton have produced meaningful results by taking the concept of the Kondratieff wave and applying it to progressively vaster continuums of time and territory. Of particular value has been the effort of Rondo Cameron and others, in their research on the Middle Ages, to posit a logistic curve of one hundred to three hundred years' duration. However, I feel that when wave theorists attempt to reduce every aspect of reality to something that can be quantified, in order to fit it in with their overall concept of measurable waves, they necessarily abandon any notion of a theory of social change on which a model of the future might be based. Moreover, I can't help thinking that to take a wave theory derived from observations of industrial society and apply it to the medieval experience is a perilous enterprise. To take for granted that our modern experience, bound up though it is with the particular conditions of industrial society, has a universal relevance is revealing of just how arrogant inhabitants of advanced nations can be. The present work is an attempt to move beyond the limited perspectives and stagnant visions that seem endemic to the futurologists of our era. I count myself among those who believe that a truly new society is about to come into being. Using history as a guide, I will attempt to posit the structure, the paradigms, and the norms of the society that will come after the industrial society.

Since what I am attempting to describe is the society that will supplant industrial society, it does not seem valid to use modes of analysis and statistics based solely on the industrial era; nor do I think it useful to accept the intellectual systems and assumptions of our age as givens. An effort must be made to see beyond the scholarly approaches of the industrial era and to adopt a perspective based on observations and analysis of human civilizations over the long term. To create a true model of social change—as it has occurred over the millennia—requires that I create new concepts and perspectives commensurate to the material. Although every effort will be made to present and define these in the simplest and most easily understandable way, I hope you can forgive me for the inherent difficulties in presenting this theory, and concentrate on the theory itself.

THE ZENITH OF INDUSTRIAL SOCIETY:
The Postwar Petroleum Culture

A World Enveloped by Rapid Growth

Let us begin with our most recent past, the period since the end of World War II. Unique to this era, especially the nearly thirty years through 1973, is the enormous rate of growth experienced throughout the world economy, particularly by the Europeans, North Americans, and Japanese.

It is easy for Japanese of my generation, who have known nothing but extremely rapid economic growth their entire lives, to assume that such growth is a natural state. Any state of affairs that persists long enough ceases to seem like an aberration. Take the example of the ancient Egyptians, who no doubt came to believe that the natural state of man was to be divided into monarchs and slaves. Seen from our present vantage point, this Egyptian concept seems singularly odd, but when viewed against the backdrop of human history, it turns out to be less unprecedented than the phenomenal rate of growth Japan has experienced since World War II! Not once in the six thousand years of recorded human history has any other good-sized national economy managed to sustain thirty years of growth at an average annual rate of 10 percent or more.

For today's Japanese, who have grown accustomed to living under such conditions, the annual average European growth rate of 3 to 4 percent seems rather sluggish. Yet when viewed from a long-term historical perspective, an annual growth rate in the 3 to 4 percent range is a tremendous achievement.

When an economist attempted to calculate what the average economic growth rate for Western Europe had been over the roughly two thousand years that have elapsed since the birth of Christ, he came up with an annual real rate of only 0.2 percent—despite the fact that Western Europe was in the forefront of continental industrial achievement throughout this period. Even the increases brought on by the Industrial Revolution were not extreme enough to bear comparison with current rates. Look at the so-called Roaring Twenties in the United States, when the drastic increase in automobile production helped create a new consumer life-style and fueled vigorous growth in oil and chemical production, telecommunications, and other new industries like radio and film production. Although this decade has assumed mythical proportions as an upbeat, raucous, prosperous era when growth rates soared so outlandishly that worldwide depression in the 1930s was the inevitable result, a comparison of its rates to current ones is sobering. According to Simon Kuznets's calculations, the U.S. GNP increased by 42.4 percent over the period 1920–29, which means the average annual rate was less than 3 percent.

Furthermore, all the fruits of that growth were suddenly wiped out by the Great Depression that began in the fall of 1929. The U.S. GNP in 1933 was only 1.2 percent greater than it had been in 1920 and exactly the same as that reported in 1919. Therefore, when population growth for the intervening years is factored in, productivity is seen to have undergone a major decline through 1933.

When the U.S. GNP for the entire twenty-year period between the two Great Wars in Europe (1918–1938) is compiled, the overall growth amounts to only 40.7 percent, for an annual average considerably under 2 percent. And the economic growth rates for the European countries over the same period were far lower.

Against this background, the twenty-some years of nearly continuous economic growth that followed World War II is truly breathtaking in scale. The pattern held true not only for vigorous economies like those of West Germany and the United States, but even for the relatively stagnant United Kingdom. Add to this the case of an economy that grew at an annual average rate of around 10 percent for nearly thirty years, as Japan's did, and we are off the historical scale. How could the postwar world possibly have sustained such unprecedented growth for so many years after the war?

Naturally no single factor could be expected to account for such an all-encompassing global phenomenon, which in fact took place over decades. For that matter, every single one of the many phenomena others have cited as factors actually did play a role, namely, developments in technology both during and after the war, the breakdown of class barriers that had restricted social mobility, increased expertise in economic policy, and the superior postwar international financial system.

Yet none of these could actually be called the decisive factor in and of itself. Technological development is regarded by many as the driving force behind our postwar prosperity, but such development took place during and after World War I as well, on a scale not vastly different. After all, the industrial technologies that contributed mightily to the industrial economy after World War II—those to produce automobiles, home appliances, synthetic chemicals, and films, among others— were all developed either before or after World War I.

The breakdown of class barriers in the West, particularly in the United States and Germany, is another precipitant of growth that had already gained momentum during and after World War I. While some believe that enlightened economic policy and an improved international financial system were what sustained the years of stable prosperity after World War II, more likely it was the high growth rate that kept things running smoothly. Once the potential for growth fell off in the late seventies, most national economies faced severe financial duress exacerbated by balance-of-payments problems, and it in fact became clear that postwar financial policy would continue to be a source of enduring problems for years to come.

Overall, then, the factors just cited may have contributed to growth in large or small ways, but they do not loom as decisive factors in that growth.

What really sets the years following World War II apart from those after World War I is the unprecedented abundance of low-priced mineral resources, energy, and agricultural products available since 1945. That such abundance is what made possible the phenomenon of prolonged growth throughout the world economy is incontestable.

It Began with Petroleum

From the 1930s and on into the 1950s, gigantic oil fields were discovered in rapid succession in the Middle East (see Chart 1). Their scale dwarfed that of the fields being pumped in the United States, Mexico, and Indonesia. Great quantities could be drawn from a single well and at an extraordinarily low cost: the cost to produce a barrel of crude oil from the Middle East's largest oil field around 1970 was ten cents, and even in the mid-1980s production costs for that area were less than one twentieth of the figure for a typical American oil field.

The low-cost petroleum drawn from these gigantic fields spilled over into the international market, creating a surplus and pulling the price down. At its lowest point in the early 1970s, the going rate worldwide for a barrel of crude oil was

Chart 1: Amounts of Petroleum Discovered and Produced
(Each Unit Equals 100 Million Barrels)

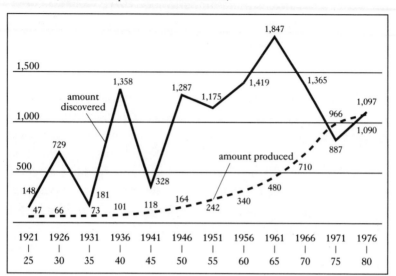

Source: M. P. Halbody and J. D. Moody, "World Oil," *Oil & Gas Journal*

$1.30 or less. This was literally cheaper than the price charged in the 1920s—and if we adjust for inflation, the 1970s rate is a mere one-sixth of the 1920s rate.

Mankind knows no shame when it comes to exploiting a resource that is cheap and abundant, and this was certainly the case with petroleum. It was used extensively as a raw material by the chemical industry, and of course as an energy source. Among the new technologies developed to take advantage of petroleum's low cost were those involving synthetic chemicals, petroleum-based synthetic fibers, and plastics.

The surfeit of cheap petroleum helped to create a glut of other material resources and agricultural products. The massive amounts of synthetic fibers coming onto the market brought about surpluses of cotton, wool, and jute, which led cotton farmers in Texas and Louisiana to start growing wheat and soybeans instead, creating an abundance of these commodities as well. Australian farmers, meanwhile, switched from sheep to cattle production, and soon there was more beef and butter available than people knew what to do with.

Agricultural productivity in general rose substantially due to the impact of chemical fertilizers and other petroleum-derived agricultural chemicals that could now be mass-produced cheaply. Even land-poor countries like Japan, where the historic commitment to maximizing agricultural output had been assiduously pursued since ancient times, saw rice output skyrocket by 50 percent after World War II, so that the stockpiles of unsold rice mounted even as total farm acreage remained unchanged. On a global scale, the surge in per-acre agricultural productivity is even more pronounced. The world population has increased 2.4 times in the past fifty years, yet the rate of increase in total food production has gone up even faster, creating excess supplies of food all over the world. This development is also the result of cheap petroleum, which made it possible to supply plenty of fertilizers and agricultural chemicals at low prices.

Thermally generated electrical power is another product cheap oil has made globally available on a massive scale. Rates for use of such power naturally reflect the influence of oil prices. Since the oil shock in 1973, Japan's electric power charges have nearly quadrupled, but even so the present rates are only about 240 times those of 1936; the overall inflation rate in Japan for the same period is some six times greater than that for electric power. Before the oil shock, overall inflation was some ten times greater than the inflation in the charges for electrical power.

Dramatic reductions in the cost of electricity mean lower prices for items where electricity powers the manufacturing process. Aluminum, expensive to produce before the war, is a case in point. Today it is treated as a virtually disposable entity, used extensively to produce cans, window frames, and electrical cables. Cheap aluminum has, in turn, driven prices down and supplies up for tin and copper.

Fuel costs for cars and airplanes have inevitably been lowered by cheap oil, making these forms of transportation, once considered luxuries, part of the life-style of average citizens. A consequence is that land that was once inaccessible is now being fully exploited, both for industrial sites and for agricultural production and processing.

It should be clear from this list of examples how the endless supply of cheap petroleum has stimulated developments in energy use and the creation of synthetic chemical products that have in turn created an oversupply of everything from material resouces to agricultural products. These mounting stockpiles of raw materials have themselves stimulated technological advances geared toward exploiting them.

A case in point is nylon. By the 1930s the technology for producing nylon was already in place, but the price of petroleum at that time was too high for this synthetic product to compete with natural fibers, so nothing was done with it. But when petroleum prices plummeted after the war, nylon became viable, and a host of new synthetic fibers were soon developed and produced. Where there is no foreseeable practical application, technology in the abstract commands little interest from investors, but once the sure prospect of making a buck off a branch of technology exists, we can be sure that the funds necessary to pursue the topic will be committed and knowledge in this field will advance.

It was the same for electrical appliances, automobiles, and airplanes as it had been for nylon and synthetic fibers; cheap oil made technological development of these products an attractive investment. If technological development took off after World War II with an intensity and enduring impact that has tended to dwarf the boom that followed World War I, it is safe to say that the difference is largely due to one factor: cheap oil.

The Country Whose Greatest Advantage Has Been
Its Lack of Resources: Japan

As should now be clear, the superabundance of petroleum helped raise the ceiling for economic growth around the world and continued to drive that growth to greater heights and duration on all fronts.

The world economy quadrupled in size in the quarter century after the war, and it was only around 1970 that it ran into its first serious bottleneck. Besides contributing to a superabundance of agricultural products and material resources, the availability of cheap petroleum stimulated the manufacture of automobiles, tractors, and other heavy implements, which opened up whole new areas of the environment to exploitation. Because development could conveniently spread out into large areas and because the pollution from petroleum is subtler in its effects than that from coal, the environmental impact of this industrial development was initially more muted than had been the case at the turn of the century, when soot and smoke pollution were a palpable scourge upon major urban areas.

But as much as petroleum-driven growth may have been a boon, the beneficial effects it provided were not distributed equally among the nations of the world. The countries that imported raw materials and agricultural products got more out of the boom than those that exported them; the importers, of course, were the countries that had advanced industrial economies. They could use their existing facilities and human resources to exploit the cheap and abundant raw materials provided by the less advanced nations. No people derived greater advantage from this situation than the historically resource-poor Japanese.

It is a universally recognized economic principle that those who can take advantage of a surplus and procure from any source gain the most. In times of scarcity, the greatest advantage accrues from procuring needed raw materials from within one's own company or from partners or affiliate organizations; but when there is a surplus, one gets the best price by flashing cash and bargaining with all sellers to drive the price down. In such circumstances, a party willing to sell below cost will always emerge.

This is especially true of the international marketplace. Because Japan was limited in resources, geographically isolated, and starting from scratch geopolitically after the war, it could freely buy the cheapest raw materials and food from anywhere in the world. It helped itself to petroleum from the Middle East, coal from Australia, iron ore from western Australia and Brazil, timber from Malaysia, wheat and corn from the United States, sweet chestnuts from China, buckwheat noodles from Canada, and so on.

Japan was also blessed with ports suitable for bulk maritime transport, another factor that helped keep the costs of raw materials down for the country as a whole.

The other advanced nations were in a position, at least hypothetically, to profit from such factors, but they were prevented from taking full advantage of the situation. The United States, for example, continues to produce ten million barrels of petroleum domestically each day, making it the second-largest-producing nation on earth (after the USSR); until the 1960s, the United States was virtually self-sufficient. But while the plenitude of American oil fields is certainly a blessing to the economy, each tends to be small, which drives up production costs. To maintain the commercial viability of American petroleum, which would have been drastically impacted by an unrestricted flood of cheap oil from the Middle East, the U.S. government restricted petroleum imports for many years, up until the oil shock. This meant that U.S. consumers paid over twice as much for their oil as was being charged on the world market.

Both the United Kingdom and West Germany had domestic coal industries and protected these by using local coal to generate the bulk of their electricity and the gas used for heating in the larger cities. Relying on local coal to generate their electricity during the 1970s meant paying out sums for this power equivalent to paying seven dollars a barrel for oil for the same purpose. The consequence was that electricity charges in the United Kingdom and West Germany, especially for home use, were much higher than in Japan.

France lacked petroleum or coal resources but was locked into a long-term contract for petroleum imports from its former colony Algeria, obliging the French to go on buying high-priced Algerian oil even after world oil prices plunged. In fact, both France and Great Britain were obliged to encourage industrial development in the former colonies of their empires by such binding contractual arrangements, despite the fact that the raw materials and food procured thereby were over-priced.

For better or worse, Japan was bound to no such arrangements, nor did it feel the need to make such restitution. Whatever it sought, it purchased at the cheapest price the marketplace could offer, without being compelled to recognize historical relationships, geographic proximity, political alliances, or past assurances, promises, or contracts. The disappointment expressed by many developing countries toward Japan (especially in Southeast Asia), countries that had hoped for more from a non-Western power, was unquestionably reinforced by this kind of behavior, and is behind the branding of the Japanese as "economic animals" in parts of the world;

but the behavior itself was indispensable to the sustained high growth of Japan's economy.

That Japan's "no holds barred" approach to procuring resources contributed mightily to its growth is attested to by the fact that the industries that developed fastest during the boom years (1960–1974) were those that depended most heavily on resources: the steel and petrochemical industries, shipbuilding, and the like.

But what boded well for the Japanese put the developing countries in an extremely disadvantageous position. The core of the matter is not that agricultural production, the economic mainstay of developing countries, lacked the growth potential of manufacturing, nor that "demand" for primary products, all the third world could produce, "failed to grow sufficiently." What really happened during the years that cheap oil flooded the market was that product substitutes derived from oil put the third world countries that produced primary products at a drastic disadvantage as demand for their exports sank, while the resultant low prices for such products worked very much to the advantage of the advanced nations, especially Japan.

Take the example of synthetic fibers. Their appearance on the scene dramatically reduced the demand for cotton and wool and led to the near-total destruction of the jute industry; jute had been the most important export for India and Bangladesh. Southeast Asian producers of natural rubbers likewise suffered from the introduction of synthetic rubber, while chemical products were developed that depressed the market for vegetable oils from Asia and Africa and fish oil from Peru. As previously mentioned, cheaper electricity from oil-powered thermal generators made aluminum an economically viable substitute for copper, which plunged the economies of copper producers in South America and Africa into depressions. Ironically, the producers of the only primary commodity for which demand grew at a tremendous rate—petroleum itself—also saw supply for their product outstrip demand, so that they, too, saw their profits undercut to an extent by falling prices.

Naturally, most of the developing countries derived some limited benefits from the worldwide phenomenon of economic growth. But they gained a great deal less than did the advanced industrial nations; while resource-poor countries like Japan stood only to gain. That is why, since 1960, there has been an ever-widening gap between the northern and southern hemispheres in economic terms.

Enlightened Self-Interest, or the Empathetic Impulse: How We Know When We Must Recognize the Other Side's Needs

Major economic forces such as those I have just described cause attitudes, tastes, and life-styles to mutate in response.

To understand the basis for economic and cultural change, it is important to remember that human beings are, essentially, clever animals who have managed to survive by using their brains. Alertness to their own self-interest—an inherited trait—dictates that human beings, no matter what their cultural background or historical setting, must develop an ethics and an aesthetics that favor exploiting fully those resources that exist in abundance, and economizing on items that are in short supply.

The instinct that drives men to find it manly and proper to address shortages of a necessary item by getting rid of bottlenecks in the supply pipeline, creating substitutes, or searching for new sources, also drives them to develop an empathetic impulse toward their environment that convinces them to hold off on things in short supply while making a point of using up whatever there is lots of. In operation, this empathetic impulse gives rise to thought and behavior that transcend the simple working out of the economic principle that what exists in abundance should be cheap and what is in short supply should be expensive. In other words, a point comes when the evolving aesthetics and ethics go beyond the logic of the marketplace.

We can see this principle at work in recent Japanese history. Before the war, when the giant oil fields of the Middle East had yet to be discovered, most Japanese perceived the world as lacking sufficient resources and food. What was thought to be true for the planet at large was perceived as being acutely true for Japan, with its limited land area, its dearth of mineral resources, and its chronic shortages. Thus it was that "thrift" and "upkeep" (taking good care of what little one had) were the prime virtues celebrated before the war. The ethics textbooks of the time are filled to bursting with anecdotes about people who took good care of what they had.

If possessions and resources were in short supply, labor was anything but, and wages were therefore very low. To employ as many people as possible became the goal of those who wished to show off and present themselves in the best possible light. The terms used to describe "a family that is wealthy and worthy of respect" were numerous, but all contained the implication that the household so described employed many servants. Wealthy families of high status who did not subsidize a few students and other hangers-on as live-ins were considered by their peers to be either lacking in compassion or eccentric.

Simply convening a large staff on special occasions was not enough if one wished to avoid the stigma of being dismissed as merely nouveau riche. The truly elite life-style was one that could be maintained only by employing a large number of servants on a permanent basis. An irreproachable mansion was one that needed many hands to nurture it.

Such estates featured a Japanese garden covering many acres, surrounded by a long fence. When it comes to labor-intensive enterprises, nothing can compare with a Japanese garden. Each tree must be twisted and tortured into an exotic and entirely artificial shape every spring and every fall. Let nature take its own course in such a garden for even two years and the damage is irreversible. Therefore, large-scale gardens in impeccable condition presented irrefutable evidence of the property owner's having maintained a formidable staff over decades. One could not possess such a garden without being of the elite.

A mansion that featured such a garden would also have very long corridors running alongside the garden for viewing purposes. The entire length of one side of such a corridor would consist of walls that were actually movable wooden shutters on tracks (*amado* or "rain doors") that would have to be opened every morning and closed every evening. The task was laborious and, depending on the scale of the mansion, might constitute a full-time job for one of the maids, who would literally be obliged to bolt down her lunch in order to complete the process of closing the doors by nightfall. One of the classic compliments employed to acknowledge truly lavish and prestigious establishments before the war was the statement, "It takes all day to open and close their shutters."

The ethical and aesthetic values of Japanese society changed dramatically after the war. Confronted with a new world in which surplus production was a global phenomenon, and able to gain access to and purchase from any and all markets, Japan made it its business to accumulate cheap materials and foodstuffs from all over the planet and process these in the enormous factories it built along its coastlines; the revenues from such mass production transformed Japan into a materially wealthy society. Those who grew up in these heady postwar years tend to chuckle when prewar slogans that allude to the need to be thrifty and take good care of possessions are mentioned in their presence.

The years of rapid economic growth in Japan since the war have created a situation in which manpower, rather than resources, has become the commodity in short supply. That is why so much emphasis has been put on the propriety of conserving labor and making the most of it. The manager looked up to today is the manager who succeeds in reducing manpower needs by rationalizing and simplifying the production process.

If prewar textbooks made much of individuals who were thrifty and scrupulously took care of irreplaceable machines and possessions, the postwar textbooks are notable for deifying managers who have rationalized industrial processes so that fewer hands are needed. It is amazing to see how the aesthetics and ethical precepts cleaved to by the Japanese have shifted in response to a changing environment.

It follows that the life-styles that earn respect in Japan today are also different in essence from those admired before the war. Abuse and contempt are heaped on households that employ too many domestics, while any estate where it took all day to close the shutters would be considered a dilapidated relic. At present, a typical swanky domain is likely to be a thousand-square-yard spread built of ferroconcrete and glass, with its air conditioning, shutters, lighting system, and curtains fully automated and capable of instant manipulation from any number of conveniently placed outlets and switching systems. When it comes to defining luxury, conspicuous consumption of materials and energy has become the name of the game, and the ultimate symbol of having arrived is to have an elevator installed in one's home.

Cost is certainly not the sole issue when it comes to deciding what real luxury is. Today it seems that even those for whom price is no object show little enthusiasm for employing large contingents of domestics. Were a corporation to dispatch a fleet of, say, ten servants to the estate of the new president, his wife would be sure to send them packing with cries of, "Who needs the uproar? No, thanks!" Frankly, when people nowadays see a household with that number of men and women serving as on-site staff, they are likely to start speculating on what sort of "special business" the family is involved in.

The most chic of the conspicuous consumers have clearly shifted their preferences in the direction of resources and energy and away from manpower. Examples of this change in tastes abound. Before the war, if one sent a gift of some fancy, expensive confection, it had to be delivered in a handmade cedar box that had clearly taken many man-hours to fashion; today it is de rigueur for such items to reach our hands wrapped in layer after layer of lavish wrapping papers and other diverse materials. When researchers at a Japanese university chose to look into this matter and methodically investigated some 1,086 confectionery items marketed as "high class" fare at various locations around Japan, they made the startling discovery that the number of caloric units of energy expended on the packaging exceeded by four times that which had gone into creating the confections. That the products were for the most part traditional regional delicacies appreciated for centuries made no difference; their manufacturers could not securely present them to modern consumers as high-class fare without the lavish packaging.

Leisure and modes of transport are two more areas where one could go on forever citing examples in which the prodigious expenditure of energy and materials is equated with consumer satisfaction. But the trend reaches its ultimate expression in the notion of the "disposable" product. Created through automated mass production to be used once and then thrown away, disposable products carry the notion of zealously conserving on labor while unabashedly using up material as far as it can go.

The shift in emphasis from conserving resources to conserving manpower, which so transformed society's notions of what is proper and attractive after World War II, was a global phenomenon, yet no country experienced it with quite the startling intensity that resource-starved Japan did after 1945. Although the Western nations and the developing countries may not have been subjected to as abrupt and radical a redefinition of their values and priorities, they did undergo a similar transformation.

The anecdotes I have presented so far to underscore the differences between the Japanese prewar and postwar conceptions of the proper relation between manpower and material were meant as shocking and therefore easily understood illustrations of the change that took place. They are oversimplistic to the extent that they fail to acknowledge that a shift toward greater consumption of resources was well under way in Japan before the war. The industrialization of the country may not have been complete at that time, but the Japanese people's worship of products and material things had already surfaced with sufficient intensity for prewar textbooks to start propagandizing against this trait. That their authors found it necessary to hark back to older values clearly indicates that the change was already well under way. But since the process was incomplete and resources continued to be dear and labor cheap until after the war, lip service was still given to the feudalistic virtues of thrift and respectful upkeep of one's possessions.

The Japanese prewar situation forms quite a contrast with that of the United States, where there was much land available but only a trickle of immigrants to exploit it. Under these conditions, Americans arrived much earlier at a consumerist ethic that dictated that men should conserve their labor but feel free to use up resources. The cowboy featured in the typical Western was in truth probably just as hard up as his peasant counterpart in nineteenth-century Japan, but observe how much he consumes with impunity. He has his own horse to ride, his own gun to shoot, and can smash up furniture and covered wagons when the mood seizes him. If he wants to roast some meat, the firewood is right there for him to burn. On the other hand, the idea of employing somebody to cut his hair or launder his clothes never seems to occur to this cowboy. He cooks for himself, and when it comes to clothes or a place to live or pots and pans or the like, the cowboy likes to keep things simple and makeshift.

American life today, with its cars and far-flung suburban homes, is the cowboy tradition carried to its extreme. Americans do not stint on materials when throwing together a product or building or a piece of equipment, but many of them hate to be bothered with attending to the fine points or little details of production. One of the reasons American culture had so much worldwide impact in the years after World War II was that a world suddenly awash in petroleum-induced surpluses could key in to the American emphasis on quantity over quality.

Later I will show how this type of materialism, in which using up a lot of "stuff" becomes an end in itself and a kind of dogma, is endemic to industrial society; it forms its spiritual core. It was in the boom years after the war, when the economy of the whole world was transformed by the influx of cheap petroleum, that the American-style industrial society reached its zenith of development and became the model that every nation aspired to imitate.

"The Merit of Scale": The Economic Advantages of Increasing the Scale of an Operation

The availability of huge amounts of cheap raw materials and agricultural products naturally had its impact on the modes and systems by which items were produced and distributed. Cheap petroleum did more than make the chemical industry and thermoelectric power plants economically viable; it caused a monumental expansion in the scale of production facilities and distribution networks for all kinds of products. Before long, it was thought that massive consumption of resources and agricultural products was "good form," especially for those nations and individuals already positioned to consume; and soon the idea began to be advanced that all the people in the world ought to be able to practice such consumption habits; "justice" demanded it. One would expect such an idea to develop under the circumstances, along with the corollary notion that any increase in output per worker would, by increasing the volume of products available for consumption, inevitably lead to greater social justice and a more equitable world. Once that logic had been generally accepted, it is not surprising that all policies that seemed likely to increase product output were adopted without a struggle.

The first such policy to be adopted held that by limiting the variety of goods to be produced—creating a single "standard" product rather than tailoring products to specific needs—volume could be increased without adding to the manpower base. Given the producer's economic imperative to use up a maximal amount of cheaply acquired resources while holding the line on labor, mass production of standardized products offered obvious advantages. By limiting themselves to turning out a standard "one size fits all" product on an assembly line, manufacturers could cut back on the amount of time spent developing new designs and blueprints, and eliminate the downtime that would have been needed to retool to turn out variations on the product. In an industrial society, standardization of all types of products is encouraged, for economies of scale can be realized even when it comes to foods and various types of services. Japan after the war poured its strength into achieving these economies, with the government pulling out all the stops to encourage the effort. For the Ministry of International Trade and Industry (MITI) in particular, pushing companies to increase volume by standardizing was an important priority for a long time.

Expanding the scale of the facilities and equipment used to manufacture and transport products was a second means by which worker output could be driven up. Industrial production is by its nature a process where increasing the size and capacity of the facility usually does not require a staff increase of comparable proportions. So if a company expands the scale of its operations to the extent permitted by the market, its capital, and technical factors, it can reasonably expect output per worker to increase. For Japan, realizing such economies meant that the economy grew, market share and the yield on investment shot up, and each successful expansion of scale led to another. Tanker tonnage, for example, increased by a factor of twenty over two decades, and blast-furnace capacity also grew incrementally; but even the expansion in scale of facilities in these two fields is dwarfed by that undergone by petrochemical plants.

Production output per worker could also be driven up by increasing the speed of an operation. This meant raising the pace at which a vehicle moved or a machine performed its function; it applied equally to processes as diverse as operating a steel mill or flying an aircraft. The fact should be kept in mind, however, that in most cases where it was a question of balancing the gains in output to be had through speeding up an operation as against those that came from increasing the size of the facility or vehicle, the advantages of size have tended to predominate. It is possible, for example, to increase tanker capacity or the length of commuter trains more dramatically than vehicular speed.

But the fourth and most important means of improving output per member of the work force has been through having either a machine or a resource fulfill the step in a process previously carried out by a human being. This is the most direct method of substituting material resources, which exist in abundance, for manpower, which is in short supply. What began with simple steps in mechanizing processes previously entrusted to men on the assembly line has now grown to encompass tasks as complex as inspecting products to assure that quality control is being maintained. Needless to say, introducing robots into the process has been more easily achieved, economically speaking, when standardization and increases in the scale of the facility have been simultaneously introduced.

Taken together, all of these techniques and operating principles are variations on the theme of pursuing what we Japanese call the "merit of scale." Eventually such thinking was carried over into areas other than manufacturing. Applying the technological advances and the "Think big" approach first developed in the manufacturing sector to other fields of endeavor enabled workers in those fields to enjoy their own versions of the merit of scale. Farmers, for example, were able to drive up agricultural productivity both by introducing ever larger and more efficient tractors and machines and by treating their fields and crops with chemical fertilizers and pesticides. When it came to distributing the flood of agricultural products newly available, modern supermarkets were introduced that took advantage of cheaper packaging materials and the mechanization of the food-packaging process itself to offer standardized products on a self-service basis; this offered economic merits of scale to customer and distributor alike. The

field of leisure has also been transformed by the standardization of the services it provides through a growing number of
chain outlets that are now heavily automated and computerized. Domestic life-styles have been altered almost beyond
recognition by the fact that the soaps and detergents and electrical appliances we use and the food products we eat can be
cheaply mass-produced; moreover, an increasing number of
citizens actually live in prefab homes or apartment buildings
that consist entirely of standardized units constructed at minimal cost. So-called instant foods are perhaps the most extreme example of the tendency toward mass production and
distribution. The value systems and notions of taste that dictate that we should consume as many resources as we can
while working as little as possible have even transformed the
methods by which we carry out household chores, despite the
fact that those methods are not dictated by the demands of
the marketplace (since the labor we are bent on conserving is
in this case not hired, but our own).

It is important not to lose track of the fact that underlying
all these rapid changes is the fundamental change I earlier
described in the way the consumer approaches consuming itself. It is only because consumers have been thus far willing
to accept on their own terms products that are nothing more
than standardized, mass-produced items made to be bought
up, used quickly, then thrown away, that it has been possible
to implement the production and distribution systems that we
have today.

Faced with this uncomplaining acceptance of the current
system by consumers, the temptation is to take the acceptance at face value and declare, "But of course they accept
these mass-produced products, because after all, mass-produced products are cheaper and that's the whole point." Such
a conclusion would be too simplistic. Look at all the people
who deliberately throw things away before they're completely
used up, or pay extra for frivolous, fancy packaging that serves

no purpose, or waste good money at the gas pump on cars much larger than they need; even a cursory glance at such behavior makes it clear that people don't mind paying big for things that have nothing to do with their innate practical needs. The fact is, human beings cannot be counted on to act coldly, loyally, and calculatingly in their own economic self-interest at all times. If human behavior can in some sense be viewed as rational, it is only when such behavior is viewed in the context of whatever the social consensus of the era declares to be orthodoxy—that is, right and proper and attractive for those times; this is as true for economic behavior as for any other kind, and consumer orthodoxies certainly do mutate from era to era. For those of another time and place who may not be privy to these received ideas, the behavior in question may seem absolutely inexplicable, irrational, and bizarre.

To sum up: the postwar environment, being blessed with an abundance of cheap raw materials and agricultural products, gave rise to a consumerist philosophy according to which it was sensible and even "chic" to use up lots of products and resources while making every effort to conserve on manpower; and the postwar generation, by adroitly matching this consumerist ideal with the technical advances and new administrative systems needed to make it real, created the matrix out of which an enormous increase in the scale of economic operations and the rate of economic growth could be sustained over a very long period. Since the civilization that accomplished this took as its point of departure the sudden abundance of cheap petroleum, and made it its business to develop ways to exploit this resource, I shall refer to that civilization hereafter as the "Postwar Petroleum Culture."

The Basic Spirit of Industrial Society

I believe that in Japan the postwar petroleum culture reached its culmination during the mid-1960s. The domestic coal industry had pretty much shut down by then and the shift toward relying on cheap petroleum to meet every kind of need was well under way by this time, although the full impact was not felt in all sectors for another five years or so. During this period, industrial complexes were going up all along Japan's shoreline, ever larger plants and factories were being built, electrical power lines reached virtually every household in the country, and private ownership of automobiles became a trend. Supermarkets began opening in every region of Japan, instant foods and prefab homes came into their own, and streetcars began disappearing.

As it turned out, Japan's version of the petroleum culture reached full flower some five or ten years later than the Western European versions did. In America, historically a culture with a preponderance of resources and a shortage of manpower, most sections of the economy were already reorganizing themselves along "petroleum culture" lines by the 1920s, although the process wasn't really completed until after World War II, around 1950. In any case, it is clear that the process that commenced with the discovery of the Middle Eastern oil fields and ended with the development of a petroleum culture by every advanced nation was completed at a frenetic pace. Such rapid transformation could occur because the ways of thinking that are characteristic of the petroleum culture are in fact simply extensions of the ideological assumptions of industrial society.

The ideology of industrial society holds that it is tasteful and attractive to consume resources in abundance, and that to provide the opportunity for such consumption to all the peoples of the world is to do them justice. These aesthetic and ethical assumptions, taken together, constitute what I would call the basic spirit of industrial society.

What finally became the industrial society began with the Renaissance, then went through a long period of incubation during which it prepared itself for the transformation into a society oriented toward the things of this world. The phenomenon that finally provoked this fundamental shift was the industrial revolution.

When we speak of the industrial revolution, what exactly do we mean? As an historical phenomenon, the industrial revolution began with the introduction of the steam engine as a source of industrial power, which in turn led to the dissemination of machines built along the larger lines that steam power made practical, and finally culminated in the full-scale development of factory production. In the larger sense, the industrial revolution refers to the drastic and rapid increase in man's ability to produce, process, and transport the things he makes from raw materials and agricultural products. As such, what the industrial revolution really means, in an ultimate sense, is the condition of plenty it made possible, the phenomenal abundance that characterizes our age.

So whether what is being looked at is the industrial revolution itself or the technical or industrial progress that came out of it, the common thread that unites these stages is that each has managed to create a condition where those who experienced that stage can say, "We have more available to us today than we have ever had before." It is also important to note that the particular machine that the steam engine was devised to power was a water pump used in mine shafts. The year in which the Englishman Thomas Savery put this pump into practical operation was 1698. Inevitably the introduction of the first steam-powered machines led directly to an increase in the supply of mineral resources, particularly coal. Such availability changed attitudes and tastes. Before the industrial revolution, people did not believe that using up as much as possible was desirable or attractive, but under the new circumstances the notion quickly gained in popularity. By the time the eighteenth century was over, the ascetic medieval philos-

ophy that rejected greed and sought beauty in restraint and
the repression of desire was on the way out. As industrialism
deepened its hold and progressed to more advanced stages,
medieval values disappeared almost completely.

Today, as we find ourselves immersed in the ethical and
aesthetic assumptions of the industrial age, it has become utterly second nature for us to believe that in any situation
where justice or fairness is being addressed, the discussion is
going to involve enabling people to consume more material
things. Take the concept of economic growth. As members of
industrial societies, some of us may be of the capitalist per-
suasion while others believe in socialism, but both sides work
on the assumption that economic growth is inherently desirable. The issue then becomes, What kind of economic growth
do we want? Whether we speak of the gross national product
or per capita consumption, our main concern is increasing how
much we consume.

Certainly nobody would dispute the fact that the Japanese
economy has grown since World War II; but, given that, what
is it that the Japanese can now consume that they could not
consume before the war? (Before answering this question, let
me observe that there are three basic types of physical consumption practiced by individuals: consumption of the labor
of others; consumption of space; and consumption of material
things.) When it comes to consuming the labor of others, Japanese consumption on a per capita basis has sunk to nearly
half what it was before the war. Japanese per capita consumption of space has also gone down; this is not due simply to the
increase in population, but also reflects the fact that much of
the land used either for farms or housing before the war has
now been given over to other purposes. The only type of consumption where we have witnessed any increase in the per
capita figure is consumption of material things. And the fact
of the matter is, if we examine our operating concept of eco-

nomic growth, we discover that it is defined precisely in terms of the increase in the number or amount of material things we consume.

There is a way to compare the advanced industrial nations that have grown economically with the underdeveloped nations that will make this clear. The commodity that the consumers of "prosperous" advanced nations consume more of than those of "hard up" underdeveloped nations do is not labor or space, but only hard goods.

In prewar Japan, an environment where the spirit of industrialism had not yet completely taken hold, the average citizen did not talk about the annual rate of growth or what the GNP was likely to amount to for the year. Elementary school students in those days were taught that Japan was a good country or a strong country; they were not taught that it was an affluent country or a country with a high rate of economic growth. Japan before the war was, in fact, still so far from becoming the consummate example of an industrial society that the classic operating principle of such societies, the notion that "increasing material prosperity is the way to achieve greater happiness," was suppressed on both the conscious and unconscious levels.

Attitudes toward productivity were likewise far different from those held today, when we take for granted that to increase productivity will make the world a better place. When we talk of increasing productivity we refer specifically either to increasing the amount of raw material or agricultural product each worker processes, or to driving up the value-added factor for a product in some other way. Of course, in the competitive market of today we tend to end up doing our best to hold down the charge for whatever value-added factor we are able to develop, in order to achieve market share; in the end we are still forced to try to turn out as many products as cheaply as possible. Therefore, what we mean when we speak of increasing productivity is nothing other than doing our part to increase the material consumption of society as a whole.

Devotion is another concept that, at least in Japan, has had its meaning altered to serve the purposes of industrial society. All devotion means today is giving your all to devising means to derive the maximum economic yield out of a production process; but it can also refer to working as hard as you can at your job, whether that involves turning out products or offering services. In either context, what is valued about devotion is its positive impact on the value of the products the individual or society is able to consume as a result. In the old days, *devotion* was a word that implied an ascetic or otherworldly commitment to a truth that transcended the merely material, but today one rarely hears phrases like "studying with genuine devotion" or "he is devoting himself to God." Yet such usage was but recently a part of our everyday discourse.

Today's society, a product of the industrial revolution on the most fundamental level, seeks above all to increase the volume of goods to which it has access, believing that anything done to achieve this goal is by definition a contribution to justice and man's well-being. Technological research and academic study are subordinated to this purpose of maximizing output, and the economic system and most of society's substructures and organisms are shaped to accommodate this goal. Anything that contributes to this purpose we have come to deem "rational," while other activities tend to be dismissed as "irrational and anachronistic" and worthy of bemused contempt.

Having reached this stage, is it safe to say that our postwar petroleum culture, by making more goods available than at any moment in history, has succeeded in fulfilling to a remarkable degree the ideals of an industrial society? Should our culture be regarded as representing the apotheosis of what an industrial society might hope to achieve?

Perhaps. But increasing the supply of goods available for consumption is not the only form of happiness known to man. Human history is rife with examples of eras and regions inhabited by peoples who would have defined happiness quite differently. As I will show in detail later, there have been periods in history when the peoples of the more advanced regions did cleave to ethical and aesthetic systems not unlike those of our postwar petroleum culture, but there have also been eras when absolutely opposed notions prevailed throughout the whole world. The belief that more is better, which is so characteristic of industrial society, is anything but an immutable truth revered by man throughout all history; even at present it does not command universal credence among the peoples of the world. Rather, it is a belief shaped by an environment in which more things, more goods and resources, are available than has ever been the case before; as such, it's a distinctly modern phenomenon and nothing more.

Today there are a number of advanced nations in which a significant portion of the citizenry subscribe to religions and/or social beliefs that are opposed to, and stand in the way of, economic growth and increased productivity. Citizens of advanced nations who are caught up in the value systems of their own industrial societies are often inclined to attack such beliefs as irrational and anachronistic, but they should not forget that those living in advanced nations that have not industrialized may still subscribe to, and desire to uphold, utterly different ethical and aesthetic systems. We can see examples of this in the Middle East, where aristocratic leaders have fallen in love with everything Western and have fervently struggled to industrialize their domains, only to end up being dumped and sent into exile, as happened so dramatically in Iran's Islamic revolution.

The cultural values of today's advanced nations are based on the ethics and aesthetics of industrialism. Some prefer to refer to these values simply as "modern Western civilization." In any case, to ascribe universality to these values is a grave error. And to go even further and assume that those values can serve as an absolute and immutable basis for interpreting either history or the future, is to allow oneself to succumb to the worst sort of smug, myopic complacency.

HARBINGERS OF A NEW SOCIETY

The Truth Sinks in:
The Supply of Resources Is Finite

We return to the question of whether the society to come will simply be a more advanced version of the one we live in now, or something truly new. Put another way, will the industrial society continue as such for very much longer? Will people still want to consume more and more material things, as the agenda of the industrial society has dictated? Will our tastes and ethics still be determined by the assumption that ever greater consumption is in the best interests of the world?

Having the questions put before us in this order makes it that much easier to recognize the fact that certain trends and traits have emerged, particularly since 1980, that are highly relevant to the issue of which direction society is going to take. After all, a flood of examples can be cited that suggest that the once-unqualified desire for more and more material things is weakening.

What brought this all to a head for most of us was, of course, the matter of oil.

The two oil crises of the 1970s made it only too clear that our faith in an unendingly abundant supply of resources and food was misplaced. Even (or should we say, especially) the Japanese, comfortably and confidently ensconced in a life-style based on cheap imports of food and resources, are now tormented by pangs of uncertainty regarding future supplies. Any rumor of a tanker being sunk in the Persian Gulf sets off a furor of Japanese speculation as to whether what we now face is major oil crisis number three; likewise, if snowfall over the course of a winter seems to be running light, dire warnings that this year's rice crop will be short are promptly sounded. Though this alarmism resulted in Japan's finding itself awash in oversupplies of both food and petroleum throughout the 1980s, the fears of impending shortfalls, and a general sense that we must regard supplies of resources as finite, are with us to stay.

When it comes to the long-term outlook, most Japanese are even more pessimistic about whether the supply of resources, energy, and food will hold up. Many genuinely believe that over the long haul we will start to see oil fields drying up and that supplies of other resources we have exploited heedlessly will likewise dwindle. Not a few worry that the havoc wreaked on the environment by man will turn enormous tracts of land into desert and that this, combined with drastic deforestation worldwide, will lead to critical food, paper, and wood shortages. Many entertain comparable fears with respect to precious metals and other environmental resources, or see the population explosion in the developing countries as portending future famines. In the course of little more than a decade, the perception that the pool of resources is shrinking has taken hold even among average citizens.

Once doubts arise as to whether the supply of food and resources is really all that plentiful, man's instinctive empathy for his environment warns him that this environment can withstand only so much exploitation; a nagging sense that it is in his enlightened self-interest to stop consuming copious amounts of whatever exists in abundance makes itself felt, and he ceases to believe that such unbridled consumption is desirable or tasteful. In other words, what I earlier referred to as man's "empathetic impulse" sends a clear signal that restraint is called for.

Mankind received such a signal during the 1980s. People at work in any number of fields underwent a change in outlook that led them to redefine what they thought of as tasteful, desirable, or attractive.

Through the 1970s, reigning concepts of what was high-class in the West and in Japan tended to revolve around size: big was almost always deemed better. If a car was big, it was classy; if a car was classy, it was big. The same went for furniture, or refrigerators, or television sets, or even magazines. The marketing of food products also proceeded on the assumption that bulk formed the basis of product appeal. The bigger any product was, the more resources it took to make it, and that, by definition, lent it greater allure.

This outlook was manifest in the approach the Japanese took to housing issues after 1965. When asked what was wrong with their homes, those questioned invariably griped that their units were too small. In other words, quality was defined in terms of square footage. Quantity and quality were indivisible in their minds. Further questioning made it clear that for most, a quality home would not only have to be spacious, but would also need to feature built-in air conditioning and heating, more than one flush toilet, and plenty of light fixtures and outlets; in other words, quality domiciles were those that needed prodigious amounts of material and energy to construct and maintain.

Had a participant in the survey described his or her home by referring to it as a one-story unit of about 500 square feet, built of wood in the old style, which "may lack air conditioning and central heating but is very, very classy nonetheless," most Japanese would have pitied the respondent as someone compelled by false pride to defend the indefensible. Yet a home so described would have constituted, to a prewar Japanese, the very essence of class and high living.

"Light/Thin/Short/Small" and
the Postmodern Aesthetic

The prevailing outlook changed as the 1980s began. "Light/Thin/Short/Small" was the slogan that defined a new aesthetic that made light, compact products all the rage. Suddenly the era when "big" and "beautiful" were practically synonyms was at an end.

Year after year until the late 1970s, automakers had introduced ever larger and more powerful models, restrained only by the parameters set by Japan's Road Traffic Act and any restrictions the tax authorities might impose. The rules of the game changed, however, as Japan entered the 1980s and began working to create lighter, more fuel-efficient cars. Though consumers in the 1970s had bought the notion that each salary raise was best celebrated with the purchase of a bigger automobile, many are now proud to own compacts and consider the outsize American models more crude than luxurious. Gas guzzling is considered such poor form these days that bicycles and motorcycles, which until recently no adult who wasn't a sportsman wanted to be caught dead riding, are now enjoying a boom; even the middle-aged are biking these days and it is hard to remember the time, little more than a decade ago, when each commuter railroad station was not surrounded by a mass of parked motorcycles and bicycles.

Trends in the marketing of furniture and electrical appliances appeal to the same logic. The makers of quality furniture were turning out larger pieces each year through the end of the seventies, when they did an abrupt about-face. This change in direction coincided with a sudden shift in emphasis in commercials for refrigerators, where the magic words "bigger and wider" were suddenly replaced by a new formula: "slim and energy-efficient." And when it comes to marketing electronic calculators or videocassettes, the war that equates "thinner" with "irresistible" is by now being fought over millimeters.

This trend was not confined to Japanese consumer behavior. Everyone knows that in 1980 the bottom dropped out of the American market for big cars with low fuel efficiency and that smaller models from Japan took their place. While the sudden jump in gasoline prices certainly affected this choice, changes in consumer taste had an even larger impact. The downfall of American automakers was their failure to foresee how consumers were redefining what they found attractive in products.

Visiting Detroit early in 1982 when the recession was at its most abysmal, I called on one of the Big Three automakers and was shown the results of a survey they had run back in 1975, when impact from the first oil shock was still strong. The survey results astonished me. Despite the fact that the respondents were told to assume that gasoline prices would rise to at least $1.40 per gallon (the peak price along the Eastern seaboard after the first shock) by 1980, the vast majority of those surveyed insisted that they would go on buying big cars and that the American love affair with large automobiles would continue as always, regardless of what gas cost. That Detroit did not get behind small cars in a big way at that time was the result of such feedback. But the American consumers who reassured them in 1975 betrayed the automakers in spectacular fashion in 1980, when they discarded once and for all the notion that any car that wasn't large had to be a loser.

If by 1983 the combination of economic recovery and sinking prices at the gas pump, plus the surge in the cost of export models due to the voluntary quotas imposed by Japanese automakers, had seriously undercut the strictly economic argument for purchasing a smaller car, this did not translate into renewed viability for the larger models. Though sales of the latter recovered some of their lost momentum, the market share was nowhere near what it had been before 1980. Detroit's habit had always been to anticipate consumer buying patterns by introducing new lines of larger cars to replace the old ones every few years, but the changed structure of the market and the shrinking share for the larger models have now been accepted as inescapable reality.

Another symbol of postwar society's drive to consume more and more resources is the disposable product and our general tendency to discard things sooner. There has been a reversal of this trend, with car owners and others tending to hang onto products 20 or 30 percent longer than they used to; at the same time, the kind of life-style where one holds onto a product for a long time as a measure of one's appreciation for its quality is now considered more tasteful than a life-style based on using up and throwing out lots of disposable items.

Architecture is another area where there has been a drastic reappraisal of what is in good taste. Up until a few years ago, the epitome of the fashionably modern in architecture was the hermetically sealed "glass box" design. That this style was considered the archetype of the modern is suggested by the fact that when illustrators were asked to depict Tokyo in the twenty-first century, they almost always drew an urban landscape in which enormous automobiles ascending on two- and three-tiered highway ramps wound their way through forests of colossal glass towers.

What is it about airtight glass boxes that makes them seem quintessentially modern? It's the fact that the design eats up energy and resources on an unprecedented scale. Windows that can't be opened mean that year-round air conditioning is required, while having the building encased in a thin sheath of glass rather than solid walls ensures that heat will be dissipated through the glass in winter and absorbed through it in the summer. Since to maintain spring temperatures in every room throughout the year means running the air conditioning system full-blast at all times, the design succeeds brilliantly at squandering an absolute maximum of energy.

Lately, however, airtight glass-box designs have become strictly old hat. Japan's current rage is for buildings lined with brick tiles, with small windows, any one of which the occupant can open or close at will. The insulation provided by the brick tiles helps to efficiently moderate temperatures, while the restricted surface area of the windows functions to limit the dissipation of heated or cooled air. Tadao Ando, whose residential designs enjoy current preeminence, has even gone so far as to create interactive interior environments in which the function of air conditioning is played down and external air is fed in to allow seasonal variations to be felt. Like the revival of interest in bicycles and handcrafted objects, these architectural designs underscore the emergence of a new perspective that opposes itself to industrialism.

Expressions of this perspective are being heard outside Japan as well. Though forests of glass towers have been constructed in the United States, a major proportion of the new American designs are for buildings with concrete or stone facades. If a series of designs by Michael Graves and Hans Hollein have tended to exemplify this trend, the ATT building by Philip Johnson, an older architect of long-established eminence, sounds a very similar note. It is remarkable that the field of architectural design, which more than any other art form owes its most pronounced development to the unique conditions of this century, is expressing its break with the values of the postwar petroleum culture in such a prominent way.

The name by which this movement is known in the art world is Postmodernism. No conclusions can yet be reached as to the ultimate direction Postmodernism will take, and it may well turn out to be the type of movement where no clear consensus as to its direction is ever reached; now is too early to say. But one thing we can be sure of is that its perspective will be totally different from that of Modernism, an artistic movement that adopted the philosophical agenda of the industrial society from which it sprang, and so sought to be ever more functional, and to achieve a measurably greater quotient of pleasure by consuming massive amounts of resources and energy.

In viewing the economic changes wrought by the 1980s, we must not forget that our redefinition of what is attractive or beautiful has had more impact on the economy than any other single factor. Having understood that, we must also realize that we cannot understand the transformation of the functions and purpose of the manufacturing economy if we view it only as an isolated mechanism whose specific facets and operations can be viewed out of context of the whole. If we really hope to understand its workings, we must view the economy as a facet of, and a force operating in relation and in response to, civilization as a whole.

The Petroleum Culture in Decline

The idea that to consume ever more products is attractive forms the basis for the notions of taste that have prevailed in the postwar "petroleum culture." This outlook has been with us ever since the industrial revolution brought the industrial society into being. But during the 1980s, we have seen the aesthetic that equates quantity consumption with good taste starting to lose its hold. What this really means is that the postwar culture based on plentiful petroleum is itself on shaky ground, with industrial society as such past its peak and moving into a new phase that will alter its essential outlines.

When the global recession of 1980–83 beset the industrialized nations, the industries hardest hit were in fact those that, because they depend on prodigious consumption of resources in order to function, are most characteristic of the postwar petroleum culture and have been the linchpin of its economic viability. During the turbulent economic expansion after World War II, companies could confidently go on building newer, larger facilities based on the assumption that people would still want to acquire more and more products. But now many are saying that "it ain't necessarily so" that more is better. The rules of the game have changed, and in the aftermath of this discovery, demand has not kept up with the burgeoning productive capacity of the linchpin industries, those most geared toward consuming large amounts of resources to create their products. So a gap has emerged.

The ones hardest hit were those whose operations were the least sophisticated, meaning the manufacturers and agricultural producers who limited themselves to turning out basic commodities in volume. The 1980–83 recession had particularly woeful consequences for companies involved in the basic processing or acquisition of agricultural products, steel, and other basic resources. Even a country with an economy as fundamentally healthy as Japan's saw its demand for resources of various kinds dip precipitously, forcing factories that processed steel, nonferrous metals, petrochemicals, cement, timber, oil, and related products to curtail drastically their operations. Processors of raw materials in the United States and the European nations were even more hard hit. The industries that service the processors of raw materials, meaning those involved with marine shipping, construction, and shipbuilding, also were depressed. Overall, the most salient characteristic of the 1980–83 recession is that it hit most strongly the manufacturers of basic materials (see Table 1).

By the summer of 1983 the world economy, led by the United States, was starting to get back on its feet once again. But many facets of the economy that emerged from the recov-

Table 1: Petroleum Consumption by the Major Nations
(In millions of barrels)

YEAR / COUNTRY	United States	England	France	West Germany	Japan	U.S.S.R.	China
1960	3,577	343	204	230	241	869	62
1965	4,201	544	398	588	635	1,318	84
1970	5,366	763	690	887	1,405	1,934	226
1971	5,522	763	748	953	1,526	2,427	288
1972	5,975	818	814	1,007	1,591	2,226	232
1973	6,318	840	883	1,066	1,851	2,398	409
1974	6,077	781	825	953	1,810	2,559	504
1975	5,957	683	781	916	1,642	2,727	577
1976	6,373	679	832	989	1,741	2,792	613
1977	6,727	686	814	1,037	1,909	2,986	668
1978	6,880	675	792	1,113	1,876	3,092	661
1979	6,756	704	872	1,121	2,000	3,132	675
1980	6,277	632	825	989	1,810	3,252	668
1981	5,826	585	725	891	1,680		638
1982	5,567	606	712	884	1,565		
1983	5,382	560	686	854	1,602		
1984	5,545	672	666	856	1,665		

Source: U.S. Department of Energy, Energy Information Administration, *International Petroleum Annual* (Washington, D.C.: various years) and *1981 International Energy Annual* (Washington, D.C.: 1982); 1981–82 data are preliminary estimates by Worldwatch Institute.

ery process were markedly different from their counterparts in the economy of the postwar petroleum culture. Recovery of demand for raw materials and resources did not keep pace with the rate of recovery of the economy as a whole. Nor was there much growth in the demand for basic materials like steel, nonferrous metals, or cement in either Japan or the United States.

A sustained slump in the international commodities market for resources, agricultural products, and raw materials was another unprecedented feature of the postrecovery economy. In the past, a recovery in world commodity prices was considered inevitable once the global economy started to regain momentum. This time prices did not follow the familiar pattern; on the contrary, as recovery for the economy at large went into full swing in 1984, commodity prices actually sank, and some plummeted so far that the bottom went out of the market and chaos set in. Petroleum was no exception, with prices dropping to unprecedented depths despite OPEC's resistance; the same held true for gold, silver, tin, timber, sugar, wheat, and corn.

There are few if any precedents for this phenomenon in previous business cycles. Insofar as economists had based their theories on knowledge of the behavior of industrial economies as these had behaved up till then, their forecasts were largely off the mark. Virtually all had foreseen U.S. commodity prices climbing much more than they did; they did not foresee that the prices of resources and raw materials would remain in a slump.

A third facet of economic behavior for which no precedent could be found involved interest rates. This striking phenomenon was mainly observed in the United States. In past business cycles, it had been typical for investment and consumption to really start to climb again only after interest rates reached a low level; the rates would then rise as recovery was achieved, but only after a certain time lag. In the early 1980s, however, a rapid recovery swung into high gear even as the interest rates in metropolitan banks remained as high as 13–14 percent; and, even after full recovery was achieved, interest rates remained low.

American economists also erred by badly underestimating the rate of economic recovery in the first half of 1984, probably as a result of their outdated preconception that no serious economic growth could occur while interest rates were over 10 percent. At this point, an economics founded in theories based on observation of industrial society is not only proving inadequate for those seeking a foundation for sound economic policy; it will not even suffice as a basis for short-term business forecasts.

The fourth and final unprecedented aspect of the economic phenomena observed in the early 1980s was in fact the driving force behind the others: it was the booming prosperity of certain smaller businesses. These have also enjoyed gains in Europe and Japan, but the archetype of this new phenomenon is to be observed in the United States. Even in the darkest hours of the early 1980s, small businesses were being started up there at a rate ten times that seen at any time during the 1950s. That these did not service the moribund producers or processors of raw materials nor the giant industrial corporations goes without saying. The great majority were active in electronics, both in hardware and associated software; the remainder dealt with service, distribution, information, or design-related occupations. Japan has also seen new growth industries spring up at an unprecedented rate in these categories, despite the retarded rate of overall economic growth that set in after the oil shock.

It is the small to medium-sized businesses, operating in the above-mentioned fields, that played the major role in the business recovery of the 1980s, even as those linchpins of the petroleum culture, the industrial giants that processed raw materials and turned out machines and therefore depended upon the economy of scale, have found themselves gradually being phased out. It is clear that the issue of who among the major players in the industrial economy will play the dominant role is resolving itself differently than it has in the past.

While there is no doubt that there will continue to be waves of prosperity and recession in the future, and that demand for resources and raw materials will fluctuate in response to this, we can rest assured that over the long term, demand for these items is not going to keep pace with the rate of economic growth. Once people began to distance themselves from the notion that "using up more and more stuff" was in good taste, it became a foregone and virtually irresistible conclusion that demand would drop.

The peak of the postwar petroleum culture is behind us. We have begun the descent.

Signs That the Industrial Society Is Dying

The postwar petroleum culture, the zenith of everything the industrial society stands for, has passed its peak and is going downhill fast; this tells us that the industrial society itself is in its death throes. We can say this because so many things happened during the 1980s that represent a complete reversal of the tendencies most characteristic of the industrial society, including the direction of technological development itself.

Ever since the industrial revolution, most technological development has been devoted to maximizing the scale, volume, and speed of production. Blast furnaces, chemical plants, and the presses used to turn out machine parts have been built on an ever larger scale, even as ships and planes got bigger and bigger. Office building and hotel construction has cleaved to the same pattern. Most of the emphasis in computer development through the 1970s was on enlarging mainframe capacity. And while we might take it for granted that industrial technology development would set its sights on expanding scale and volume through mass production, it seems that such expansion was also the target of developments in entertainment, information, and "life-style" products and services.

Maximizing the speed with which an operation could be completed was another major goal of technology during this period. Engineers recognized no limits in the pursuit of greater speed of operation for everything from looms to steel mills and airplanes. For those running companies devoted to products whose heyday of development was clearly past, like the railroads, increasing the speed of operations was a way to move forward and try to capture the imagination of the consumer; the like held true for the makers of electric stoves and other appliances, who scored a big hit by introducing the microwave oven. Whenever people talked about what to look forward to in new technology during this period, the discussion would include the prospect of even faster supersonic jets and Japan's dream project of developing magnetically suspended high speed trains.

There was, of course, some technological progress devoted to increasing efficiency in order to save on energy consumption, but the resources and staff allotted to such research was less than a tenth of that committed to increasing the scale, volume, and speed of operations during the same period. In the late 1970s when I worked at the Industrial Technology Institute of the Ministry of International Trade and Industry, what most captured the imaginations of our top researchers was still technological research into how to achieve greater volume and speed; energy conservation research was still considered the province of second- and third-rate researchers willing to do on-the-spot fieldwork.

The picture was not much different in the research labs run by the universities, in the telecommunications firms, the national railway system, or private companies. Over 70 percent of the budget for research and development at the Technology Institute operated by Japan National Railways (JNR) was spent on its efforts to create an ever faster bullet train and to bring to fruition its pet project of a magnetic "hover train"; only puny amounts were committed to improving the parts of the system already in operation. Under such circumstances, to be involved in speed research at JNR was the pinnacle for researchers and technicians.

For Japan and for the West as well, the prevailing outlook on these matters underwent a singular change in 1980. No longer do we see significant energy devoted to developing giant blast furnaces or tankers that can carry more than fifty thousand tons. Developing a train that can travel over 700 miles per hour no longer seems realistic, and even in aeronautics, a field where finding ways to get there faster is its reason to exist, the race to develop an aircraft even faster than the Concorde is on hold; indeed, the Concorde's viability as a form of transport is itself being questioned.

Even in weapons technology, where economic feasibility is not the driving force, the push for bigger, faster weaponry has ground to an almost complete halt. No plans are afloat to build a warship larger than the Nimitz line of aircraft carriers, nor is a program under way to develop fighter planes that can fly faster than Mach 3. Even nuclear weapons, which only seemed to get bigger and bigger with the years, are now designed for systems that emphasize numbers over size, so that warheads with force greater than a megaton have come to seem anachronistic.

Current research and development tends instead to revolve around finding new ways to save energy, to create more adaptable and multifunctional products, and to disseminate information. The steps taken to reduce weight and conserve on energy in automobile and ship design are already well known, and similar advances aimed at energy conservation in building and home design are being sought and achieved. The introduction of sophisticated industrial robots into the factory production process and the use of LSI (large scale integration), IC (integrated circuits), and computer technology to create "intelligent" products have made possible far greater diversification and flexibility in terms of what reaches the customer than was the case when greater economy through standardization was the ruling principle. In the computer field itself, efforts to develop supercomputers with even greater capacities have not ceased, but what is spectacular about the last decade is the rapid development and diffusion of increasingly sophisticated and reliable models for use in offices and homes. During the 1970s, the dream that in the future a single, gigantic computer could be linked to terminals in every corner of Japan that would then access it through a complex system of time-sharing seemed practical and worthy to virtually everyone; but this is another case where an idea founded in "big" thinking has been discarded as grandiose and unrealistic.

Dubbing this move toward a new kind of technological innovation a "shift from a hard to a Holonic path," Professor Takemochi Ishii of Tokyo University has suggested that it marks a major break with the notions of technological progress that have prevailed in industrial society. Since until now, such progress has been considered mankind's greatest achievement in the twentieth century, any major reassessment of its purpose and direction must be accorded the utmost significance as we attempt to predict what sort of society is to follow this one.

One point we must not overlook is that this change in what people expect from new technology has not come about simply as the direct and inevitable consequence of technological progress itself. That computers and industrial robots have done much to make diversified production a possibility is indisputable. They have also made it much easier to achieve energy savings and to disseminate information. But one should not construe this to mean that once computers were introduced into the factory, producers could adapt and diversify their products without incurring additional costs; in fact, producers in areas where computers cannot be relied upon much to control the costs of diversification have nonetheless felt compelled to diversify.

As an example, consider that in Japan over the past ten years the number of types of containers in which beer is sold has shot up from eight to over 130 types. It is said that as a result, the costs involved in brewing and distributing beer in Japan have increased by some 20 percent. Since this tendency to diversify product offerings has been even more pronounced what it comes to fast foods and designer clothing, it is not unreasonable to suppose that those who produce these products have incurred yet higher costs in diversifying. Even in the case of that most representative product of the mass production phase of the industrial era, the automobile, so many more variations in available body styles, interior decor, and colors have been introduced that the costs of these have outstripped the savings achieved through robotization of the assembly process to an extent that is anything but negligible.

These facts suggest that diversification of product lines first became a trend not because this was suddenly an economically feasible option due to technological progress, but because what customers wanted—their notions of what was tasteful—changed. Producers then adapted to these needs by developing the requisite technology, with the consequence that consumers, having found out how easily their desires could be accommodated, were stimulated to develop yet more specific and diverse desires, and so on back and forth, creating an entirely new kind of business environment. The global business environment has thus come full circle, reversing the logic of the business environment that had prevailed during the boom years of the industrial economy, when consumers believed that more was inevitably better and producers pulled out all the stops to accommodate them by maximizing size, volume, and speed. In his 1988 book, *The New Realities*, Peter Drucker painstakingly collected numerous examples of 1980s phenomena in any number of fields that cannot be explained in terms of the economic and administrative principles we now use. Should this trend continue, not only will the end of the industrial society be its inevitable consequence, but a truly different society is certain to emerge.

Enlightened Self-Interest Once Again Comes into Play

The time has come to ask, What next?

My main purpose here is, after all, not simply to forecast the demise of industrial society, but to give a sense of its sequel, the society to follow. And while I intend to concentrate on providing a detailed answer to this question in chapter 4, I feel that at this point a rough outline of the transformation of society, and the worldview that will emerge from it, are called for. This is, of course, no simple task. Theories and research based on observations of industrial society are of little use in this context, and existing concepts fail to provide sufficient illumination. The fact is, if one hopes to come to grips with an entirely new type of society, an utterly different conceptual framework must be developed. The painful and awkward task of creating a new vocabulary and theoretical framework must be embraced. At the very least, we will need to look into the vicissitudes and transformations undergone by the civilizations and economic social orders that preceded the industrial society, hoping to find there a broader perspective than our current one.

To prepare us for this task, I wish to consider the workings of that empathetic impulse that acts as the agent of the most basic and profound social changes.

Earlier I described how it was enlightened self-interest, guided by the empathetic impulse, that led man to find it becoming and tasteful to use up plenty of whatever existed in abundance. History shows us that in all times and places, the empathetic impulse is a driving force. It was the workings of the empathetic impulse that brought into being not only the postwar petroleum culture, but the industrial society itself.

It follows, then, that if we wish to know what kind of world is in store for us as society enters the next phase, we would be wise to ask the question, What commodity or item will exist in abundance from here on in? The answer to that question should tell us a great deal about the society to come.

What we are likely to possess a bountiful supply of is wisdom—defined in the broadest possible terms so that "knowledge" and "information" are included in its range of meanings.

The stores of what we call wisdom increase as human knowledge and experience accumulate, and are disseminated through the education systems and information and communication networks we have developed, even as the ways in which people perceive and discern this data are perpetually adapting and reforming what we call wisdom. Now, however, we have suddenly arrived at a stage where, due to wave after wave of breakthroughs in computer and communications technology, the means exist to store, process, and disseminate wisdom on an incomparably vaster scale than was possible before. Particularly in the last several years, as personal computers and office computers and the communications technology to link them have been developed and integrated into our lifestyles, there has been a virtual explosion in the amount of information we find ourselves dealing with at home and at work.

The commodity of which we now have an abundant supply is, in other words, wisdom. It therefore follows that in the new society that is now forming, the life-style that will earn the most respect will be one in which the owner's conspicuous consumption of wisdom (in the broadest sense) is displayed, while the products that will sell best will be those that reveal their purchaser to be a person "in the know." Such products, which more than anything else manifest their owner's access to the best knowledge, information, and accumulated wisdom to be had, possess what I will hereafter refer to as "knowledge-value." It is my contention that we are entering a new phase of civilization in which the value attached to knowledge is the driving force, and that is why I have dubbed this next phase the era of the knowledge-value society.

Products That Function as Containers or Vehicles for Knowledge-Value

How shall we account for the value of wisdom as a component in a product's manufacture? What exactly is knowledge-value? These questions are currently provoking much consternation among economists and other commentators, including critics. Not a few of them emphasize the importance of something that corresponds to knowledge-value in their writings, but most perceive it as a factor only in products created to meet the needs of consumers in the education or information industries, and describe it in terms of moving from hardware to software, or into intangible goods. Describing what is in fact a major social transformation in such a simplistic manner makes it that much more difficult for people to grasp; furthermore, it provokes those in the establishment media with a vested interest in the status quo of the industrial society to lash out against a trend that seems sure to threaten their holdings.

Certainly there is no disputing that the "education and information industries" (keeping in mind that such vague and ill-defined usage blurs vital distinctions) are in the business of selling a brand of knowledge-value. As such, they can be expected to prosper in the years ahead. But the prosperity they enjoy and the share of the economy they will command, as industries selling knowledge-value per se, is not going to be all that much greater than that enjoyed by other sectors of the economy where literal knowledge-value is not the commodity being offered.

But in the vast majority of cases, the demand for knowledge-value will be met, say, by products in whose unique designs it is manifest, or by procurers of highly specialized services that can draw on a long tradition in order to respond precisely to customer needs.

Assume that one is about to purchase a necktie. If the product chosen has a world-famous brand name like Hermès or Dunhill and the purchase is carried out in Tokyo, the price could run to over 20,000 yen ($135). Buy a generic necktie made from the same material, however, and the price drops to 4,000 yen (about $27). Even without going to the extreme of requesting something highly unique and unusual, it is possible to encounter a discrepancy in price of 500 percent between two neckties made from the same type of material. Yet a close examination will reveal little if any difference in terms of the energy or resources expended to make the product or in the weaving, dyeing, or stitching that went into its manufacture. Nor will the Hermès necktie turn out to be three times longer, or specially embroidered, or otherwise notably different. Yet it commands five times the price. And many are more than willing to buy such neckties, although nobody is forcing them to do so. That a brand-name necktie should cost $135 is, in other words, a socially recognized fact.

The necktie contains something of value in excess of the costs expended on its materials or manufacture. What is it?

It is the fact that when one buys a necktie from this company one can be secure in the knowledge that the product's image is recognized to be excellent and that its superior design will reflect the collective wisdom of those associated with the firm that has created it. The brand name, in other words, has knowledge-value; one is recognized as wise for having purchased a product that reflects the accumulated wisdom of its makers.

Comparable examples could be presented for products that manifest new technological breakthroughs or unique new materials, or have capabilities as yet unavailable in other products. When products are acknowledged to possess some unique new technical feature, it is not at all unusual for them to be sold at a price many times what it costs to turn them out. With some products, the manufacturers have been able to double or triple the asking price simply because they have conspicuously deployed some unique new material in a few small but noticeable spots. Other products which cater to the fetishes of consumers obsessed with possessing "cutting edge" technology can command absolutely surreal prices by incorporating some minor function no other company is yet offering. The service and entertainment industries also present many instances where a unique or distinctive service is marketed with great success despite the high cost. Each of these examples is a manifestation of the premium attached to knowledge-value.

That people have increased their appreciation of knowledge-value as a variable in product appeal does not necessarily mean that they are rejecting material things as such. I will address this issue in greater detail later, but for now let me state that the significance of material goods as containers or vehicles for knowledge-value is undeniable. The issue for us is to measure the extent to which knowledge-value has surged in significance in the perception of what a product is worth.

At this point, some readers are probably saying to themselves, "Wait a minute, this is nothing new. Economists have always looked at how art objects and jewelry are priced, which also has almost nothing to do with the physical cost of producing them, and they recognized that such products were exceptions to the usual principles involved in pricing. It's obviously happened before."

I have no quarrel with this statement. But in the knowledge-value society that is emerging, such valuation will no longer be the exception but the rule; it will not be the occasional product that commands a high price because it has knowledge-value; virtually all products will be evaluated on this basis. It will be the standard rationale understood and acknowledged by everyone, the assumption on which the social structure is founded and in accordance with which individuals behave.

People sense that wisdom or information (that is to say, knowledge) is the commodity that exists in greatest abundance now, and are thus driven by enlightened self-interest to make the most of it, for they can safely assume that if they draw on the supply of knowledge, there will still be more where that came from.

What gives a society its identity, what makes it what it is or determines what it becomes, is not simply the sum of what it has or what exists in it, but what it has in it that it considers important. What is the general paradigm of that society? is the question that must be asked if we wish to comprehend its essence.

Harbingers of the Knowledge-Value Revolution

Even in the industrial society we have known up to now, the prices for certain items such as works of art, high-fashion clothing or accessories, or cutting-edge technology bore little or no relationship to the basic costs of the materials or the manufacturing process involved; those who produced them have been able to demand much higher prices than if they'd based pricing on manufacturing costs. These goods could thus be said to possess a kind of knowledge-value.

However, such products have been rare and extreme exceptions to the general rule and have only tended to manifest themselves under unusual circumstances. But in the type of society we are moving toward, a society where everything revolves around knowledge-value, it is likely that the major portion of the value or price ascribed to a product will be based on knowledge-value factors, and those who hope to create products that draw a good price will be mainly concerned with incorporating as much knowledge-value into a product as they can.

Such a change will fundamentally alter the world in which we live. To begin with, there will obviously be a shift away from standardized production of standardized goods, toward a system that will turn out a greater variety of goods but will turn out each type in smaller quantities. Knowledge-value in a product derives, after all, from factors that tangibly set it apart from other products available in the marketplace. Furthermore, whenever a producer succeeds in making a killing by cultivating a new form of knowledge-value into his product, we can be certain that his competitors will soon leap into the fray trumpeting other forms of knowledge-value that they will insist are "better yet"; the inevitable consequence of such competition will be a system that offers ever increasing diversification of product lines in conjunction with a tendency to keep reducing the costs involved in offering new product lines. Such intense competition is likely, at the same time, to create an environment in which the "boom" enjoyed by any popular product or technological innovation keeps getting shorter and shorter. Our world will be one in which new designs, technological innovations, and products that offer new and unique combinations of functions are constantly being introduced only to be superseded by yet newer offerings, so that knowledge-value itself, like petroleum before it, becomes a disposable commodity to be used up and thrown out as rapidly as possible.

The surge in product diversification and information technology that ushered in the 1980s can be seen as the precursor of a major shift away from standardized mass production toward a manufacturing sector that is more heterogeneous and where individual operations tend to be smaller in scale. We can see evidence for this trend in the proliferation of smaller firms (known in Japan as "venture businesses") that have recently enjoyed enormous success and rapid growth by developing products with knowledge-value. In the cultural sphere, the iron grip of modernism has been broken, while the tendency for a particular star or the latest trend or fad to utterly dominate the public imagination seems to have weakened considerably. There are, in other words, enough signs on the horizon for us to safely declare that the great transformation into a knowledge-value society that has given this book its title is well under way.

Why should this now be the case? Because knowledge-value, by its very nature, requires a highly subjective society in order to take hold. We must remember that the resources, agricultural products, raw materials, and other basic commodities that formed the very foundation on which the industrial society was created all tend to have fixed, stable values. For example, the use to which one puts a bushel of rice, say, or a ton of steel, or a bolt of cloth tends to be the same all over and therefore both the utility and the value of such commodities or products is more or less stable and fixed, even if the price may fluctuate in response to supply and demand factors. It follows that if at some point the price rises far out of proportion to the genuine value of such commodities, it is very likely to afterward drop in rough proportion to the extent that the product was previously overvalued. In other words, the value of the products remains more or less centered in the long run, even if their prices hop up and down in accordance with market fluctuations. That the long-term pattern will be a stable one can be safely postulated.

If the main items being produced are either resources and raw materials of the type I have just described, or mass-produced standardized products created by processing such materials, then the means by which they are produced—the facilities and the processes being carried out in those facilities—will also have a value in and of itself, to which a more or less stable price can and will be ascribed. Certainly this is the case with the fields in which rice is grown, just as it is for the blast furnaces in which steel is produced or the looms on which cloth is spun. Whether or not a recession at a given moment means that the producers of cotton or steel incur some losses in the short run, it can be assumed that before long there will be a recovery that will make producing these commodities once again profitable.

However, the same cannot be said for knowledge-value products. Take the designer neckties that were fashionable last year and commanded a price in the range of 20,000 yen at the time. If such ties are no longer trendy, there's a good chance they will turn up in the bargain basement on sale for something like 4,000 yen. In other words, the knowledge-value for which consumers were once willing to pay an additional 16,000 yen is now of no worth whatsoever. Under such circumstances, it is safe to presume that even though the price has dropped to one-fifth the level of a year ago, nobody is going to swoop in and buy up huge numbers of these ties in the expectation that they will once again be worth five times the price they currently command.

What is true for fashion items like neckties also holds true when it comes to the marketplace for new technologies and functions. Even if a company rakes in large profits by intro ducing some spectacular piece of new technology, the time will soon come when a competitor does them one better, at which point the price commanded by the suddenly obsolete product will abruptly drop through the floor. With products like software for personal computers, this sort of thing is in fact happening all the time.

In short, not only is knowledge-value a variable subject to intense fluctuation, but each of its manifestations tends to be a transitory, one-shot phenomenon. And even more important: the figures who create knowledge-value tend to lose their viability and value due to changing trends in fashion and technology.

Take the case of a designer whose designs were well received at one time. For a company to have grabbed up such an individual and experienced thereby a tremendous surge in growth that established the firm as a major force in the fashion business is not a rare occurrence. But if the designer's creations lose their appeal after a number of years have passed, not only can the firm find itself with a lot of goods it can't sell; the firm itself can lose its credibility and lose its chance to have any role in creating further knowledge-value.

The same can be said for virtually any type of operation involved in generating knowledge-value, whether it be developing new technology, or products, or corporate planning, or artistic production, or entertainment, because each of these functions involves creativity. The transitory nature of knowledge-value is linked to the transitory nature of the creative process itself.

In a society in which the limitless diversity and transitory nature that characterize knowledge-value form the strongest current, the economic environment will be harsh and unforgiving, characterized by a boom-or-bust psychology that will play havoc with lax or lackluster enterprises. However, this highly competitive process in which winners win big and losers lose everything can serve as the means to drive society to ever greater heights of achievement and to fulfill the desires of the people.

The Major Changes in Social Structure That Accompany Transformation of the Economic Order

What is unique about knowledge-value as I have described it is that human beings create it. And a unique facet of the knowledge-value society—one that distinguishes it from the industrial society—is its tendency to unite labor and the means of production.

What brought the industrial society completely into its own was the industrial revolution. First taking hold in England in the late eighteenth century, it spread to Western Europe, America, and Japan by the mid-nineteenth century in the form of factory-based industrial production, which became a feature common to all those societies. This is the generally accepted explanation of the phenomenon and one with which I concur.

There were, however, numerous major breakthroughs in technology that occurred both before and after the development of factory-based production. Thus we might well ask why this particular moment in an ongoing process is invariably pinpointed as the onset of the industrial revolution. Factory-based production was not simply a matter of rapid technological progress; rather, because it entailed the separation of labor and the means of production, it led to a fundamental transformation of the structure of society.

During the medieval era and afterward, the means of production most in use were agriculture (with farmers employing their own tools on lands they had been given the right to cultivate), handicrafts (for which the artisans possessed the needed tools), and commerce (practiced by merchants who sold out of their own stories or peddlers who owned the carts and horses from which they hawked their wares). So while there may have been quite a few exceptions, overall the dominant means of production of this period was one in which he who possessed the labor also possessed the specific right (if not the actual property in the modern sense, for the operating principles were different) to employ the land and/or tools essential to his particular method of production; at the same time, those rights he possessed also bound him to practicing that profession and no other.

But the industrial revolution that began in England in the nineteenth century and then spread to Western Europe, America, and Japan, by giving rise to a factory-based form of industry employing enormous machines driven by steam power, created a situation in which labor and the means of production were estranged from one another. This initiated the polarization Marx described between the capitalists who own the means of production and a free labor force that possesses nothing but the services it can offer.

What the industrial revolution brought about, then, was not simply a new form of technology or a shift in the means of production, but a radical, all-encompassing transformation of society. Its momentum was such that each new development—the introduction of the internal combustion engine, or electric power, or the birth of the chemical industry—did not reverse the impact of these major changes but only reinforced them. The means of production—that is, the facilities of the modern industrial factory—grew enormously in scale and cost, which made it harder and harder for individuals and family units to operate or finance such facilities, since they could not

expand to accommodate the changing conditions and requirements of operation. Indeed, for a long time after the industrial
revolution, each technological breakthrough or innovation
only tended to make society conform more completely to the
outline of characteristics particular to the industrial society;
these breakthroughs did nothing to alter the pattern that had
been established.

But what about the knowledge-value society toward which
we are moving? What are the means of production or tools
employed by those engaged in the ongoing pursuit of sup-
planting and increasing knowledge-value? A designer needs a
desk and the pencils, triangles, and other tools to draft blueprints. Cameramen and photographers need their cameras.
Most computer software designers require only a small-scale
computer to carry out their designs. The tools needed to carry
out any of these functions are not that prohibitively expensive. Acquiring them involves costs that are more than reasonably manageable for individuals. Even corporations constructing facilities to develop new technology or product lines have
been less inclined to build enormous laboratories in recent
years; more and more, they are going with medium- or even
small-scale research labs, and building them in town rather
than in gigantic industrial parks at the edge of nowhere. The
direction and prevailing notion of technological progress is
moving away from the "big science" that was obsessed with
maximizing scale, volume, and speed, toward a notion of technology in which diversification, efficiency, and integration of
multiple functions is to be desired.

In the end, the most important means of production for
creating knowledge-value is the individual mind, and those
who are charged with generating it must strive to bring to bear
as much knowledge, experience, and perception as they can.
Creating knowledge-value is a pursuit in which labor and the

means of production have become inseparably wedded; the worker *is* the means of production.

Assuming that the number of workers involved in the task of creating knowledge-value is going to increase, it is likely that the opposition between labor and the means of production that has been an enduring feature of the industrial revolution will now start to break down and reverse itself, so that a new conception of production in which the two elements are reconciled and consolidated will prevail in society in the future. This means, of course, a reversal of everything the industrial society stood for. How it will alter the structure of society is a point I will address in detail in chapter 4, but it goes without saying that the change will have enormous ramifications for the various economic institutions and for the way people view the government.

I contend that the changes that began the 1980s portend not simply a more advanced industrial economy but the beginnings of a transition toward a new kind of society, because I believe that the transformation that has now begun will not be limited to technological innovations or changes in the industrial structure, but will fundamentally alter the very structure of the society itself. In that sense, the changes now under way in Japan and the United States amount to the most important transformation that has occurred in the two hundred years since the industrial revolution began. This is why I have chosen to refer to this transformation as the knowledge-value revolution.

The events of the last several years, since the first (Japanese) edition of this book was published in December 1985, seem to me to accord almost entirely with my forecasts then.

Interest rates in Japan shot up in the fall of 1985, whereupon those industries that rely on raw materials went into a tailspin, while consumer demand for the highest-quality brand names and products skyrocketed. At the same time, the consumers' tendency to demand greater variety in products intensified, and the trend toward offering numerous variations (with a shorter production run for each of the variants) on a product became that much more pronounced. At this point in time (1990), Japan's greatest economic difficulty is that it lacks the system and the ability to easily diversify the products it supplies to accommodate the greater specificity and diversity of consumer demands. As I will explain in some detail in later chapters, the social structure that Japan has evolved, which ideally suited it for modern industrial mass production, ill-suits the country when it comes to cultivating the type of individualized creativity essential to developing the diverse forms of knowledge-value it will need to compete effectively as we move into the next phase.

The American experience during the second half of the 1980s was somewhat different from Japan's. That the dollar weakened as the yen and the Deutschemark climbed in value gave American industry a competitive advantage in the international marketplace. In spite of this, however, the productivity and employment figures for American industry did not grow to the extent anticipated. Even after the dollar fell, increases in employment and productivity were largely confined to the sectors of the economy where white-collar workers are involved in producing knowledge-value; I am referring to research and development, communications, the information industry, finance, design, and real estate. These increases are probably due to the fact that in America, which is further along in the knowledge-value renovation than Japan is at present, rolling up one's sleeves and going to work in a factory environment devoted to turning out commodities or standardized products is a prospect that is losing its appeal for young Americans entering the work force.

The second half of the 1980s was a period of worldwide economic prosperity. Nevertheless, the growth and surpluses in the supply of resources and agricultural products did not mean that the prices for these commodities once again underwent the volatile fluctuations of the 1960s. Though prices for many resources did come down, people did not revert to thinking that the life-style which involved maximum consumption was the epitome of good taste, as they had believed in the days when the industrial society was at its zenith.

On the contrary, as can be seen from the growing concern over global environmental issues, the sense that there is a material limit on how much we should produce and consume is getting stronger. If Iraq's behavior in Kuwait results in genuine uncertainty about the oil supply (something that can only be judged over the long term), this sense of limits on consumption is likely to be powerfully enforced.

But if we are looking for the single most powerful illustration of the fact that the tastes and beliefs of the industrial society are on the way out with the end of the 1980s, the collapse of faith in the socialist administrations of the Eastern bloc and the Soviet Union probably provides the most potent example. As I will describe in greater detail later, socialism, and its sacred trinity of idealism, the planned economy, and one-party rule, was one of the ultimate expressions of modern industrial ideology in that it believed that mankind could evolve into an *Homo economicus* ("economic man") capable of behaving with objective rationality. The socialist system was an attempt to implement concretely this vision in administrative terms and as such, it proved ill-equipped either to create knowledge-value, which relies to a great extent on subjectivity, or to deal with the diversification of consumer demands that is characteristic of the emerging knowledge-value society.

The Knowledge-Value Revolution Has Begun

When we survey the various phenomena that occurred during the second half of the 1980s, it appears that the knowledge-value revolution is spreading throughout the world. Like any major social and economic transformation, this revolution is not likely to run its course quickly; we should expect, rather, that it will take years before the knowledge-value revolution is completed in any absolute sense. There will in all likelihood be some periods when the changes come thick and fast and others when they grind to a halt; there may even be times when we seem to be reverting to the values of the industrial society. But I am certain that when we look at the big picture, the overall movement will be one that is carrying us away from the industrial society and toward a knowledge-value society.

We have postulated that the industrial society began with the industrial revolution. This does not mean, however, that at the onset of this revolution, the cumulative value of industrial production exceeded that of agriculture, or that workers outnumbered farmers. Rather, the industrial revolution served as the trigger whereby the modern factory-based production system became the mainspring of economic growth and capital accumulation. The first step was taken down the path toward industrial society.

When the transitional process is viewed in this light, can it not be said that the knowledge-value revolution began in the 1980s? I do not mean to imply that the volume of knowledge-value products will soon exceed the volume produced by traditional manufacturing; nor am I saying that the number of workers involved in creating knowledge-value products is about to become greater than the number working in manufacturing, or that such production, geared toward generating knowledge-value, is likely to emerge as the dominant form of production in our society in the immediate future. What is meant is that, as a result of the changes that occurred in the 1980s, the creation of knowledge-value is becoming the mainspring of economic growth and corporate profits, and that we have already begun to move away from the industrial society toward a knowledge-value society.

Changes in the resource environment, in population figures, and in technology will precipitate a rethinking of our notions of taste and ethical values, which in turn will induce a fundamental transformation in our social structure. Because such a structural transformation will give rise to enormous problems, the most critical issue to be addressed here is what sort of transformation it will be. In the knowledge-value society, we can expect to encounter patterns utterly different from those of the industrial society we have grown up in, which means that our current system of knowledge, predicated as it is on observations of the society we know, will be of little avail. At the least, we must broaden the range of our research to incorporate observations and consideration of the human civilizations that preceded the industrial society.

What we must be prepared to undertake, then, is a journey back into history to seek out the factors that set the patterns for various human civilizations and to examine closely those "disruptive elements" that act as catalysts to overthrow and replace such patterns for particular societies. To free ourselves to perceive the conceptual outlines of the society that is emerging, we must be prepared to transcend the limits imposed by the matrix of "common sense" and theory of the industrial society from which we sprang. To this end, I believe it is important to examine those societies that existed over a long period of time with parameters very different from those of the industrial society.

2

Seeking Out the Disrupters of the Established Order

THE UNCERTAIN FUTURE

The two oil shocks of the 1970s made that decade a turning point for the idea that resources are finite. Suddenly the notion that energy, resources, and agricultural products existed in boundless abundance became untenable. Many people, feeling we were about to enter an era of chronic shortages, were overcome by dread every time the news reported a short-term bottleneck in the supply of some item. Environmental problems on both the regional and global scale put further pressure on people to recognize the limits on material consumption.

The empathetic impulse that impels man to find attractive the idea of using up a surfeit and economizing on a scarcity proved acutely responsive to the new situation. By the 1980s, the orthodoxy of the postwar petroleum culture went into decline. The thirty years of infatuation with "faster, bigger, more" peaked and reversed gear: consumers were suddenly anxious for "light/thin/short/small," and companies worked to increase the amount of variety and intelligence built into their product lines.

In various fields of art there had already been something of a critical and artistic reaction against the emphasis on physical comfort and convenience characteristic of modernism; but under the label Postmodernism, this reaction grew to mainstream status. On both the technical and artistic levels, the drive to burn up ever more energy and resources has died out, and the main thrust has shifted toward a concentrated effort to fulfill internal, psychological needs.

As people of the modern age we have called anything that made possible the supply of more material goods *modern* and *rational* while disparaging and casting out anything that did not as *archaic* and *irrational*. Our political and educational systems, our business organizations, and our families have all concurred in adopting such attitudes. Since we were taught about the industrial society and its social paradigms as soon as we became aware of things, any inclination we might have developed to question these assumptions was nipped in the bud. Indeed, we have been drawn into thinking of the modern form of civilization, based on the social paradigms of the industrial society, as eternal, unchanging, relevant, and universal for all people throughout the world.

However, the fact that our drive to use up more energy, resources, and farm products began to fall off during the 1980s means that the very underpinnings of industrial society—its notions of taste and its ethical norms—have been discredited. This is not a matter that will end simply by changing our modes of production and product lines or the directions in which science and the arts are developing, although such changes are already under way. The social paradigm itself must in the end be fundamentally transformed. That change, when it is realized, will mean the end of the industrial society and the emergence of a different society.

What will the society to come be like? The time required to complete the transformation is likely to be so great as to need to be calculated in terms of centuries, which makes the attempt to elucidate what form it will finally take—based on the few short years of changes we have witnessed so far—seem a daunting and somewhat rash undertaking. I believe that there are, however, important clues that can aid us in this task.

Man possesses a recorded history stretching back some six thousand years during which he has experienced comparably great changes many times.

If we scan the extensive records of this history in search of the factors that accompany significant cultural transitions, we may, by observing these factors under current conditions, arrive at a sense of the next society's basic outline. What we are really looking for are those prophetic disrupters of the established order whose "desecrations" of civilization began to appear when a major change was in the wings. By sizing up the state of these disrupters today and what desecrations they seem likely to wreak, we can make some educated guesses about the future.

The society to come will not be an industrial society. Accordingly, it will be impossible to predict or comprehend the form of the society to come on the basis of observations or standards or the intellectual systems proper to the industrial society alone. Nor will the standards or intellectual systems of societies that preceded our own be of much use. The best we can hope for is to get an understanding of how the disrupters of the established order that precipitated change in particular civilizations came to trigger the transformation processes, and then to understand and identify the processes themselves.

If we succeed in drawing up a model of these interactions and the processes by which they evolve, and feed into the model various factors that represent the current status of the disruptive elements, we should get some clear signals as to what lies ahead. There is no disputing that this is a most unreliable method, but in a period of such cataclysmic change I feel that in spite of everything an effort must be made to meet this challenge.

A Viewpoint from Which to Approach Social Change

It soon becomes clear to any reader who tries to unravel the strands of human history that a number of distinct civilizations have come into being over the course of mankind's long travail and that each has evolved its own unique type of society. Modern historians have chosen to refer to these as "stages of development." Implicit in this choice of words is an attitude that is typical of modern man, the assumption that history is a progression, that human society is constantly advancing in its development. Despite this view, most historians feel obliged to designate the several hundred years of the early Middle Ages, the years after the fifth century A.D., as the Dark Ages, the decline of the glittering Classical Age. For no matter how positive a light any modern, industrial-age historian tries to cast upon the early Middle Ages, there is no way he can make them out to have been a period of "progressive development."

The standards applied to reach the conclusion that the period in question was one singularly lacking in positive ramifications are, of course, unique to modern man. To label the Middle Ages the "Dark Ages" is to judge the period by the ethical norms and notions of taste of modern man, which means defining progress as the increase in the volume of goods produced and consumed. For nothing about the Middle Ages was particularly well suited to the enterprise of increasing the volume of material things—not the thought, nor the code of conduct, nor the social system.

As far as the people of the medieval era were concerned, the greater material prosperity of the classical age was only part and parcel of what made that era "the dark age of godlessness." Their own tastes, ethos, and social paradigm were utterly different from those of modern man. It was not due to ignorance or sloth that the people of the middle ages forsook the scientific techniques and rational spirit of the classical age. It was, rather, that they aspired to what they perceived as a "more advanced state" that accorded with the "higher purpose" of existence to which they subscribed; to reach it, they had to discard what they felt were the vulgarities of the classical era.

The medieval perspective on the classical age that preceded it is important for us to bear in mind as we ruminate on the society to come after the industrial era. If the new society truly transcends the present one, then it cannot be judged by the standards and criteria of industrial society. We must rather try to imagine the ethics and tastes of those who will live in that next society.

In approaching history from the viewpoint I have just described, we must constantly bear in mind the importance of not letting ourselves get too caught up in the small details and minutiae of each era. Because so many individuals lived through the particular eras we will be examining, there will be a diverse body of facts available from each of these eras. One does not imagine that all the people alive in a given era had the same thoughts and behaved in the same way. For that reason, no region or era we choose to look at will present one single ethical outlook or one operative notion of taste that functions to the absolute exclusion of all others.

Nevertheless, for each of these diverse societies there is a dominant theme that we ought to be able to think of as the single governing paradigm for that society. For example, since modern society is dominated by the aesthetic principle that to consume more things is attractive, and by the moral principle that to supply more things is good and just, it conducts its business transactions on the basis of parity, or the principle that there should be a universal fixed price for each item, as opposed to barter. In reality, however, exceptions to this rule abound. Exceptions on the grand scale come about, for example, due to efforts to redress inequities among nations at the international level, while the small divergences from the parity principle can be glimpsed in such cases as political contributors or patrons of sumo wrestling, who give generously without knowing specifically what, if anything, they can expect in return. That such exceptions exist does not provide us with a basis for seriously questioning the notion that modern industrial society thinks of parity exchange as the proper basis for operating businesses as part of the social paradigm it has established.

It is the broad social paradigms that in this sense exemplify each era that we must seek. Since that is our purpose, I will limit my presentation to key periods in which particular societies reached their most characteristic form, and argue simply that those I present are good representative examples.

The period during which human societies and civilizations (even in those advanced regions that are in the vanguard of a particular era) assume the form that best exemplifies that epoch is actually quite short. Most of human history consists of a succession of stages in which the transition from the preceding society to the society to come is ongoing, and what I refer to as representative periods is no more than a momentary apotheosis in which the reality of a society most closely corresponds to a particular social concept. However, these periods of apotheosis are important to us in the current context because they mark the times when a social form based on a particular paradigm most explicitly realizes that paradigm.

Even in these terms, there are some problems with the concept of the historical apotheosis. In reality, these representative periods or apexes often do not occur at a single point in historical time. Among the various spheres of activity that taken together define a society, there are some spheres that tend to "kick in" sooner and become the forerunners of a transition, even as certain others are latecomers. Thus when the latecomer fields are finally reaching actualization of a particular social paradigm, other forerunner fields have already embarked on their transition to the society to come, with the consequence that a pure form of the paradigm is never reached.

Historical scholarship to this point has not lingered much over the issue of the relative speeds of change in various fields of human activity or the time lag between a change in people's tastes and ethical views and the emergence of manifestations of that change. "Modern" historical scholarship, with a tendency toward specialization that confines the scholar to studying one type of phenomena, seems to have closed its eyes to such issues. The fields of political history, economic history, the history of technology, and art history have all split off into fields studied on their own terms, with each content to develop its own unique periods and theories of history.

In terms of my own pursuit of paradigmatic change, I do not believe it important to dwell on the issue of the precise moment when an era reaches its peak; I will follow the specialists in treating such dates as a peripheral issue. And if, in the following pages, I seem to range freely between periods and attach little importance to the precise moments at which transitions occur, it should come as no surprise.

Oasis Farming and City-State Nations: The Origins of Civilization

For those who examine the history of mankind, it is important to decide at which point that history really begins. Since the current study is devoted to exploring the theme of disruptions and transitions in human civilizations, I would argue that a sensible starting point would be when civilization and society were first established on a stable basis—i.e., when farming began.

Primitive man mastered a number of techniques during the ancient period, but the birth of farming was of overwhelming importance in the formation of civilization and society. Certain scholars regard hunting and fishing as vital to this process and refer to such developments as the "first technological transition," but for me this seems a little too speculative. Hunting and fishing skills may be observed in other species and their development by humans is likely to have antedated the development of civilization, for the human race would have perished had it lacked them. But while it is true that stone and wooden tools were employed and that carrying out these activities did require some organization, not enough evidence exists as to the forms of hunting and fishing practiced before the advent of agriculture for us to determine how coordinated these activities were or how sophisticated the tools actually were.

Another group of scholars contends that the herding of livestock antedates the birth of farming, and that societies centered on this activity constitute the earliest form of human civilization. Certainly the care of livestock is a productive activity that cannot be seen in other animals and to the extent that its practice requires organization, continuity, and planning, it deserves to be referred to as a "civilized" activity. However, it is difficult to know what level of technological sophistication or social organization was achieved by the human beings who herded livestock in the years before the advent of agriculture. The only herding societies we have information about are those that came into being subsequent to the birth of societies based on farming and that existed on the periphery of the latter. At this point there is no basis for assuming that livestock herding as it was practiced before the advent of agriculture was necessarily on a par with that carried out later on the periphery of farming societies.

By contrast agriculture, from its inception, shaped civilizations and societies different from any that preceded them. The advent of farming formed the foundation for a social structure that assumed its own permanence, and relied upon enormous buildings, which is why we refer to this period as the "primary stage" of civilization.

Let us not, however, commit the error of equating the forms of agriculture employed at this primary stage—millennia ago, possibly more than ten thousand years ago according to some accounts—with farming as practiced today, or in the medieval world, or even during the classical age. It is not as if the mastery of agricultural technique was achieved in one fell swoop—nor has the impact of farming technology on society been uniform or consistent for all times and places.

The earliest stage of farming technology probably involved no more than knowing to plant the seeds and then harvest them. The next stage in all likelihood consisted of activities aimed at protecting the sown seeds from the ravages of animals and weeds, to ensure a better harvest.

Strong doubts persist as to whether and to what extent the earliest practitioners of farming aerated the soil by plowing it. Judging from the wretched tools excavated from various sites associated with primitive farming, it seems that the early farmers simply poked small holes in the ground for their seeds. Regular watering and fertilizing came much later, and facilities for artificial irrigation were beyond the pale of imagination.

Such farming techniques limited farmers to naturally irrigated land with soft soil that would retain water, which meant land adjacent to river banks or in oases. And so it was in the few locations that could support such farming that the earliest civilizations sprang up. Given the small amounts of arable land their inhabitants had to make do with, it was natural that each such community should form itself into a city-state.

This early stage of farming, humble though it was, did inculcate in man the concept of planning. To carry out continuous farming, after all, it was absolutely necessary to preserve a portion of the harvest as seeds for the following year.

That cannot have been easy. The proportion of their crops that farmers had to set aside for seeds in this primary stage of agriculture was drastically higher than is the case today. According to Geneviève DeCour, in tenth-century France the wheat harvest was only three times greater on average than the quantity of grain planted as seed. The estimates that one can form on the basis of Georges Duby's writings concerning the town of Wolfenbüttel in the ninth century point to even lower yields for barley—almost always less than two grains for each planted. The productivity of land along riverbanks and in oases was generally high, but it is doubtful that the yields achieved by ancient farmers greatly surpassed those of their European counterparts in the Middle Ages. Furthermore, natural disasters, climatic shifts, military invasions, and damage from insects, mold, and plant disease could be counted on to reduce drastically the harvest yield on a frequent basis.

Extreme discipline, enforced or self-imposed, must have been required to make farmers set aside one-third of each crop for the next year's planting. When one considers that in Japan a figure like Sakube of Iyo, who saved one bale of rice during a famine in the eighteenth century and died of starvation, has been venerated as an example of a "noble farmer," it seems inconceivable that men in ancient times would voluntarily have set aside one-third of their harvest. I believe that it was the vital need to enforce the preservation of seed grain that led to the formation of city-states and the investiture of authority in the monarchs that governed them and assumed the function of managing the redistribution of what was harvested.

And it should be stressed that although early farming moved man rapidly toward establishing cultures and organizations predicated on the assumption of long-term continuity, it did not immediately result in materially affluent societies. For even if a particular society in this era achieved material affluence at some point, its population was sure to shoot up over the course of a few generations and make it poor once again. Restricted to a harsh regimen of primitive farming within the narrow confines along rivers and in oases, the men who lived during the primary stage had to abstain absolutely from any kind of material indulgence and probably found it next to impossible to relax their constant vigilance against external threats.

Limited technology and resources and relations with external enemies set the terms on which primary stage cultures operated. The limited amount of arable land led to the formation of the city-states, while the necessity for conserving great stores of seed reinforced the authority of the monarchs to force members of their community to deliver up what they produced on a noncompensatory basis for redistribution.

In this primary stage, commercial exchanges in the modern sense did not exist within but between communities. Communities in which markets were opened were called towns (*machi* in Japanese) to set them apart from the other communities (*mura* or villages) in which groups *(mure)* of people simply resided; in Japanese the etymology of the terms suggests that barter exchange in the Japanese islands first began between communities rather than among the members of particular communities. The phenomenon is not unique to Japan; for virtually every early civilization for which real evidence of actual conditions has been found, barter between rather than within communities constituted the first phase. Needless to say, the concept of parity exchange had not yet come into play.

In the environment that imposed material abstinence on its inhabitants, people devoted their energy to introspection rather than the things of this world. The empathetic impulse, which drives men to develop systems of ethics and taste in which it is "good form" to use up what exists in abundance and conserve what is scarce, worked to convince the inhabitants of primary-stage civilizations that to interest oneself in the things of this world was vulgar and even evil, but that devoting one's time (the single commodity that existed in abundance) to spiritual contemplation was an act of great moral beauty.

Thus awakened to the religious impulse, men concentrated their spiritual energy on the attempt to give form to the supernatural. This can be seen in the strikingly symbolic figures of men and animals rendered as abstract patterns on pottery and copperware from Mesopotamia, northwest India, and China's Yellow River regions. If we apply to this art the standard of realism, then we must judge the cave paintings of the barbaric hunting tribes that came earlier as far more accomplished.

It may seem unthinkable that the originators of the agricultural civilizations, who developed the technology not only to erect mighty castle walls around their cities but to execute elaborately abstract patterns in their art, should prove so starkly inferior to their primitive counterparts from the hunting tribes at realistic representation. It seems that man, at this stage of his development, sensed a more noble beauty in speculative abstractions and symbols than he found in a realism based on the material world.

The Agricultural Revolution
That Gave Birth to Ancient Society

The first great transformation of agriculture—and thus civilization—took several thousand years to complete. It was concluded when the discovery of methods to break up and aerate dense soil and to draw water into dry areas provided the means to expand the range of arable land.

It is impossible to know with any certainty which disruption or shake-up of the established order stimulated these discoveries and the transformation they inspired. The stimulus may have come from the discovery of new resources, or a dramatic shift in climatic conditions. The evolution of more advanced social systems may also be considered a likely catalyst for the transformation; the Egyptians under Queen Nefertiti, for example, are known to have developed a specialized bureaucracy by the fourteenth century B.C.

But our primary suspect has to be new technology. By the early fifteenth century B.C., waterways were being constructed in the cities, along the rivers, and in the oases of Mesopotamia and northwest India; iron implements had made their appearance by 1400 B.C. Of course, it may have been the specialized bureaucracies that enabled the application on a grand scale of certain techniques acquired in relatively confined regions and thus expanded exponentially the area of fertile land. In either event, the spread of irrigation technology made it possible to farm on arid land, while the power of iron tools made it possible to till the soil and convert forest areas to farmland. (One assumes that iron would necessarily have been an extremely precious commodity at this time and that man could not have been so foolish as to use a metal so prone to rust only for weapons and ceremonial use.)

This was the grand transformation wrought by agricultural technology. Man, who up to that point could raise plants only where natural conditions permitted, was now able to improve and develop the land itself to create arable fields; the transformation thus occasioned was more far-reaching than that which the introduction of power generation and large-scale machinery during the Industrial Revolution wrought in the fields of manufacturing.

The agricultural revolution, begun around 1500 B.C. in Mesopotamia and carried forward in northwest India and along China's Yellow River valley, utterly transformed human society. Around the city-states that had developed in isolated spots along riverbanks and in oases, farming villages could now spring up and develop over ever wider areas, even as the world in which men lived increasingly consisted of societies with a growing abundance of material things. Surpluses of the items they produced encouraged men to engage in barter, which opened up traffic between far-flung regions. This in turn led to a second great transformation, one in which great progress was made in methods of transport. Development of technologies involving horse-driven vehicles and boats occurred at this time.

The living conditions of nomads and fishermen were transformed as caravans that traded in horses and cattle and ships operated by maritime merchants appeared. The new modes of transport made possible the delivery of exotic items from distant lands and also set the stage for piracy and raids. The empathetic impulse that acts to inform men where to seek their enlightened self-interest was stimulated by the new situation, with the result that men directed their attention to the things of this world. They began to make a point of observing things as they actually were. That people who found themselves exchanging their own surplus products for exotic ones turned out by peoples from distant lands should develop the habit of looking things over carefully is only to be expected. Over time this habitual and wary attention to detail would manifest itself in an artistic realism devoted to transcribing things exactly as they were, and a spirit of scientific inquiry whose main questions concerned why the things they watched so closely behaved as they did.

At the same time, the preoccupation with material things led to a preoccupation with the land that produced them. People who had confined themselves to the isolated environs of their particular city-states now changed their minds and sought control of land, extending their authority into the peripheries and eventually setting their sights on trade routes in an unrelenting drive to expand. The city-states became regional states.

The historical record tells us that political states (like those of the Hittites, or Ancient Babylon, or the new Egyptian monarchy) existed from the beginning of the tenth century B.C. While it's true that these "states" had achieved domination over a wide territory, in their initial phase these probably would be more accurately described as groupings of city-states that recognized the authority of a common ruler. Territorial states of the truly regional type described above were first established in the west by Assyria during the early eighth century B.C.; in India by the Four Powers (Magadha, Kosala, Kashi, and Vrijis) from the late sixth century onward; and in China during the Spring and Autumn period (770–481 B.C.). When Confucius notes that "the holdings of the old Chou dynasty were deemed prosperous, yet any of the seven great states of our era exceeds them in breadth," his statement can be read as an acknowledgment of the transition from city-states to regional states.

However, the really decisive factor that marks the transition to an era of territorial states was the emergence of a mode of production in which human beings were forced to work by other human beings in order to achieve the goal of turning out more products than strict survival required. To people for whom material things now held a strong attraction, who believed that an abundance of these promised happiness, the fact that the potential for opening up more arable land and forging commercial links with distant regions could create circumstances in which the individual worker could produce more than he needed to survive—and thus help to create surplus production—did not go unnoticed. Out of this came a system based on the notion that by employing people in production activities and giving them no more than they needed to survive, the employer could acquire more goods for himself; this system, which we designate slavery, soon spread far and wide.

Widespread development of slavery was a characteristic feature of ancient societies, seen throughout the West, the Middle East, India, and China. Past historians assumed that the further back in history one looks, the more cruel humans become, and that slaveowners were able to bring the system of slavery into being via the arbitrary application of brute force, but recent research largely discredits this simplistic conclusion. To establish slavery and thus achieve surplus production, certain resources and types of technology were absolute prerequisites; brute force alone would not suffice to bring such a system into being. To take for granted that the further back in history one goes, the more barbaric the human beings are going to be, and that it follows inevitably that the human needs and rights of slaves were invariably ignored, is simply to indulge in the hypocrisy of the quintessential modern man with his faith in historical progress linked to equality and humanism.

Let us put the issue another way: The widespread development of slavery is a distinguishing characteristic of the production system during the ancient period. In the past historians used the label "ancient" to cover the entire range of recorded history prior to the Middle Ages, but if the point of using such labels is to mark discrete stages in social development, using a single vague label to cover this long period is inadequate. Between what I have called the *primary stage*, in which primitive agricultural techniques tied men to the land within oases and near rivers, and the *ancient era*, which was launched by the development of techniques for creating arable lands through plowing and irrigation, the dramatic developments in agricultural technology created a new set of circumstances in which commerce between communities could develop, which in turn led to changes in political and social structures. Underlying these changes we find a radical transformation in tastes and ethics—in the values of the society—which marks the emergence of a new social paradigm.

To that extent, it could honestly be said that civilizations in the primary stage were as different from those of the later stages of the ancient era as the medieval civilizations were different from the modern ones.

The Ancient Era, When Material Things Mattered Most

Ancient society developed during a period when material things were relatively plentiful and growing ever more so. For those inhabitants of ancient civilization who lived in the more advanced areas (the so-called seminal regions), the supply of material things had definitely been growing more plentiful and diverse for as far back as they could remember. They experienced firsthand what we refer to today as economic growth and an improved standard of living.

By the fifth century B.C., or even sooner in some cases, the average citizens (excluding slaves) in the advanced center of the civilized world—meaning the Mediterranean ports, Mesopotamia, India, and major portions of China—enjoyed a lifestyle of greater material affluence than that of many of the world's poorest regions today. Moreover, new items to be traded would appear and new technological breakthroughs would occur every few decades, and the average citizen could expect some new type of product to be made available from time to time.

The empathetic impulse in men responded sharply to the reality of such affluence as the inhabitants of ancient society increasingly concerned themselves with material things and derived their pleasure from owning and consuming them.

Accounts of the ancient era abound in tales of rulers who indulged their appetites to the fullest while the people under them devoted themselves to accumulating wealth. In such accounts, the mighty rulers are inevitably rich—that is, they possess a multitude of material things; one gets the impression that the estimates of a monarch's greatness were based entirely upon how much wealth he had accumulated. Certainly there were railings against the worldliness of the age by the Stoics and the *bokka*, followers of the Chinese philosopher Mo Tzu (aka Micius [479–483 B.C.]), but such responses strike me as little more than nostalgic pining for the vanished past of the primary stage of civilization. The tenor of the times was set by the pleasure-seeking Epicurean philosophy and moving toward the pragmatism of the Chinese Legalists.

That the ancients, given their passion for things and the pleasure they derived from owning more and more of them, proved loath to sell their own goods cheap or to pay a high price for those sold by others should come as no surprise. It was when everyone was haggling to preserve the slightest advantage for themselves that the principle of parity exchange was born. This became one of the social paradigms of the ancient era and helped to establish commerce on a permanent and large-scale basis.

The scale of commerce during the ancient era was enormous. During the Peloponnesian War, Athens was able to carry on without serious shortages in the face of a blockade around its perimeter by Sparta and Sparta's allies; behind the mighty fortress walls that connected Athens to the harbor of Piraeus, the Athenians even succeeded in continuing their commercial and manufacturing activities without disruption.

For a city of over 300,000 people to remain active for years without supplies from its surrounding villages would have required shipping capacity on a grand scale, as well as substantial earnings from the products it turned out.

Such capabilities made it inevitable that the population would increase. Some speculate that at the peak of the ancient era the populations of both Rome and Chang'an exceeded one million. Though there's room to question the exactness of such figures, a number even approaching this is impressive for single metropolises, especially when the global population for the era was 200 to 250 million. For urban centers of this magnitude to develop there must be flourishing handicrafts and commercial activities on a grand scale.

There must also be a system of currency. A critical function of the state during the ancient era was to mint currency and uphold its credibility. That Han Wu Di (141–187 B.C.), the first Chinese emperor, set out to conquer all of China and unify it under one currency clearly indicates how vital the issue of currency was. Commercial powers like Carthage went so far as to establish a type of convertible currency, using hides, before the beginning of the third century.

The ancients loved and treasured coins and put their faith in them; they even accepted their function as capital to a certain extent and took it for granted that interest would be charged. In China at the close of the Warring States era (403–221 B.C.) there appeared numerous accounts of individuals who amassed great fortunes via commerce and moneylending, the majority written to express respect for these accomplishments. The historian Sima Qian, the "father of Chinese history," made a point of inserting a section of anecdotes about moneymakers, singling out especially successful parties for praise. This is a sure indication that he, like others who lived through the reign of Emperor Wu, the best years of the Former Han dynasty (206 B.C.–A.D. 9), dreamed of achieving wealth. It may be worth mentioning that sections on money-making were featured in Chinese chronicles only through the first edition on the Former Han dynasty and were dropped when the chronicle of the Later Han was composed during the Tartar partition (Northern and Southern dynasties period; A.D. 317–589); they were never featured again.

In the West as well, the Greek shrines performed the function of borrowing and lending funds and profited thereby. Gaius Plinius Secundus (Pliny the Elder), who died in A.D. 79 when he traveled to Vesuvius to witness the volcano's eruption, had a reputation as a most scrupulous man, yet he writes proudly that he raised the standard interest rate to 5 percent. If we can assume that prices were stable, such a rate is comparable to that charged today. Then as now, money was thought of as a profit-yielding asset—as capital.

Along with their emphasis on parity exchange, the manner of their economic development, and their strong interest in material things, went the ancients' pursuit of realism in art and their spirit of scientific inquiry. The fastidious pursuit of realism in art has been thought of as unique to Western, and particularly Greek and Roman, civilizations, with no parallel in the Oriental tradition. However, a number of recent excavations, starting with those of Qin (aka Ch'in) dynasty (221–207 B.C.) sculptures depicting mounted horsemen, provide proof that during the years when ancient China flourished it produced art that bears comparison with that of Greece and Rome in its zealous elaboration of realistic representation. This new evidence has forced reconsideration of the notion that the realistic art produced in India and the Middle East during this period was indebted solely to the Greeks.

It seems reasonable to read the fact that realistic representation began to appear in many unrelated locations around this time as evidence that when men—whether Oriental or Occidental—find themselves blessed with material abundance, their interest in the objects of this abundance grows and they begin to feel that exact depiction is the source of true beauty. Further, those who have become deeply attentive to things will turn to pondering the particularities of their forms and the principles and causes that produce their movements. What we call the spirit of scientific inquiry grows out of this impulse.

Here, too, past scholars have been loath to acknowledge that civilizations other than that of Greece displayed a scientific bent. However recent judgments acknowledge that in China during the Spring and Autumn (770–481 B.C.) and Warring States (481–221 B.C.) epochs medicine, agriculture, physics, and logic attained a very high level and great general applicability, as did Indian mathematics and chemistry in India's submodern age. The spirit of scientific inquiry was no more an exclusively Western phenomenon than was realistic representation in art. It is, rather, a spirit common to all peoples who develop an appreciation of material things.

Not simply in their economic principles, but in the fields of art and science as well, the ancient societies abounded in what we have come to think of as "modern" rationalism.

Ancient States That Sought to Increase Production

When we look at the major functions of the state in ancient societies, we find them to be the same as those of a modern state. The first function is to conduct military actions aimed at securing productive territories and keeping roads open. To achieve this, the ancient Greek city-states, the Persians, and the Romans all dispatched powerful armies and fleets to far-flung regions and maintained them there. Their royal counterparts in India did the same. In China the Great Wall was constructed by the Qin and Former Han dynasties to secure their territory from incursions, while the Later Han rulers dispatched Wei Qing, Huo Qu Bing and others to western China to maintain their hold on the commercial routes there.

The more highly evolved ancient societies conscripted their troops and imbued them with a powerful sense of mission by holding out the prospect of great personal gain for soldiers and their units. Driven by such dreams, Greek armies defeated barbarian hordes that far outnumbered them, and Roman troops likewise proved well-nigh invincible. As for the soldiers of the Han dynasty when that military empire was at its peak, the poets sang that "but one of our men oft smote three of the enemy." That the heights of economic and cultural development should be reached when military might was at its apex seems as true for ancient societies as for modern ones.

The state was also expected to fulfill the function of increasing the production of goods while lowering the cost of distributing them. As is the case today, states fulfilled this second function by carrying out public projects; the ancients put enormous energy into schemes for flood control, irrigation, road building, harbor development, construction of canals and waterways, and the like. The Persians and Romans constructed superb aqueducts and roads, while the Greeks and Romans built a network of harbor facilities to provide for supply and transport throughout the Mediterranean.

In China as well, irrigation and flood control projects were pursued on a vast scale, and all road were built to conform to a single standard carriage width. Perhaps the most astonishing of the Chinese projects were the enormous canals built to link northern and southern China. No canals of comparable length or width have been constructed anywhere on earth in the intervening two millennia.

A third major function the state was expected to fulfill was that of maintaining price stability and fair distribution; in effect, it had to guarantee exchange parity and a degree of consistency and fairness in the system for determining taxes. To accomplish this task, it seems to have been necessary for each state to promulgate a code of laws and a system for strictly enforcing them. It is possible to find examples of legal codes, like that of Hammurabi, as far back as the eighteenth century B.C., and there is also the early example of the Ten Commandments introduced by Moses; but not until the seventh century B.C. in the West can there be seen an ongoing system of laws subject to more or less continuous development and revision, while in China it was not until the end of the fifth century B.C. that the ideology to support a legal system came into being. By the second century B.C., such developments had culminated in codes such as Roman Law, the establishment of a centralized, administrative rule under Han Wu Di (141–87 B.C.), and India's Laws of Manu.

Taxes were also a serious issue: when people have a major stake in the abundance or scarcity of goods and consider parity exchange a guiding principle, they are likely to take taxes just as seriously. The publication during the reign of Emperor Wu in Han-dynasty China of the world's first treatise on public finance, the "Salt and Iron Treatise," bears out this point. As is clear from this example, where the state monopolized the sales of salt and iron, ancient states did not limit themselves to simple land-based taxation, but treated manufacture and production as a major source of revenue.

The functions of the ancient state, described above, resemble those of modern states to a remarkable extent. If we add to these the responsibility for public welfare, viewed increasingly as a major problem by the end of the ancient era, and leave out the question of education, then it can be said that ancient states carried out almost all the same functions, for the same reasons, as do their modern counterparts.

Readers raised in industrial societies may think: Of course, that's what states do; it goes with the turf. But we do not find states of this type in either the primary stage that preceded it or in the medieval era that followed; at the same time, the responsibility for religious matters that was the preeminent duty of monarchs during the primary stage shrank markedly in importance during the ancient era.

Within ancient societies religion was highly visible, and it was a function of states to put on festivals, but if the truth be known, these were simply ceremonial exercises, mostly entertaining "events." Transmitting the will of the gods and divining the future—viewed as vital aspects of governance during the primary stage—were not taken nearly as seriously during the ancient era, when the power of the priests to make pronouncements on policy diminished. On top of that, the number of gods in the pantheon kept proliferating, and there was tolerance toward people with different faiths.

Every type of religious current flowed into Rome, eventually making it possible for an emperor as steeped in bizarre pagan heterodoxy as Elagabalus (ruled 218–222) to hold the throne. In China, the land whose "citizens flaunt their indifference to the gods," religious faith became virtually extinct and even Confucianism was nearly pushed aside by the pragmatism of the Legalists. The first of the Qin emperors went so far as to bury Confucianists alive, while his high priests urinated on the crowns once worn by Confucianists. Not only religion per se, but any otherworldly ideology was treated with contempt. Even India, that most fervently religious of environments, tolerated a multiplicity of faiths at this time. Neither Asoka of the Mauryan dynasty nor Kaniska I of the Kushan dynasty, both kings who had converted to Buddhism, dared to suppress the Hindus. Individual rulers might make their religion part of their government policies if they possessed the clout to do so, but these religions never became the principle on which the sovereignty of the state was based during this period.

For the ancients, who revered material things and possessed a scientific spirit and a realism founded on looking at things as they were, religion was not a decisive or crucial matter. The religions that were suppressed by the ancient states were those that had originated in the primary stage or, prefigured the medieval era by repudiating worldly values and realism and denying the validity of the then-prevalent social paradigm.

The Development of Ancient Civilization and Its Limits

An aesthetic sense in which it is attractive to own more and more things; a social paradigm founded on the principle of exchange parity; a realism that observed things as they were and a scientific spirit that sought the underlying causes for why these things behaved as they did; and a state with a military establishment, public works projects, and a judicial system that acted to ensure fair dealings and equitable taxation—on any number of levels there are profound resemblances between ancient and modern societies. But on other levels there are also profound differences. The largest has to do with the means of production.

Within their spheres of influence, the ancient civilizations made use of the system of slavery in virtually every field of production. During the days of the Roman Empire, there were numerous types of slaves: some worked in agriculture, others rowed boats, or specialized in handicrafts, or worked as entertainers or artists. Indro Montanelli states that there was at least one slave in every Roman household during the second century A.D. In the areas of the Roman Empire that lay beyond the Italian peninsula, however, slaves were not nearly as numerous.

Not as much is known about conditions in the Chinese and Indian civilizations of the time, but the consensus is that there were fair numbers of slaves or menials or, in the case of India, members of the Sudra caste. Whether their situation or status was comparable to that of the slaves of the Roman empire or the Greek city-states is unclear, but we can presume that they fulfilled similar roles. While it would be a mistake to assume that all systems of production during the ancient era were slave-based, those that did use slaves played a critical role.

Past observers convinced themselves that there must have been great numbers of slaves in the city-states of primary-stage civilizations. Basing their arguments on conditions in Greek and Roman civilizations, they inferred that the building of enormous, nonutilitarian structures such as the pyramids and ziggurats would have certainly required hundreds if not thousands of slaves. Today this theory has been almost completely discredited. It is now understood that although these societies surely did include slaves, their numbers were few, whereas the force responsible for building the pyramids of Egypt and the ziggurats of Mesopotamia was the passionate religious and regional solidarity of the men of the primary-stage civilizations, who cared little about consuming or owning material things.

For slave-based production to be viable, three conditions must be met: (1) the product of the slave's labor must be of far greater value than the cost of his upkeep; (2) the workplace must be of sufficient scale to reap an advantage from slave labor (in the case of agriculture, this means broad enough tracts of arable land); (3) there must be an organizational framework, both conceptual and actual, capable of assigning and directing the slaves in carrying out the simple and repetitive actions fundamental to slave-based production. Due to the primitive agricultural technology, the shortage of arable land, and the lack of task- or function-specific organization during the primary stage, it was next to impossible to establish slave-based production. Making effective use of large numbers of slaves who lacked both the personal motivation and the aptitude to improve their performance on either the technical or managerial level cannot have been an easy task.

The ancient form of civilization first developed by societies in the Middle East, northwest India, and the Yellow River valley of China during the eighth and seventh centuries B.C. persisted and expanded for roughly a millennium. During that time, many new techniques were discovered, the centers of civilization repeatedly shifted, and great political powers arose and fell repeatedly. But the essential features of ancient civilization I have described, however much they may have been reinforced or diffused over increasingly larger areas, did not alter significantly during the course of that period.

As ever greater tracts of land were brought under cultivation, production increased, trade spread over wider areas, and links were formed over longer distances. The representational arts became more refined and the sciences reached a higher plateau; and slavery-based production was practiced on an ever larger scale, until it became a standard feature of the era.

With the passage of time, the territories of the nation-states grew vaster and, in the end, gigantic unified nation-states emerged. Alexander's short-lived hegemony marked the midway point in a process that culminated in the West with the unification of the entire Mediterranean region under the Roman Empire and in the East with China's transition through the Warring States period into a unified nation under the Qin and Han dynasties. In India a comparable unification was achieved under the Mauryan and Asoka dynasties. As they achieved unity, these enormous new empires put their energy into consolidating and expanding the territory under their domination, maintaining secure trade routes, executing public works projects, and establishing equitable and effective legal systems.

However, the fact that the ancients relied on a slavery-based mode of production imposed clear-cut limitations on them.

If one thinks of slavery as a form of labor it can seem inexpensive. But if one thinks of the slave as a tool, with the source of power to drive the tool built in, as it were, one comes to realize what a tremendous expenditure of managerial attention and operating costs are required to exploit this tool. No matter how callous and indifferent an owner might have been, he still had to provide the slaves with a roof over their heads and food to eat if he hoped to use them for any length of time. Slaves needed eight hours of rest and generated large quantities of waste that had to be disposed of. They also raised the specter of revolt or sabotage. A system of technology that relied on such an inefficient power source for its operation had inherent limits, and it was the fate of ancient civilization to be defined by those limits.

Ancient civilizations attained high levels of achievement in the representational arts, science, and philosophy. They had refined techniques in architecture and engineering and also in some kinds of handicrafts. The level of technical accomplishment that prevailed in general industry, however, never achieved comparable excellence. This necessitated heavy reliance on slaves and land, and it was this reliance that ultimately set limits on the growth of ancient civilization.

With each individual continuing to seek material plenty for themselves to the extent possible within those limits, it is hardly surprising that the distribution of wealth eventually loomed as a political issue. As the pace of development in the Greek city-states, Rome, and the Han empire slackened, social welfare emerged as a decisive issue for the state. Moreover, the dimensions of this perceived responsibility tended to mushroom over time, since implicit in the mind-set that associates beauty and taste with material plenty is the wish for goods to be fairly distributed. What constitutes "fairness" is, of course, always a subjective matter.

When a society is driven by its attraction for material things to make the principle of exchange parity one of its social paradigms, the predictable result is that cheaper forms of production spring up and products from areas where production costs are lower flow into the society. This fact drives the society to greater technological innovation and social development, up to a point. But the other side of the coin is that it gradually undermines family farming and other traditional forms of production that are inefficient, causing their collapse. Inhabitants of the civilized regions gravitate toward the cities in search of greater convenience, material affluence, and the ease and status that sedentary occupations in urban centers seem to promise. As a result, the large families and regional communities that support traditional agriculture break down and are replaced by urban societies with the smaller households appropriate to sedentary workers, who maintain much less contact with their neighbors.

Such changes mean that the well-being of families and regions alike suffer. Once a man moves to a city to find material wealth and a sedentary job, he loses the small circle to which he can escape at times of adversity.

However, being raised in a culturally advanced area or possessing citizenship in an advanced country or city does not automatically confer on one the abilities or the type of personality or the good fortune needed to land a sedentary job in an urban center. It is splendid when what society demands in goods and services promptly shifts to coincide with those goods and services that people most wish to be engaged in supplying, but that is not always the case. If the demand for the goods and services produced by those who work in sedentary occupations only grows at a limited rate while the number of citizens who wish to work in such jobs shoots up dramatically, it is obvious that there will be a large number of drop-outs who do not get to do what they want. The only remaining route for those who have lost the small circle to which they can escape is to rely on the political power that comes to them through their sole remaining asset, their citizenship, and seek public welfare.

When this happens, academic theories are certain to appear that conclude that it is only just to meet these demands, and politicians who seek to increase their own influence hop on the theoretical bandwagon. The latter are in most cases members of an echelon of society for which welfare was never an issue. For those who are more than financially satisfied themselves, showing compassion for the poor is an easy way to satisfy their drive to be famous while reinforcing their consciousness of themselves as elite. In opposition to them emerge politicians who enlist support from a coalition of the well-off (those blessed with the talent and the luck to succeed) plus those recalcitrant individuals who refuse to forsake their inefficient, privately run farms and other enterprises. When a society bent on the pursuit of material affluence reaches its zenith, we are certain to see this pattern of dramatic confrontation between the old and the new, with demagogues emerging on the fringes of both left and right.

A more serious issue is the decline in military power that results from the breakdown of family and community. The problem is not simply that those engaged in sedentary occupations in the city are physically less suited to be soldiers than those used to tough physical labor. It is that once they leave their large families and regional roots behind, they no longer need concern themselves with family honor or keeping up appearances before the other villagers, so that they lose the burning need to fight that would drive them to risk death. Even the Roman battalions that boasted invincibility and the crack units of Han troops who were praised for being a match for a foe three times their number quickly weakened with the disintegration of the farming-village-based society. The only thing the army of a "civilized" nation has going for it once this point is passed is better equipment and superior organization.

This is why the ancient societies of the period around the middle of the second century B.C.—at the point they could be said to have reached their zenith—found themselves facing a political crisis. It is from this point that the transformation of ancient society commenced, a transformation that led to such political phenomena as the collapse of the Mauryan dynasty in India (180 B.C.), the crumbling of the Roman republic (27 B.C.), and the usurpation of the Han empire by Wang Mang, who poisoned his predecessor and declared himself emperor (A.D. 8).

These crises were overcome by the prompt imposition of new systems (although not in the case of India, where the circumstances were different), but the means by which this was achieved involved reinforcing the authority of the emperor by expanding the ranks of those entitled to citizenship and reorganizing the army so that mercenary troops formed its core. Thereafter, the ranks of those granted citizenship in Rome and in the Han dynasty swelled virtually without limit, as the privilege was sold at a discount, so to speak, to outlying tribes on the periphery. The original citizens of these empires had to endure watching the value of the citizenship they had once prized cheapened and desecrated, and accept the welfare they received as their compensation.

The Symptoms That Foretell
the Decline and Fall of a Civilization

The reorganized ancient empires—Imperial Rome, the Later Han, and the Āndhra Dynasty in India—were certainly vast empires and at times achieved a luster that brooked comparison with or even surpassed their earlier greatness. But the ancient form of civilization had clearly passed its peak as the intense disintegration that ultimately leads to the demise of a society proceeded with ever greater speed. First to go were resources, as the limits of available land were reached and energy shortages began to be felt.

By the time Rome, the Han empire, and the Mauryan dynasty achieved their peak of expansion, they had literally arrived at the ends of the earth they knew. Beyond lay only barren deserts, dry, frozen tracts of uncut forest, and uninhabitable tropical rain forests—land unfit for habitation or exploitation with the tools then available. To the civilized man of the ancient era, the frontier—in a material sense—had been reached around the time of Christ. Imperial Rome would later expand to the north and east roughly a century and a half later under Emperor Hadrian, but it would not yield fruits that would go very far toward satisfying the worldly ambitions of the citizens. That is why the next emperor, Antoninus Pius, abandoned a fairly large portion of his territory. Even the most committed of imperialist rulers will find it impossible to persist for long in demanding large sums to defend territories that produce nothing that his people want. The leaders of the Later Han and Āndhra dynasties were wise enough to appreciate this fact without having to learn it the hard way; the Later Han empire actually seemed to turn its back on its own general, Ban Chao, by cutting loose its western territories.

Methods did not then exist whereby the output of material goods by any of these empires could have been increased through further territorial expansion. Not only were the resources themselves exhausted, but the land that was left could not produce enough food to feed the slaves needed to exploit it. If slaves were, in a sense, the "powered tools" of ancient civilizations, those civilizations had reached a stage where increasing the number of tools was problematical.

But even more critical was the energy crisis. Forest resources, the one and only energy source for ancient man, were becoming seriously depleted around the first century B.C. In the West, the areas that boasted the oldest civilizations—from Mesopotamia to the Mediterranean perimeter, and particularly the north African coast—presented the most striking examples. The Cedars of Lebanon from which the Phoenicians constructed their great fleet, the giant Tunisian forests that nurtured Hannibal's elephants, and the deep woods of the Greek mountains where the Olympian gods were said to reside gradually disappeared.

In China as well, the forests of the Ordos zone were lost as denuded mountain peaks stretched far into the north. Northwest India also grew increasingly arid and desertlike. The regions of the world that had been the sites of the oldest civilizations had begun to dry up, although they were yet to reach the advanced stage of deterioration that can be seen today.

How did this come about? There are several theories to explain it. Some blame climatic changes; some point to excessive deforestation; others point to the primitive agricultural methods practiced by unassimilated tribes on the perimeters who set fire to their fields after the harvest. Each of these factors undoubtedly played a role, but it was allowing cattle and other animals to graze on cut lands that was most responsible for rendering deforestation irreversible. The most pernicious ravager of the landscape was the meek and lowly sheep.

The energy shortage caused by deforestation delivered a decisive blow to industrial activity. Production of metals and the baking of tiles fell off, farm implements were reduced in quality, and it became problematical even to find the materials to keep the irrigation systems in good working order. Under such straitened circumstances, shipbuilding and construction suffered.

The ancients, who had never stopped striving for greater material affluence, must have been overwhelmed with despair by the spectacle of such realities. Technology as it then existed could not find an energy source to replace timber. The axis of civilization shifted toward the areas with more available forest land: northern Italy, Gaul, Hispania (the Iberian peninsula), southern and central China, and central India.

Population Decreases in the Advanced Regions

The second symptom of malaise was the decrease in population in the most culturally advanced regions. According to the estimates Jean-Noel Biraben has made on the basis of calculations by John D. Durand, during the four hundred-some years leading up to 800 B.C. when ancient society as such was evolving into its most characteristic form, global population hovered around 110 million (see Chart 2). It then began to climb, reaching a peak of roughly 300 million around the time of Christ, an increase of 2.5 times in roughly eight hundred years. The most striking surges (in some cases, to as much as six or ten times the previous level) took place, predictably, in areas where the ancient form of civilization was the most highly developed—the Mediterranean coast, central India, and China's Yellow River valley—and could produce the food and healthy conditions under which population growth most often occurs.

The trend began to reverse itself, however, in the first century B.C., with population in the advanced regions suddenly undergoing a precipitous drop even as it began to climb along the less developed peripheries. After a dip during the first

Chart 2: Global Population Patterns from 1600 B.C. to the Present

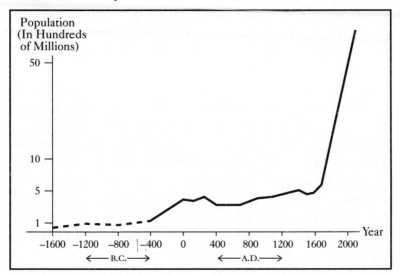

Source: Jean-Noel Biraben

century A.D., it began climbing again, building to another peak during the second century before beginning a startling decline that was sustained for some four hundred years. It was not until the eleventh century, during a period that might be called a kind of pseudo-modernization, that the peak reached around the time of Christ was finally surpassed.

That the poorer, less advanced regions should sustain a surge in population while the more prosperous advanced regions should see a falling off may seem paradoxical, but we can seek the causes for this in the type of atmosphere that is created in the final stages of a civilization whose ethical and moral outlook is based on the desirability of material plenty. If continued technological progress and an expanding supply of resources seem assured, even those who desire material affluence will not cavil at population increases; they can maintain the faith that more hands will mean greater production.

Once people start feeling that the supply of resources has its limits, however, the picture changes; people discover that the most expeditious way to ensure that one is blessed with relative material wealth, in a world with a shrinking supply of resources, is to limit the number of family members to whom this finite supply must be distributed.

This notion, founded on the assumption that more is better, means that the loss of frontiers will make birth control popular. If family farms are on the way out and the family as an institution is falling apart, the trend toward birth control really kicks in. For sedentary workers in cities who do not depend on a large family-based work force to sustain their income, nothing is more certain to guarantee a larger share per household member than keeping the family small. To have too many children becomes anathema; having none at all becomes an attractive alternative. After all, urban offspring cannot be counted on to see their parents through old age and the parents can usually expect to make it through without them. When civilization reaches this stage, the state usually sees to it that citizens are provided with "bread and circuses." Social welfare also does its part to reduce the population and undermine the institution of the family.

That sexual morality breaks down when the ties that bind families are cut and men and women are free to act on their desires seems to be a universal human principle applicable across boundaries and eras. In Rome after the era of imperial rule ended, varieties of lurid sex flourished. How the famous of those times repeated their marrying, divorcing, philandering, and indulgence of every perversion! Those considered wise men—Julius Caesar, Pompey, Augustus, Pliny—were among them. Yet for all the sex, most were childless.

Cato the Younger censured the sexual aberrations of his political foe Caesar, calling him "every woman's husband and every man's wife," but this was when things were still at a relatively benign stage. By the time 150 years had passed, no one would have dreamed of taking Emperor Hadrian to task over his proclivity for collecting pretty young boys.

Women were a match for the men. Rumors of orgies and promiscuity bordering on the pathological have attached themselves to nearly every queen or empress who reigned during this era. Even Emperor Marcus Aurelius, regarded as "virtue incarnate" in his own time, had to close his eyes to the licentious behavior of Empress Faustina. These were times when a lucky husband was one whose wife had merely two or three lovers.

The "Roman way" had one good thing going for it during this period: no aged, childless person of wealth needed to fear being left lonely in his dotage, for all were besieged with males and females after their legacy. Such a practice merely served to reinforce the trend toward childlessness.

The common citizenry did not lag behind their social betters in this respect. As the ties that had once bound regional societies and family units together continued to atrophy, the burden imposed by the state's commitment to provide "bread and circuses" to the uprooted got bigger and bigger. Given the situation, one could not expect decent soldiers to emerge from the ranks of the citizenry. The army came to be composed entirely of mercenaries, including large numbers of barbarians and emancipated slaves. The pressures on public finances to provide their sustenance became enormous. Even the mighty Roman Empire found itself facing financial disaster, giving rise to such creative thinkers as the Emperor Vespasian, who obtained revenue by constructing public lavatories and charging a fee to users and a fine to nonusers. Not surprisingly, the fines were pitched higher than the fees.

China appears to have reached a comparable stage even earlier. The demise of the self-supporting farmer at the end of the Early Han era resulted in the spread of enormous plantations operated by powerful clans. The farmers who had lost their stake either worked as farmhands or private soldiers for the clans or became drifters who joined marauding bands of robbers. So many joined the mercenary forces hired by the clans that the title that had once described a private in the army attached itself to these clan hired guns, who became an absolute necessity as their employers were increasingly threatened by the bands of drifters. As things fell apart in China, the poorer Chinese survived by fighting for one side or the other in this struggle, which was the only way both sides could be sure of having something to eat.

It is worth mentioning that the title that described the hirelings of private clan armies became official legal usage during the Tang dynasty (A.D. 618–906) and designated a status level above that of servants but below that of free citizens (it was roughly equivalent to that of a farmhand). The evolution of this usage reveals the trajectory these clan "hired guns" had followed, starting out as farmers and full-fledged citizens during the late years of the Former Han dynasty, then losing their land and having to sell their own freedom to survive in the Later Han, when they became drifters and ultimately hired mercenaries. That the ranks of such disenfranchised people had grown so large as to approach a majority indicates that the transition to a medieval society had already commenced.

The forces that arrayed themselves against these developments and sought to return to past glories were formidable. It was precisely to achieve this idealized return that Wang Mang (ruled A.D. 9–23) seized the Han throne and declared himself emperor of what he chose to literally call the Xin ("New") dynasty (aka Hsin). This usurper of imperial status eliminated the former regime's retinue of Han lords and set out to emancipate the citizens and redistribute the lands that had been the property of the great clans, while also attempting to cancel the debts of the free farmers. Wang Mang offers the example of a man in whom the rational spirit was so strong that he ordered vivisection for purposes of medical research; at the same time, his hankering for material goods was such that he had his army collect every type of weapon mentioned in the treatise on the sixty-three types of military tactics. He was the very essence of the cultivated man of the ancient era, which was probably why those farmers who still possessed land had turned to him for help when faced with the threat of extinction.

Yet despite his progressive goals and rational spirit, for reasons we cannot know, Wang Mang somehow lost his way once he established the Xin dynasty; gripped by nostalgia for the remote antiquity of the primary stage of civilization, he gave himself over to practicing astrological divinations and mystical rites. Things were only made worse when he rushed his program of reforms through on the basis of haphazardly conceived plans that were further undercut by the bureaucrats, most of whom had formerly served the clans Wang Mang had opposed. These bureaucrats did what they could to sabotage his dynasty, which soon collapsed; Wang Mang himself was murdered.

That those who perpetrated the overthrow were armies of clan hirelings from the provinces, abetted by bands of drifters like the "Red Eyebrows," indicates clearly how much Chinese society had changed. Free citizens no longer possessed the power to keep their own choice on the throne; nor did they have the will to bring about reform.

In China, where upholding one's family and worshiping ancestors are deeply rooted concepts, it is not surprising that the consciousness of family links on the part of the upper class was still quite intense during this period; still, it was not unusual for kinsmen of the Han imperial family or the several lords to have younger brothers or cousins who were paupers. Average Chinese were even less prone to acknowledge family ties at this time. The heroic figures in the Chinese classic, *The Romance of the Three Kingdoms (Sanguo Yanyi)*, who are of common origin, hardly seem to know who their real brothers are. Although the three main characters feel bound to one another as "brothers" or comrades in the story, we are never told anything concerning their actual brothers, even though there is no reason to believe that they were each single offspring.

Under conditions such as these, the birthrate fell and the population declined, even in China. Population statistics were being compiled there even before the era in question. According to figures listed in the "Book of Han" (a dynastic record) and the "Notes on Geography," there were roughly 12 million households and a population of 59.6 million in the Former Han era (c. A.D. 2), but by the year (146 A.D.) that Emperor Zhi died in the Later Han era, the figures had shrunk to roughly 9 million households and 47.6 million persons. The number of households had shrunk by 24 percent in a century and a half, and the population by 20 percent.

But the numbers for A.D. 57, the year Guangwu Di, one of the first Later Han rulers, died, are roughly 4 million households and 46.5 million people—the all-time low for both categories. Some argue that after a decline in the population due to the poor rule of Wang Mang and internal strife, the population recovered considerably during the peaceful times of the Later Han dynasty. However, this is conjecture based on unreliable numbers: knowing that the then emperor, Guangwu Di, planned to emancipate the slaves, the clans apparently suppressed the count for their households in census reports, thereby drastically reducing the overall figure. Mere civil unrest and a government in disarray could not account for such a drastic reduction in the population.

By contrast, population in the less advanced regions on the periphery increased dramatically. The influx of technology, goods, and ways of doing things from the advanced regions was accompanied by a surge in the birthrate, which produced the population increase. But to have technology and goods flow in is one thing; to alter fundamental concepts of taste and morality is not as simple. Due to the influence of the advanced regions, the economies of the later-developing regions did in fact grow, but only to see the effect of any increases in their productive potential absorbed by increases in their population. Despite the fact that there was not enough to eat, the number of people just kept climbing.

The increasingly precarious imbalance between the situations of advanced regions with plummeting birthrates and the less developed regions where the population kept soaring, eventually resulted in the predictable grand migration from the overpopulated climes of the latter to the undermanned environs of the former. This movement prefigured the successive waves of migration that would ultimately spell the death of the ancient form of civilization.

The Final Stage of the Ancient Era — A Shift in Aesthetic Values

When did the ancient era end? This is another question on which opinions diverge.

Although most histories of the West assert that the ancient era ended with the collapse of the Western Roman Empire in A.D. 476, some see the era ending much earlier, in 313 with official recognition of Christianity, or in 375 with the Visigoths invading Roman territory and launching the first of the great migrations.

Among historians of the Orient, there are those who cleave to the theory that the ancient era lasted until the start of the Tang dynasty (618), but the most powerful support is currently given to denoting 316 — the year that the Western Jin fell and ushered in the period of upheaval sometimes called the Tartar Partition—the end of the ancient era. There are yet others who see the retreat south of the Eastern Jin in 420 as lying on the cusp between ancient and medieval, or who mention the year 439.

Making such a determination for India or the Middle East raises an especially complicated set of issues, not the least because of the many gaps in the historical record. The majority of historians have chosen to abandon the ancient/medieval dichotomy in dealing with these regions and feel that the emergence of Islam as a dominant force signals the onset of a "New Era": in the Middle East, with the fall of Persia's Sassanid dynasty in 641; in India, with the death of Harsha of Kanauj (606–646), who brought about the great temporary unification. While this leaves some seventy years of confusion and schism until the year 712, when the Islamic armies led by Mohammed Bin Qasim commenced their attack on the Sind region, it does not seem inappropriate as a demarcation point for the end of the ancient era.

In any event, for our purposes it is not strictly necessary to point to a single moment as marking the instant when the ancient era came to an end; the transition process is, as I indicated earlier, protracted and multiform and, in the case of the ancient era, its brand of civilization and its social paradigms had been gradually disintegrating for quite some time. The crisis that beset the ancient civilizations of the West, China, the Middle East, and India around the time of Christ touched off a major process of transformation. What sustained and accelerated this process, until it became irreversible, was a fundamental change in the ethical values and the notions of taste which had formed the matrix from which ancient civilization had developed. The social paradigm on which ancient society had based itself now began to disappear from every facet of that society.

Two phenomena served to undermine this fundamental paradigm. The first was the change in the basic outlook of those who lived in advanced nations like the Roman Empire or Han China. At the moment around the time of Christ when, for all practical purposes, Rome and Han China ran out of frontiers, the depletion of their forests deprived them of the ability to increase their productive capabilities. Moreover, the supply of slaves—in economic terms, a source of energy as well as a tool of production—began to shrink. The weaker the empires became, the less they were able to convince barbarian tribes that fighting for the imperial army served any function, which drastically undercut imperial power. Thus deprived of the essential ingredients of land, energy, and tools, the ancient societies could no longer augment their productivity, and this forced the citizens to face the fact that the days of plenty were coming to an end.

In the hearts of the ancients, the empathetic impulse went to work. The powerful obsession with material things began to taper off. By the second century A.D., people in both the Orient and the Occident were increasingly drawn toward an introspective rather than a material ideal, and modes of thought began to spread that condemned and demeaned the seeking of social status and material wealth as vulgar attachment to the things of this world. In the Roman Empire, the burgeoning popularity of pagan cults that praised those who kept themselves "poor but pure" was evidence of this new trend, which in China manifested itself in the spread of Taoism and the secret arts and ascetic practices of hermits.

In Rome after the passing of the "five good emperors," only Philistines shameless and grasping enough to toady to emperors as monumentally foolish as Caracalla and Commodus were allowed into the inner circle that held the reins of power. Likewise, in China after the second century, the Later Han rulers frequently sold court appointments to raise revenue and the eunuchs were able to exert considerable authority. Self-respecting men of principle gave public office, family life, and the pursuit of wealth a wide berth, preferring to drown their sorrows in bouts of wine drinking and otherworldly discourse that transported them to the realms of fantasy. "The Seven Sages of the Bamboo Grove" were representative of this time. Their retreat from reality was a way of turning their backs on the ethics and tastes of ancient civilization.

There was also a dramatic decline in the sciences, once the pride of ancient civilization, with literally no scientific progress taking place in Rome or China after the second century. As for the arts, which are the forerunners of change in any epoch, the pursuit of realistic representation had completely degenerated. Although artists of the Mediterranean basin had produced brilliant realistic sculpture in great quantity and quality, their work is of little interest after the second century. In China as well, artists in the tradition that produced outstanding representational depictions of horses and soldiers during the Qin and Former Han eras turned out work that is oddly crude and artless during the Later Han.

One cannot imagine that man abruptly lost either his capacity to think creatively or the talents required for realistic depiction. The giant empires were still secure, most of their territories were at peace, and their economies were not in great disarray. Conditions sufficiently stable to allow scientists and artists to immerse themselves in the labors of research and creation still existed. But scientific research and realistic art were practically abandoned nonetheless: artists, thinkers, and citizens had lost interest in material reality and forsaken the scientific spirit and aesthetic sense that exulted in observing and recording "things as they are." For by this stage, the values of the coming medieval era were already latent in the hearts of those who lived in the advanced regions.

How the Middle Ages Began:
Shifts in Population Patterns

One other element was working to undermine the tastes and ethics of ancient civilization. It was the enormous influx of people from the less developed peripheries into the advanced regions spurred by the discrepancies in wealth and population between the two.

Earlier I described how population began to shrink in the advanced regions and to surge along their peripheries around the time of Christ. This led to a situation where those who were too poor to eat forsook the underdeveloped regions to head for the more advanced areas where prosperity reigned and population was on the wane. It was not simply a matter of the "excess populations" from outlying areas hurling themselves willy-nilly into the advanced regions, for virtually all residents in the "center" now aspired to perform sedentary labor in the major urban areas, making it necessary to bring in individuals willing to do farmwork or construction. During the initial phase lasting until roughly A.D. 200, the vast majority of the "barbarians" who made such moves in Rome and China worked either as slaves or at menial physical labor.

Yet as time passed, some of these new arrivals came to own their own farms and businesses or became scholars or amassed personal wealth. And some of them, of course, intermarried with the local population.

The quickest and easiest way for the outsider to gain acceptance was by becoming a mercenary. The locals, supported by welfare or their sedentary jobs in the affluent and convenient urban centers, had no desire to enter the armed forces. To build up the military strength of these empires, hiring barbarians was the only alternative.

In any age, the ultimate foundation of a nation's authority is its military. Without the allegiance of the army, neither monarch nor parliament can maintain status and authority. In an age of mercenaries, an apparatus involving preferential treatment is a necessity. Funds are raised for bonuses and incentives; land is promised to the soldier after his demobilization. These privileges cannot be denied on the basis of the soldier being a "barbarian."

It is only to be expected, of course, that over time these steps foster the economic self-sufficiency of the non-native community. As such individuals succeed in establishing themselves economically, their "dependents" (others of the same background who rely on them for support) emerge in force. If these find employers or sponsors who speak the same language and observe the same customs, the trauma of cultural adjustment need not be faced. Like an avalanche gathering force, their numbers grow until their ideas and customs permeate the lower stratum, or base, of the society. Even so, the immigrants themselves continue to respect and yearn for the prosperity and easy living of the "higher civilization" and do all they can to "fit in"—rather like immigrants from developing countries presently in the United States. For all their efforts, however, such assimilation remains superficial. They change the clothes they wear, study the language, conform to the life-styles and "system," and try to follow the principle of parity exchange as they make a go at living in the new environment. These adaptations, however, cost them great hardship.

For the Germanic peoples, the Mongols, and other tribes from the northern reaches who had been living in undeveloped forests and plains, life up to this point in time had been based almost entirely on hunting and herding; so far they had been largely untouched by ancient civilization. Thus they had little inherent interest in materialism or the trappings and products of ancient civilization.

Of course these people required material goods and wanted

more of them. But unlike their "civilized" counterparts, they did not possess an aesthetic outlook that equated happiness with the quantity of things they owned, nor were they committed to a moral outlook in which everything was sacrificed in an effort to increase the number of objects that constituted such plenty. The social paradigm that presupposed the principle of parity exchange remained foreign to them. Deep in their hearts, vestiges of the tribal, communal values that antedated the tastes and ethics of ancient civilization must have persisted. If some momentary provocation brought such impulses to the surface, these less than completely assimilated people no doubt found themselves awash in expressions of contempt and alarm from the natives around them.

However, as the numbers of such immigrants increased and they acquired financial influence, they formed their own neighborhoods. Within these enclaves there was no need to strictly observe the customs and systems of the advanced region. One did not have to hide one's tastes and mores; indeed, cleaving to the "old ways" was approved: if assimilation went too far, there were neighbors ready to denounce one as a "race traitor" or "toady" or "sell-out." This phenomenon can be observed today among some groups of Hispanics and Asians in the United States.

The greater the preponderance of such "societies within the society," the greater their political and social clout; they begin to exert an influence upon the systems and way of life of the advanced regions into which they've moved. At the least, original inhabitants must learn to live with a variety of overlapping customs and practices. Inevitably some of the members of the advanced society find these unfamiliar cultural elements of interest and make a positive effort to appreciate and comprehend them. Before long, the society finds itself overrun with "progressives" who maintain that there is much to be learned from the less advanced cultures; and now there emerge droves of that superficial breed of people who imitate everything foreign. Take the example of Rome under Diocletian (ruled A.D. 285–305), when Roman troops actually wore trousers. Or Later Han China, when those who could afford it slept in Western-style beds. Society itself began to reflect this hodgepodge of influences, and the social paradigms became composites of these influences.

In short, the massive numbers of partially assimilated immigrants from underdeveloped areas caused shifts in population patterns and power within the ancient empires, which served to speed them down the path to transformation. Even an empire such as Rome, which had prided itself on its pragmatic rationality, found that by the end of the second century religion had become such a potent force in the political arena that the state had to choose between either actively suppressing it or making it the basis of the state's own authority. So too Rome's equally down-to-earth counterpart, Later Han China, was riven and weakened by uprisings of the "advocates of the Great Peace" (T'ai P'ing) even as Rome was tearing itself apart over the issue of the merits or horrors of Christianity. The Sassanid Persian empire established early in the third century had designated Zoroastrianism as its state religion and thus was already a semimedieval state, yet it, too, had to agonize over how to deal with the form of Christianity practiced by the Nestorian sect and by Judaism. Insofar as a defining characteristic of medieval society is its preoccupation with matters of the spirit, the transition to a medieval state was already well under way.

In both the Occident and the Orient, then, the ancient form of civilization was disintegrating even before the Western Roman empire and the Western Jin dynasty were toppled. The events that led to their political collapse simply delivered the finishing blow.

How India's Ancient Era Persisted—
A Link Between the Classical and Modern Eras

India presented a somewhat more complicated situation. To begin with, the Indian subcontinent has on only rare occasions experienced anything like political unity. It has come close on only three occasions: under the Mauryan dynasty at the time of King Asoka (274–236 B.C.); at the peak of the Mughal empire (c. 1600); and under British rule in the modern era. The fact that the subcontinent was consolidated during the colonial era that persisted into this century makes it easy to misconceive what the history of the region has been. Riven by political schism and strife, it more closely resembles Europe than China in its geohistorical pattern.

Another point to bear in mind is the way in which India's fertile land attracted hordes of nonindigenous peoples to the area during the ancient era. The Indo-Aryans who gave birth to Hindu culture were themselves a people who had migrated in remote antiquity, while the Greek forces left behind by Alexander were another nonindigenous group who entered during the ancient era; they were succeeded by the Huns and the Parthians or Pahlavas. India, like the Mediterranean and northern China, also attracted "excess" people from less-developed regions as these saw their populations surge. The last group of northern invaders of India, the Rajput clans, emerged as serious contenders for hegemony around the seventh century, when they succeeded in breaking up the great kingdom that Harsha of Kanauj had once built up.

On the other hand India, with its warm and humid climate, is said to have suffered the depletion of its forests at a later date than did the lands of the Mediterranean basin, the Middle East, or China, from which we might safely infer that the changes associated with an energy shortage were likewise delayed on the subcontinent. On that basis, I believe it is reasonable to regard India's version of ancient civilization as having persisted into the mid-seventh century, up to the point when Harsha of Kanauj died (A.D. 646).

As for the arts, India continued to pursue a voluptuous realism long past the point when Western and Chinese artists had distanced themselves from a purely representational approach. Nor were the Indians as quick to forsake scientific pursuits. With pagan tribes a growing presence on the subcontinent, however, art forms increasingly pandered to mere sensual stimulation, and by the Chandella dynasty during the era of Rajput domination in the ninth century, Indian art had come to consist of such works as the enormous and grotesquely sensual nude reliefs carved into the walls surrounding the Khajuraho temple. The phantasmagorical imagery unique to Hindu statuary also developed during this period.

Indian science at this juncture likewise turned from the material world to the realm of the purely theoretical, and made great strides in chemistry, astronomy, and mathematics. One of its surpassing achievements was the formulation of the mathematical concept of zero. It would be a long time, however, before this concept inspired any practical applications in technology or production. One might refer to Indian society during this era—from roughly the fourth to the seventh centuries—as representing either a "protracted ancient stage" or a "semimedieval stage" of civilization.

India's protracted ancient stage has exerted a profound influence on the history of human civilization. The persistence in India of a form of rationalism (which nomads and migrating tribes carried along the Central Asian corridor through the Himalayas to China) stimulated the development during the Song dynasty of what we might call "Song rationalism," which in its numerous applications launched what could fairly be designated a "protomodern age" in China.

In the West, what revived interest in material things was the influx of exotic oriental goods that pilgrims and Crusaders visiting the Holy Land brought back from the Middle East, starting in the eleventh century. In China, in contrast, the stirrings of such a rebirth were already being felt in the seventh century. That was only possible, I believe, because the "exotic items" brought from the West (in this case, originating in India) by Sogdian traders plying the routes between Iran and China provoked a similar resurgence of interest in material things on the part of the Chinese. When as a consequence the Chinese in the tenth century disseminated technology based on the use of coal throughout their empire, the resultant excess production stimulated massive development.

The narrow trade routes linking India and China geographically also served as a bridge between epochs—the protracted ancient era that persisted so long in India and the protomodern age that arrived so early in China.

TRACKING THE "DISRUPTIVE ELEMENTS" THAT UNDERMINE CIVILIZATIONS: WHERE THEY STAND TODAY

The "Disrupters of Civilizations": Changes in Technology, the Resource Supply, and Population

Previously I described how the ways in which the members of a society define beauty and ethical responsibility form the foundations for those social paradigms that give that society its particular identity. But it should be understood that the manner in which a society perceives beauty and moral truth is not the outcome of chance or of the propagandistic machinations of particular groups or individuals, but of elements I choose to call the "disrupters of civilization."

The first disruptive element is technology. The fact that technology plays an important role in bringing about social and cultural change has already been pointed out by Joseph Schumpeter and others. However, Schumpeter's consideration of the innovative effects of technological development, which relates them only to the business cycle and social progress within industrial society, is conceptually far too narrow. Even so, Schumpeter's thoughts contain important elements. Specifically, the prevailing historical outlook has too often considered technology as a result rather than a cause or formative element in the development of a civilization. The typical expression of this outlook runs along these lines: "Since civilization attained such a high level, technology also advanced." Schumpeter's presentation addresses this misconception and, in refuting it, makes a number of key points.

Claiming as we do that technology is one of the "disruptive elements" capable of triggering a new form of civilization, we must also acknowledge that a technological advance can occur in a society before that society has itself reached a very advanced stage of development. Societies at a quite limited stage of development have frequently served as the launching pads for a major breakthrough in vital fields of technology. This was the case when the technology of refining iron ore was developed at the beginning of the ancient era; when coal-utilization technology was diffused throughout China in the ninth century; and when use of steam engines spread through eighteenth-century England. None of these societies was considered to represent the vanguard of civilization at the time the breakthroughs occurred; they were considered peripheral cultures far removed from the centers of the civilized world.

That technological innovation is very often nursed into being by just such straitened circumstances is something all will acknowledge. "Necessity is the mother of invention": Innovation occurs when conditions propel the human intellect to shoulder a given task. But this does not mean that all inventions are the children of necessity in the sense that they fulfill a particular social desire. Key technologies that trigger full-scale social transformations are more likely to be chance discoveries. They resemble mutations in the course of biological evolution.

Furthermore, a technology may be born of necessity in the eyes of a society and nonetheless prove to be a disrupter of that society. A technology may progress by such extraordinary leaps that its actual applications outstrip the wildest dreams envisioned for it. For thousands of years men have dreamed of flying through the skies like a bird, but none dreamed of flying hundreds of persons over the Pacific at the speed of sound. The presence of airborne vehicles among us has drastically raised the expectations we make of them.

For this reason, a dramatic technological advance may generate an excess in one type of commodity even as it fosters shortages of others, creating a new environmental balance in which man's empathetic impulse will goad him to redefine his needs and change his patterns of consumption. The result of this process will be a new social paradigm predicated on that particular technological system. The distinguishing features of ancient civilization, for example, were linked to the irrigation technology that made cultivating land for agricultural use a possibility, while modern civilization derives its identity from its access to factory-based manufacturing. However, it would not be correct to describe technology as the sole potential disruptive element capable of provoking a social transformation, for transformation can occur even when technological progress is not being made. At the time when the ancient form of civilization went into its death throes, for example, technology as such was in a stagnant phase.

The second potential disruptive element is the supply of resources. This variable could also be referred to in broader terms involving the variables of environment, climate, and the natural features of a particular landscape.

The Japanese are very committed to the notion that the physical and climatic environment exerts a formative influence on any racial group's cultural identity. Japanese often explain the character of a civilization—or even the characters of particular individuals—in relation to the features of the region that brought them into being. Without a doubt man's empathetic impulse—the instinct that most defines cultural forms in its responses to surpluses or shortages of commodities—is most often activated by factors in the physical environment. No amount of advanced technology is likely to assure, for example, that the inhabitants of desert cities will be blessed with as cheap and abundant a supply of water as is available in Japan.

However, if one wishes to discuss cultural variations in terms not of differences between regions but of changes that take place in a given culture over time, the definition of "environmental variables" should not be limited only to those that involve climatic, topographical, or other natural conditions, but should be broadened to include other factors that affect the supply of resources. After all, the supply of any given resource in a particular environment is likely to vary significantly over time.

Variations in the supply of particular resources have their own sets of causal factors. Technological advances will often dramatically increase the supply of particular resources; and economic growth can drive up demand. But it is also not unusual for supply and demand to fluctuate drastically through the chance discovery of a major new source or due to a cataclysmic upheaval in the natural environment. I have already mentioned how the depletion of forestry resources in the ancient civilized zones brought about their decline and how the discoveries of huge oil fields in the Middle East enabled the postwar petroleum civilization to take shape.

Population factors constitute the third potential disruptive element.

Economists long spoke of population as the consequence of economic forces. The gist of this outlook was simple: "Where there is food to eat, population increases." There was even a school of thought that held that economic growth could be monitored by direct reference to population increases or decreases. Its adherents would look at the fact that population growth did not occur under the Tokugawa shogunate during the second half of its reign and would then proceed to place more emphasis than necessary on the economic stagnation that was a facet of this period.

One need only glance at the situation in today's advanced nations, however, to realize that not only is the statement that "population increases where there is food to eat" not always true, but neither is its converse—that "population decreases where there isn't enough to eat." Currently the birthrates in Japan and Western Europe—where people have clothes on their backs and more than enough to eat—have declined greatly from what they were, even as population has exploded in the far poorer developing countries. The phenomenon is not unique to our times; the late stages of the ancient era show a comparable pattern.

Population change can itself become the disruptive element (the sole perpetrator, so to speak) that precipitates the transformation of a civilization; it can also be a passive by-product (the victim, as it were) of such transformations.

There are other variables beyond these three (technological change, changes in resource supplies, and population shifts) that may also be considered potential disrupters, acting alone or in concert to induce a social transformation. Prime among these is what I would call the "ethnic environment"—the type of relationship (hostile or smooth, and to what degree of intensity) that exists between the peoples who live on the peripheries of a major civilization and those who live at its center.

The Japanese culture evolved in an archipelago so isolated from other countries that its inhabitants might as well have been living on the proverbial desert isle. As a result, the Japanese tend to turn a blind eye and a deaf ear to problems that involve diplomatic and military considerations. This accounts for their heightened sensitivity to ways in which the "natural features" of an environment influence a culture and for their tendency to downplay ethnic environment as a factor. In nations that are part of a continental land mass or on contiguous islands with other nations as near neighbors, the movements of surrounding groups loom much larger. The presence of a powerful and hostile race as a neighbor requires enormous expenditures of resources and time, forces a people to change their ways of thinking, and creates a state of heightened tension.

There are epochs during which a culture is deeply conscious of the presence of other peoples and of cultures essentially different from itself, and other epochs in which their presence is less deeply felt. The system, or map, according to which other cultures are perceived and classified can also mutate from age to age.

For the inhabitants of ancient civilizations, the distinction between civilized peoples and barbarians was vital. The Qin and Han dynasties and the Roman empire absorbed tribe after tribe of alien peoples, granting them citizenship after a generation if they acculturated. In contrast, medieval man placed importance on differences in religious beliefs. For modern man, the focus is race. The expenditure of resources and the type of consideration allotted to military defense in a given era rest on these sorts of distinctions.

Thus, certain facets of the ethnic environment—the types of relationships existing among various peoples or tribes coinhabiting a particular region in a given era—were established by the form of civilization then prevailing. I have a strong feeling that the prevailing ethnic environment is in its turn capable of inducing changes in a society and civilization, but analyzing the form and extent of these changes is a task for which my lack of knowledge disqualifies me. I hope that others will explore this topic.

Another potential "disruptive element" is the issue of organization. The process of change in a society or civilization also alters the function, character, and structure of its various organizations. Differences between forms of organization tend to enable or restrict a society in making effective use of a particular technology. Therefore, organizational changes that may evolve during a period in which technology itself remains unchanged have the potential in and of themselves to induce a transformation in a society or its form of civilization.

A minority of scholars contends that the transformation from the primary stage to the ancient form of civilization had more to do with an increased capacity to organize than with a spectacular technological leap. We also have Adam Smith's suggestion that the major breakthrough in the development of modern industrial technology was the acceptance as an operating premise of the concept of the division of labor—that is, the concept of function-specific organizational division. Smith's point seems incontrovertible.

It is impossible to explore this issue in further depth because the level of scholarship by historians specializing in the history of organizational development is far less advanced than is the case in the other subspecialties of history. So I will confine myself to making the point that a social transformation must also decisively transform the principles of organization in a society; it is an inevitable result.

Population Explosions in Areas Where There Isn't Enough Food

Ancient and modern societies resemble one another in a number of ways. Both champion notions of taste and ethical systems that define *happiness* in terms of a plentiful supply of goods, and *justice* as anything that contributes to such plenty. Both also proceed on this basis to establish exchange parity— the principle of a fixed price for a given good—as a social paradigm (even if, in the case of ancient societies, their capacity to enforce the paradigm is inhibited by the state of their technology and information networks).

We have already discussed those disruptive elements that foster the birth of new forms of society and civilization and hasten the demise of those that have run their course. The next question is, Where do things stand with these disruptive elements at the present moment? The answer should provide us with important clues about the fate of modern industrial society.

Let us begin with population, where changes have been the most striking.

As previously noted, J. N. Biraben estimates that global population began falling rapidly in the second century as the ancient era was ending; launched into a conspicuous recovery starting in the tenth century; suffered a temporary but precipitous drop in the fourteenth century; but surged fiercely in the next (see Chart 2). By then the onset of the modern era was under way. Unprecedented acceleration thereafter became the rule, particularly once the industrial revolution in the late eighteenth century commenced the full-scale shift to an industrial society. According to estimates prepared by the United Nations (see Table 2), the figure for world population (around 900 million in the year 1800) reached 1.65 billion in 1900, 2.25 billion in 1950, and 4.4 billion in 1980. The United Nations report expects it to reach 6.1 billion by the year 2000 and to climb to 8.2 billion by 2025. As for rates of annual increase, these were 0.5 percent in the nineteenth century, 0.8 percent in the first half of the twentieth, and should average 1.9 percent for the second half of this century (see Table 4).

On the basis of these figures, one could say that not only is population growth—a distinguishing feature of the industrial society—thriving; it is on the upswing. It is the ingredients of growth that pose the problem.

In 1800, roughly 250 million of the world's 980 million people lived in the advanced regions—Eastern and Western Europe, North America, Japan, Australia, and New Zealand—while 730 million lived in developing regions (see Table 2).

Table 2: Trends in Global Population
(in millions)

Year	Global Population	Advanced Regions	Developing Regions
1750	791	201	590
1800	978	248	730
1850	1262	347	915
1900	1650	573	1077
1950	2255	832	1693
1960	3037	945	2092

Figures from 1985 on are forecasts.

Year	Global Population	Advanced Regions	Developing Regions
1970	3695	1047	2648
1980	4432	1131	3301
1985	4826	1170	3656
1990	5242	1206	4036
2000	6119	1272	4847
2010	6988	1321	5667
2025	8195	1377	6818

Table 3: Breakdown of Global Population by Regions (1960–2025)
(in millions)

Region	1960	1970	1980	1990 (projected)	2000 (projected)	2025 (projected)
Africa	275	355	470	635	853	1542
Latin America	216	283	364	459	566	865
East Asia	722	887	1058	1204	1346	1581
South Asia	877	1116	1404	1731	2075	2819
North America	199	226	248	274	299	343
Western Europe	328	356	374	386	391	401
Oceania (island nations)	16	19	23	26	30	36
Japan	94	104	117	123	129	131
Soviet Union and Eastern Europe	311	345	375	406	431	486

Table 4: Trends in Global Population Increases
(percent)

Year	World Total	Advanced Regions	Developing Regions
1800–1850	0.5	0.7	0.5
1850–1900	0.5	1.0	0.3
1900–1950	0.8	0.8	0.9
1950–2000	1.9	0.9	2.2
1950–1960	1.8	1.3	2.0
1960–1970	1.9	1.0	2.3
1970–1980	1.8	0.8	2.2
1980–1990	1.7	0.7	2.0
1990–2000	1.6	0.5	1.8

Source: United Nations Estimates

The ratio was roughly 1 to 3. By 1900 the population in the advanced regions had climbed to 573 million as against 1.077 billion in the developing areas, a shift to a ratio more like 1 to 1.8. By 1950 the figures were 832 million and 1.693 billion respectively—a ratio of roughly 1:2—with the proportion of those in developing countries beginning to climb, but not too dramatically; however, to the extent that some of this shift represented population movement from advanced regions to developing ones (migrations to Latin America and South Africa), the overall trend still clearly pointed to greater proportional increases by the peoples of the advanced regions. Whether one uses estimates by Allen J. Wilcox or Timothy J. Carr and Susan Saunders or the United Nations report on the first half of this century, and however one chooses to factor in migratory movements, the inescapable conclusion is that population growth between 1800 and 1950 was far greater in the advanced regions. In the second half of the nineteenth century, population grew in advanced regions almost four times as rapidly as in developing regions. These conditions bear out the observation that population increases where there is food to eat.

From the beginning of the Great Depression of the 1930s, however, a new pattern begins to emerge, one which by the second half of this century amounts to a complete reversal of the previous trend. While the average annual rate of population increase in the advanced regions during the 1950s was 1.3 percent, it was 2.0 percent in the developing regions; in the 1960s, the rates were 1.0 and 2.3 percent respectively; in the 1970s, 0.8 and 2.2 percent; and by the 1980s they had become 0.7 percent for the advanced regions and 2.0 percent for the developing ones (see Table 4).

Furthermore, a large proportion of the population increases in advanced nations are now accounted for by increases in longevity and the inflow of migrants from developing countries.

If we look only at birthrates, the patterns for most nations in the advanced regions point toward decreases in population. If, as in the ancient era, there had been no increase in life expectancy during the 1980s, the population figures for people born in advanced regions would in fact have declined considerably over the last decade.

In contrast, the populations of the developing areas continued to grow rapidly, although the rate of increase itself has declined somewhat. According to the United Nations, the population of the developing areas grew at an annual rate of 52 million in the 1960s and 68 million in the 1970s, but reached 85 million in the 1980s and is expected to approach 100 million in the 1990s. We are now witnessing the tragic phenomenon of population going down where people have food and skyrocketing where they do not. The result has been a precipitous and growing imbalance between the advanced and developing countries in wealth as well as population. This is a well-known fact, as is the fact that hungry third world citizens have been spurred to migrate in large numbers to advanced nations where there is a decent food supply. This is especially noticeable in the United States, which has absorbed large numbers of Latin American and Asian immigrants.

It is estimated that 12 million illegal immigrants from Latin America entered the United States between 1975 and 1985 and that only one-third of them were arrested and sent back. Even the United States is powerless to stop this influx at the source. Indeed, some governments have publicly acknowledged that they are urging fleets of refugees ("boat people") to leave, and others vigorously resist the notion that they are under any obligation to repatriate citizens who've been caught attempting to enter the United States illegally. Things have reached such a pass that certain nations no longer regard it as a source of shame that their own citizens are willing to break laws in order to get out.

We cannot rule out the possibility that a day will arrive when literally hundreds of thousands of people from developing countries will begin to form hordes and force themselves on the advanced nations. It would not be at all surprising if this occurred before the end of the century. The possibility exists of great racial migrations in the near future.

The emerging trend toward massive population movements clearly resembles those of the Later Han era in China, the Three Kingdoms era in India (when the Sakas, Pahlavas, and Kushans ruled), and of Imperial Rome. Modern historical scholarship, which is oriented toward political history, has tended to attach importance only to incidents involving organized military invasions (such as those during the final phase of the Jin dynasty in China or the storming of Imperial Rome by barbarians from the north) that led directly to the collapse of those dominating empires. Well in advance of these events, however, the imbalances of wealth and population between the peripheries and advanced regions had precipitated a massive influx of barbaric peoples who became low-class laborers, slaves, or mercenaries in the advanced regions. This flow of poor peoples from overpopulated societies to less populated wealthy ones is analogous to the current situation in the United States and Western Europe.

The Resource Picture Changes and Desert Wastes Encroach on Once-Fertile Land

As for the second potential disruptive element: the resource supply situation also changed dramatically after 1970.

The discovery of petroleum resources in the Middle East in the 1940s and 1950s has been lumped together with the discoveries of silver in Mexico in the sixteenth century and of gold in South Africa in the late nineteenth century, as one of the three great mineral discoveries in history, but the social impact of discovering oil was by far the greatest. That abundant Middle Eastern oil should have been found at this historical moment may indeed have been a happy accident. In any event, the return-on-exploration ratio—the balance between the costs of exploration and the value of the deposits thereby unearthed—has never been so high. Thanks to this, mankind was blessed from the 1950s through the early 1970s with an unprecedented abundance of cheap energy and could enjoy an affluence never dreamed of before.

However, when discoveries of new oil fields in the Middle East began to taper off and it simultaneously became clear that even the combined might of the advanced nations was powerless to reduce the political and military instability of the region, the era of cheap and abundant energy came to a rapid close. New discoveries of petroleum resources have continued since then—in Mexico, the North Atlantic and North Pacific, and in the Arctic Circle—but the costs of exploration and production have been ten times those encountered in the Middle East.

Furthermore, reliance on the resources of coal known to exist, though they may last for two hundred years, will also involve costs ten times greater than that faced when exploiting petroleum in the 1970s. Other newly discovered alternatives, such as atomic power, will involve costs at least as great, while the estimated price tags for using geothermal heat or solar energy are likely to prove even more prohibitive.

That modern civilization would abruptly collapse as a direct consequence of depleting its energy resources is highly unlikely. Should a sustained, crippling war break out in the oil-exporting region of the Middle East and the oil supply be cut off, industrial economies such as Japan's would be sure to suffer greatly. Viewed from a global perspective, however, the repercussions of such a crisis would not bring the end of civilization as we know it, and some kind of recovery would be accomplished. In the course of human history many regions have undergone savage destruction at the hands of nomadic tribes, but no record exists of a great civilization utterly disappearing as a result.

The issue is more likely to pose itself in terms of escalating energy shortages leading to escalating energy costs, creating a situation that civilization and society can resolve only by changing their very essences. Such a transformation is already well under way today, in the 1990s. I think it highly likely that the sort of transformation which the depletion of forests wrought upon the ancient form of society is now occurring in modern society.

The fact that tensions about the oil supply relaxed somewhat during the 1980s, allowing prices to drop, may have given us a temporary respite during which it was possible to stop worrying about limited resources, but all we will have to show for having enjoyed this short-lived respite is a further shrinking of our resources. It is all too likely that the 1990s will witness a return to rising demand and escalating prices.

But loss of another resource raises issues even more serious for man than would a permanent energy shortage. This destruction is currently occurring worldwide, as more and more of our land is being turned into desert.

For those living in advanced nations, the loss of frontiers (in the physical sense) can be seen as having taken place around the start of this century. Man had moved into every sector of the remaining frontiers in North and South America, Australia, South Africa, Northeastern China, and Siberia. Urban and industrial pollution (especially from mining) had become a conspicuous part of the landscape of Europe and the Eastern seaboard at this time, swelling the ranks of a then burgeoning drive for environmental protection. It seems that for the first time man began to sense that there was only so much space for him on this planet.

As luck would have it, the emergence of oil as an alternative to coal and the introduction of newly developed forms of transportation worked to alleviate any sense of impending crisis at the time, although droughts, dust storms, and the unseasonable cold that ravaged every corner of the globe during the 1930s underscored anew the limited capacity of advanced technology to overcome every obstacle to cultivation and development of new frontiers. This recognition explains the popularity of the "ecology" issue during the 1930s.

But if a wall of resistance to the idea of "unlimited development" had begun to form in the advanced nations, the spread of chemical-based fertilizers to almost every farm and of automobiles to most households—made possible by the abundant postwar supply of cheap petroleum—seemed to knock that wall down. By 1970, however, the destruction of forests and the water table was turning land into desert on such an enormous and striking scale that the problem could no longer be ignored; at the same time, the problems created by this phenomenon are on such a huge scale that they are beyond the capacity of man's current technology and knowledge to resolve.

Every year since the 1970s, over 69,000 square miles of forests have been destroyed, while 23,000 square miles of land have begun to turn into barren desert. Far from slowing down, the process is gathering speed. Land denuded of its forest reflects solar heat and reduces precipitation. It appears that not only do these formerly forested areas themselves become deserts; the areas around them begin to dry up as well.

Currently the encroachment of the desert is most pronounced along the southern rim of the Sahara but it can also be seen in the Middle East and India. Even in Thailand and Brazil, carpeted in green until but a few decades ago, the forests have been massively depleted and the soil beneath has been exposed to the sun. By the year 2000, the proportion of forested land on the planet will sink by 17 percent, and will decline all the more rapidly thereafter (see Table 5). The more pessimistic observers predict that by the year 2020, the amount of forested land will be one-fifth what it was in 1970, while the amount of desert will have doubled.

That the lands of developing nations with rapidly increasing populations are turning barren poses grave problems. This phenomenon is the underlying cause of the famines in Africa and is forcing large numbers of people there to migrate to other areas to seek relief. Deforestation and rampant population growth may affect the earth's atmosphere catastrophically in the not-too-distant future.

At this point, man has not only run out of frontiers to develop; he must also face the fact that much of the land he occupies is becoming unsuitable for production and habitation. It can be stated fairly that the conditions that caused the breakdown and decline of the centers of civilization during the latter days of the ancient era are being replicated in the second half of the twentieth century.

To be sure, there are those who insist that the energy prob-

Table 5: Current and Projected Figures on Global Land Resources
(1975–2000)
(Units: millions of acres)

	1975	2000	Amount	Rate of Change (%)
Deserts	1,956	3,171	+1,215	+62
Forests	6,331	5,229	−1,102	−17
Irrigated Land Damaged (by salt accumulation and other factors)	275	283	+8	+3

Source: U.S. Government Special Report—*The Globe in the Year 2000.*

lem can be resolved through the liquefaction of coal or advances in atomic power technology. And there are those who
think that by relying on biotechnology or synthetic protein,
we can achieve a breakthrough in the food problem, even with
more and more land turning into desert. Whether such high-
tech solutions can in fact rescue hard-up developing nations is
highly debatable.

Technological solutions or not, there will certainly be a
growing realization by people around the world that resources
are finite. This realization will bring into play the empathetic
impulse, and a forceful repudiation of the tastes and mores of
the era of material plenty. Great changes along these lines can
be expected before the twenty-first century.

The Direction of Technological Progress
Reverses Itself

Let us now consider the third potentially disruptive element,
technology. What is its current status?

Modern man sees technology as his area of highest achievement, the field of endeavor in which his past and present accomplishments continue to most dramatically supersede those
of his forebears. Yet in this aspect too the key "ingredients"
are changing, and a major shift in direction is under way.

There was a time, especially in the 1970s, when direly pessimistic views of technological progress and man's ability to
deal with its implications predominated. One aspect of this
outlook held that the major scientific frontiers had been conquered during and just after World War II and that the pace of
new development was shrinking; thus it was felt to be increasingly unlikely that the types of research and exploration then
under way would significantly improve or alter human society.
At the same time, the dangers and fundamentally inhumane

nature of "big" science and technology were underscored to make the point that scientific progress does not inevitably lead to greater human happiness.

Lurking in the background of these attacks on science and the notion of progress was a genuine bewilderment as to the direction of science and technology.

With the advent of the eighties, however, the overall pessimism about scientific progress seemed to lessen. Suddenly electronics-related technology seemed to surge forward, new computers and communications devices popped up everywhere, reaching more and more people, and a host of breakthroughs in biotechnology and synthetics opened up a new range of possibilities. More important, technological progress itself was being redefined in a way that represented a break with the "big science" approach that had prevailed up to that point. The character and function of technological progress were no longer perceived in terms of making products faster, larger, and in greater volume. The fields of technology that now held promise and appeal were those that led to greater diversity, greater diffusion of intelligence, and more efficient use of resources.

One reason for the change of direction was that the payoff on the technological breakthroughs then pursued were growing smaller and smaller. Let us consider the potential time savings of successive technological breakthroughs in transportation. When Tokyo and Osaka were first linked by trains, the journey (roughly 400 miles) took 24 hours. Since covering the same distance had previously required 12 days on foot, rail travel shortened the journey by 11 days. Fifty years later, the newly introduced *Tsubame* ("Swallow") superexpress train was making the trip in 7 hours, achieving a reduction of 17 hours. The next stage—the *Shinkansen*, or "bullet train"—undoubtedly represented a great leap forward in railway technology, but compared with its predecessor, it achieved a savings of a mere four hours. In the future, the most a super-high-speed (230 km/hr) train, such as the floating electromagnetic "HSST linear motor car," can hope for is to shorten the travel time by about one and a half hours—hardly a radical change.

In medical research as well, once dramatic results—such as the discovery of the antibiotics that cure tuberculosis—have given way to more attenuated and less conclusive achievements, such as the various therapies that have achieved partial success in suppressing cancer. Whereas treatment for tuberculosis—by assuring complete recovery for patients in their teens and twenties—can extend life expectancy for potential victims by as much as fifty years, cancer therapies more typically protract the lives of elderly patients by something like a decade. While the technological breakthroughs involved in the latter achievement may be on a massive scale, the social impact is far less dramatic.

When it comes to nuclear fusion or the generation of electric power through solar energy, the direct impact on society is even less immediately perceptible. The end product is the same electric power produced by hydroelectric or oil- or coal-burning plants.

The reader may feel I place too much emphasis on society's attitudes toward technological progress, and that this emphasis may simply be wrong. It may be a mistake to declare that a period of technological stagnation is already upon us. But I feel it is just to assert that the impact on society of technological progress is no longer as decisive as it was around the middle of this century.

Ever since the industrial revolution—nay, even in the period leading up to it—the main direction of technological progress has been toward greater size, quantity, and speed. This was "progress" aimed at increasing the volume of material goods in order to enable people to consume more and more of them. However, the social impact of progress conceived along such lines has steadily diminished in terms of its ability palpably to increase man's sense of satisfaction, and that reality has brought with it a sense of loss. The bewilderment over where technology might be taking us that set in during the 1970s no doubt reflects the fact that simply increasing volume, speed, and quantity are no longer goals that make sense to people.

By contrast, the types of technological advances that occurred in the 1980s represent a change of direction more appropriate for satisfying the desires of those who feel the supply of resources is finite. Scientific progress today is moving in a direction more in line with the desires of society at large, and this has resulted in more cheerful forecasts of its utility and impact.

Once more, for emphasis: the drive to enlarge, expand, and accelerate production—the main thrust of technological progress ever since the industrial revolution—began grinding to a halt during the 1980s. In its stead, the most striking recent technological breakthroughs have been those that produce greater diversification of function, greater diffusion of intelligence, and more efficient use of resources. Our goals, in other words, have begun to shift toward creating a greater variety of goods and services in response to individual preferences and fashion trends; the economies of mass production are no longer so compelling.

If we assume that technological development is pursued for the purpose of fulfilling and satisfying the desires of the people, the changing shape of consumer demand sends an important signal: it tells us that the very essence of the tastes and ethics of the consumers who make up society is being transformed and that civilization itself—which is ultimately the product of those tastes and ethics—is also being fundamentally transformed.

Art as a Leading Indicator of Change

Certain trends that asserted themselves as the 1980s began were clearly more than ephemeral phenomena. These were the growing popularity of a subculture devoted to conserving resources, increasing customization, diversification, and individuation of product lines, and the strong tendency for pricing to be based on the subjective appeal of such products rather than the stark fact that they offer a particular function at the lowest price. I believe that these changes are representative of a historical current that will prevail no matter how many outbursts of resistance and retreats may occur in the years ahead.

Further corroboration of my belief may be discovered in the arts, a field of human endeavor that tends to be in the forefront of any imminent social transformation.

Art, which was extremely symbolic during the primary stage of civilization and at times even veered toward abstraction, shifted with alacrity to a realistic mode at the very beginning of the ancient era. In their willingness to look at the things of this world on their own terms and to try to reproduce them objectively, without any infusion of their own subjectivity, these artists anticipated the rational and materialistic spirit of the ancient era.

Conversely, as ancient civilization began to exhibit symptoms of decline, representational expressions in the art world rapidly lost their vibrancy and turned to formalism and symbolism. The abstract patterns of medieval Islamic art are, for example, a gorgeous distillation of the powerful faith and the hints of a higher reality that characterize the spiritual life of that society.

In a like manner, the return of realistic representation in the fifteenth century anticipated the flowering of modern civilization. Botticelli and Leonardo da Vinci both attained their peak of activity around A.D. 1500, and it was in 1508 that Michelangelo began painting the ceiling of the Sistine Chapel. The activities of all three men predated Copernicus's *De Revolutionibus Orbium Coelestium* (1543) and Luther's 95 Theses (1517); Botticelli and Da Vinci were born over one hundred years before Galileo, Michelangelo almost ninety years before him. England's Glorious Revolution (1688), its Bill of Rights (1689), and Thomas Newcomen's invention of a steam engine for use in draining mines (1711) lagged behind the return to realistic representation in art by two hundred years.

Of the various phenomena described as "modern," the trend toward realism in the arts commenced before religion and science entered their modern phases and very far in advance of comparable transitions in politics or technology. This was no accident. Insofar as the roots of modernization may be found in the rational spirit that observes and seeks to understand things as they are, it is only natural that such observations would begin with external appearances; the impulse to record accurately the results of this contemplation of the external facets of things was thereby born, and with it realistic representation.

This effort to portray accurately the external forms of objects eventually led to curiosity about their interior anatomy and the principles governing their movement. It is telling that vivisectionists in fifteenth-century Venice should have belonged to the artist's union. The demand to conduct autopsies in order to better understand human anatomy arose among artists earlier than it did among physicians.

These studies of anatomical structure and the principles underlying bodily movement formed a linkage with the concerns of science and drove scientists to push for reform against the restrictions imposed by the church, which was opposed to study or contemplation of the world of matter on its own terms. For this spirit of reform to have practical consequences—for it to bring change in the political order—required not only recognition of the need for such reform throughout society, but the political power to implement it. And for the rational spirit in science to produce technological breakthroughs and industrial development required engineering skills, capital, and managerial competence. It goes without saying that a good deal of time is required to nurture these various elements to fruition.

It is not only that artists can accomplish their ends merely by manipulating externals, but that they, who possess the most acute sensitivity, need less time and money to achieve their purpose than do other members of society. They are free to create the conditions that allow them to be the first to anticipate and announce cultural transformations.

In this respect, it is worth noting that the tradition of realistic representation in art was already breaking down by the end of the nineteenth century. The masterworks of the Impressionists are more subjective than objective, more fervent than rational in approach. The abstract works of Paul Klee and Vassily Kandinsky, completed early in this century, are ultimately vehicles for intuitive glimpses of a higher reality. One may discern in the works of these geniuses an unmistakably noble beauty—but one that is far from the literal-minded rational spirit of the modern age.

In truth, the ranks of artists who are acknowledged as the masters of the Impressionist and Expressionist movements include several whose visions are idiosyncratic in a way that goes far beyond the usual stereotype of the rash and stubborn "eccentric artist." Not a few of them were alcoholics or suffered from psychological maladies of one sort or another. The fact of an artist's character or personality being "offbeat" should not lead to the work being devalued, of course. My only point is that in praising what some might call the "abnormal beauty" of these works, the twentieth-century art world is clearly being swayed by something other than the rational, materialistic values that created the modern industrial society. The most keenly sensitive individuals within modern industrial society, those least constrained by social and economic pressures, had already begun moving beyond the industrial society one hundred years ago.

And it is no accident that these antirationalist artistic movements should have flourished about the time that the frontier was disappearing.

What started in the fine arts has since expanded its range to encompass every other artistic domain and is now spreading into other fields, such as design, that directly affect our lifestyles.

Music that follows no clear system, films with plots that make no sense, hallucinatory or illusionistic photographs, fashions neither sumptuous nor comfortable (but marvelously expensive), long beards and hair—all these seemingly bizarre fads are part of the attempt to subvert rationalism and develop a postindustrial perspective. The revolution in popular culture symbolized by the Beatles and Mary Quant was by no means a short-lived fashion trend. The movement away from industrialism toward a knowledge-value society is not something that popped up out of nowhere during the last decade. The harbingers have been visible for a long time on any number of fronts. What has been missing is a unified vision of the new society in creation.

What sort of society will it be? What will be the social paradigms under which the new order will operate? Our attempts to answer that question require that we go back and look at history once again. To examine carefully what befell the world after the collapse of the ancient civilization that so resembles our modern industrial society seems to me the best means of grasping what may lie ahead. However circuitous this approach may seem, I don't believe it is wasted effort. For if we look at how another civilization, the medieval one, threw out a whole system of ethics and tastes based on the idea that an abundance of material things could bring happiness and developed and operated by a different set of paradigms, it may offer us indications of how a highly advanced civilization may be very different from the modern one we have known.

I would never say that the future is going to be the same as the past, and it follows that I have doubts about our ability to infer a future society from observations of medieval society. But we are too deeply immersed in the concepts and knowledge systems of modern industrial society; to recover our freedom of thought, I believe it necessary for us to get to know this very different society. It is on this basis that I proceed.

3

Is What Lies Ahead a High-Tech
Version of the Middle Ages?

The Birth Pangs of a New Society

Today, surrounded on every side by the advanced technology and abundant consumer goods that are part of our lives as citizens of the advanced industrial nations, we believe unquestioningly that the world we know—the world of the advanced industrial society—is the most highly evolved one human history has produced.

This cannot be categorically denied. The human race has never enjoyed such general wealth and security as can be found in today's advanced industrial nations. Our daily lives are simply awash in material goods, and the ease with which we can conduct communication, travel, and our jobs—thanks to a plenitude of modern conveniences and systems within the society—has greatly increased. There may be some specifically modern problems such as industrial pollution, contamination from numerous sources of the food we eat, frequent accidents and disasters, and the stress induced by adaptation to modern civilization, but comparing these problems with the malignant contagious diseases and parasites and marauding bandits that beset men in the past leads to the conclusion that ours is a world of considerable safety. Those who live in countries with advanced economies today can expect to enjoy unprecedented longevity.

Information today is communicated more speedily than ever before, primary education is available to virtually everyone, and opportunities to pursue higher education are increasingly open to those with the good fortune, ability, and effort to avail themselves of it. Science and technology have attained a high level of development. Social phenomena are minutely observed and analyzed in great detail. Respect for human life and protection of human rights are acknowledged social goals. Though there may be wide disparities in the wealth and influence of different members and constituencies within the society, it is clear that poverty and oppression do not jeopardize life to the extent that they did in preceding eras.

However many flaws and problems one may be able to point to within the advanced industrial societies of today, the number of areas in which they are superior to any society of the past is still far greater. In this sense, humanity has definitely progressed in its development.

However, when we look at human history over the long haul, we see that man has not progressed or advanced in a straight line from remote antiquity to finally achieve the type of society that exists today. Even if we confine ourselves to examining the seminal regions to which I earlier referred— those regions that produced cultures that were the most "advanced" or influential (in the sense of being widely imitated)—we find that over time their cultural constructs mutate strikingly, often in directions that steer them on a course diametrically opposed to the sort of standards by which modern society evaluates progress and civilization.

Without going so far as to say that it is true for all men at all times, we can say that, in the main, man has pursued his ideals and the quest for what he believed would be a better society on a more or less constant basis. It is in the nature of the beast. I find it hard to believe, moreover, that during certain periods of history the entire human race would suffer a sustained drop, in terms of its biological capacity to intelligently and dextrously pursue these goals. And yet it is a fact that over certain sustained periods human cultures moved in directions that carried them farther and farther away from what modern industrial society regards as desirable goals. This must mean that man's ideals and operating assumptions must themselves have mutated. If that is true, then the criteria according to which we conclude that the modern version of human society represents "the most advanced stage" are not universal, objective criteria, are not eternal and unchanging for all men and all places. And there is a strong possibility that the "society to come" after this one will have ideologies and social paradigms different from those that currently prevail.

From the earliest stages of the modern era, when industrial society was still in its preparatory phase, conditions in the advanced nations of the world were ripe for the pursuit of tastes and ethics that attached great importance to material things. It was a time when people were ready to pour all their energies into pursuing such a goal. The conceptions of beauty that men in the industrial nations had pursued for so long were at last being satisfied in a big way.

But these conceptions of beauty are not the only kind man is capable of attaining. The burst of volatility that in the early 1980s animated the disruptive elements that induce major social transformations is already sending out shock waves and beginning to alter the tastes and mores that have been accepted as dogma within the industrial society for so long. The three major potential disrupters of the established order—population shifts, changes in the resource supply picture, and new developments in technology—are in such an active state of flux that they are producing phenomena never before encountered in the industrial society.

Global population, which rose rapidly after the industrial society was formed in the eighteenth century, continues to climb, but the patterns have reversed themselves since 1960. The situation with resources and the environment is similarly turbulent. Even in the area of scientific and technological development, the source of pride and ultimate priority of industrial man, technological advances to increase speed, volume, and scale have virtually ceased, and efforts to diversify, to diffuse intelligence and function, and to conserve resources have become the main focus of technological development.

This trend is likely to continue for a long time. The dynamics of the global population explosion are unlikely to change anytime soon and there are no signs that the depletion of forestry resources or the encroachment of the desert upon formerly arable land will cease. That being the case, there is no basis for believing that technological development will again prioritize enhancement of speed, volume, and scale. The real technological progress will be directed at enhancing diversity, energy efficiency, and information functions.

With the death of the industrial society at hand and the birth of a new kind of society well under way, it is incumbent upon us, as members of some of the most advanced nations of the former, to seize our historical responsibility to attempt to predict the operating principles of the future society.

Speculations as to which historical moment most closely replicates the features of our own will inevitably point us toward that dark hour when the once-triumphant materialistic civilization and rational scientific spirit of the ancient world fell into disarray and yielded to the very different spirit of the medieval civilization that followed.

As Thucydides once eloquently stated, "the history of the future, insofar as human nature continues to guide it, will unfold along similar lines even if the specific conditions to which that nature must respond are different." It follows that similar situations in the past should prove to be reliable guideposts for exploring what is to come.

THE BIRTH OF AN ANTIMATERIALISTIC CULTURE AND ITS KEY FEATURES

"Progress" as Denial of the Materialistic Civilization

In the previous chapter I pointed out that the ancient and modern forms of civilization resemble one another in a number of ways.

As a result of the agricultural revolution in which men systematically constructed and operated irrigation and drainage systems that made it possible for them to open up and cultivate vast tracts of arable land, human society found itself blessed with an unprecedented abundance of material goods. The area available for human habitation expanded greatly and, as it became possible for men to produce a surplus beyond what they needed to assure survival, commerce was established on a permanent basis to facilitate the exchange and distribution of such surpluses. This in turn transformed the systems of administration of city-states into those of regional powers.

At the same time, the potential for vastly expanding the amount of arable land and surplus production gave birth to a system that utilized human beings as "tools with motive power." The system of slavery that had existed on a very limited scale in the primary stage that preceded the agricultural revolution was now implemented on a grand scale throughout the ancient world. More and more goods were produced as a result, and more and more commerce could thus be carried out.

Man's empathetic impulse focused on the sudden abundance of material things. Operating in such an atmosphere, man's organizations and forms of governance also emphasized functions that contributed to further increasing the supply of goods. Function-specific systems and organizations were formed and carried on their operations continuously over very long periods in ancient societies.

The ideologies that made possible the formation of ancient societies also expanded the supply of material goods in order to create a materially richer world. Scientific progress, technological development, function-specific organizations, territorial expansion, public works projects, fair administration of justice, and redistribution through a system of welfare were all obligations of the state that conformed to the ideology that made greater material affluence its goal. One of the social paradigms that became firmly rooted on the basis of this ideology was the price mechanism. Members of a society who see happiness in terms of increasing the amount of material goods and define justice in terms of the fair distribution of same are likely to agree on no other method of exchange.

But the ancient form of civilization, like those which preceded and followed it, did not follow the same line of development forever; it gave way to something else. To put it in very broad terms, the ancient mode of civilization—in its essential outlines—was dying out in China by the second and third centuries, and in the Mediterranean domains of the Roman empire by the end of the third century. Even if the ancient empires managed to stay alive as political entities for some time after that, the essential ingredients that had constituted ancient civilization during its prime had already been replaced by something else.

The situation was more complicated and the transformation a good deal more protracted in India, but certainly by the middle of the eighth century, when the empire created by

Harsha of Kanauj had disintegrated, the last of the ancient civilizations can be said to have died out.

The collapse of one type of society is synonymous with the birth of the form that succeeds it. To say that ancient civilization broke down is to say that the culture of the society to come, the medieval, established itself. The second and third centuries in China and the third and fourth centuries in the Mediterranean basin constituted the formative phase of medieval culture. We would do well to remember that the breakup of the ancient (the "old society") and the evolution of the medieval (the "new society") are simply two phases of one process simultaneously unfolding.

Modern man tends to take a grave view of the collapse of the ancient civilization and to think of this transformative phase as one in which civilization degenerated and human society was in retreat. Emphasis is placed on those violent and destructive aspects of the transition that reinforce this grim view. Attributing the collapse of ancient civilization to the "invasions by barbarians from the North" and their "savagely destructive acts" is typical of this approach.

That the Western Roman empire was destroyed by invading Germanic tribes from the North, or that the Western Jin dynasty met its end at the hands of marauding nomads from the steppes along the northern reaches of China are matters of literal fact; that attacking Huns from the North and Rajputs from the South caused the dissolution of the kingdom that ruled India is also literally true. But it would be utterly erroneous to believe that these military invasions by barbarians are what demolished the ancient civilization or brought about the "dark ages" of the medieval era. The basic character and essence of these ancient empires had changed long before that; the decline of ancient civilization antedated the extinction of the political organizations and entities that had once embodied it.

In the case of the Western Roman empire, the religious influence of the East had spread and a number of small regional
powers were asserting their independence long before Odoa-
cer (434–493) restored the imperial crest to Byzantium. China
under the Western Jin dynasty also witnessed the rising popularity of Buddhism and Taoism and saw its domains beginning to split up into small autonomous territories. The conviction that good taste means consuming more goods and that
"anything that leads to more goods for the people is proper
and just" was vanishing, while the hermetic medieval spirit
that celebrated vows of poverty and a retreat into the mountains, fields, and forests of nature was catching hold.

What caused the breakdown and final extinction of the ancient world was not the overthrow of civilization by the mind-
less ignorance and savagery of barbarians from the North. It
was the change in tastes and ethics that had been under way
long before that. Only when that change had taken hold could
great empires boasting enormous financial power and overwhelming populations be brought to their knees by impoverished and barbaric minorities.

This hardly means that such an outcome was welcomed by
the inhabitants of the civilized regions at the time. Wang Yen,
the Western Jin dynasty general who had to surrender the
realm to the barbarian Shi Lo, lamented as he did so that,
"This would not have happened had I not been so engrossed
in useless esoteric discussions, but had worked instead on
building up our defenses and finances." His was a lamentation no doubt shared by many of the elite members of the
Western Jin dynasty at the time; but it should be remembered
this same Wang Yen, who had scorned common speech and
mundane affairs, had been considered a great prodigy and had
quite won over the common folk with his tone of lofty ele-
gance.

The notion of the man in charge of national defense utterly

giving himself over to the intoxication of esoteric discussions can only strike a modern mind as sheer idiocy. It would seem quite natural to us that someone so callously irresponsible would be executed after the defeat for neglecting his duties. Yet so elegant and noble was Wang Yen's bearing that even the barbarian Shi Lo could not bring himself to behead his defeated adversary; and a far less humiliating expedient to the people of that time was resorted to: toppling a stone wall on Wang Yen and crushing him to death. So by the time of the Yong-jia Uprising (311–316), when this incident is said to have occurred, the issue of how one comported oneself before others—the issue of honor, in the medieval sense—already loomed large, even in the eyes of a so-called barbarian from the North.

Numerous instances of such seemingly remarkable behavior can also be cited from Western chronicles of this period. In 452 Attila the Hun, having reached the gates of Rome with his armies, was persuaded by Pope Leo I to remove himself to the North. It has been suggested that this barbarian's failure to sack the opulent capital grew out of a fear of being excommunicated by the pope; but this interpretation is no doubt Church propaganda intended to augment the specter of excommunication. It is quite inconceivable that Attila, who was not a Christian, would fear excommunication. Rather it would seem that he, like his counterpart Shi Lo, had advanced to the medieval stage of deriving spiritual satisfaction in abstaining from (and thereby transcending) merely materialistic benefits.

In short, the ancient civilizations did not die from the destruction or regression visited upon them, but were abandoned from within as the tastes and morals of their inhabitants shifted toward other values that were progressive in a quite different sense. These values belonged to the medieval culture then in its formative phase. If one adopts the values of medieval culture when looking at the situation, one will see these ages as periods when great advances were made in seceding from the crassly materialistic values of the past and toward a "better" kind of culture—one governed by God.

Today we believe that our societies continue to progress in stages. Science and technology keep reaching greater heights and economies continue to grow. Facilities for production and living have been further improved and consolidated and information has become even more widely dispersed. But this does not necessarily mean that the society of tomorrow will be a more advanced version of the industrial society.

If the tastes and ethics of both our own and the next generation turn out to be different from those that went with the industrial society, the society that is created as a consequence of our notions of progress will likely come to possess ideologies and paradigms divergent from those of its industrial predecessor. And it would not be strange if these societies, having less available for their material consumption, were to distance themselves from the rational spirit of the past. The people of the medieval era, as a result of what they considered great advances, created a society with less material consumption and a nonrational spirit.

Medieval Societies That Emphasized Social Subjectivity

Illustrated guides to botany of the type illustrated on the following page were published in Europe late in the thirteenth century. While there is nothing inaccurate in the carefully drawn portion of the plants that protrude from the soil, the underground portions reveal such phantasmagorical features as a root in the form of a tiny human figure with a tiny dog leashed to its neck (in the case of the mandrake root) and a root in the form of a legged fish (the pike weed). Appended to these remarkable illustrations, moreover, are scrupulous descriptions of the habitats, harvesttimes, compounds of which they form a part, and the medical efficacies of each plant.

Plants with tiny figures for roots do not, of course, literally exist. Yet the botanists of the time published these illustrated guides in perfect seriousness and the populace believed in them.

If people then believed that "God created man with His hands," or, "the earth is flat and the sun and stars move in the canopy that overhangs it," the primitive tools of observation then available to men can account for the fact; even now, children would innocently accept such explanations if they were proffered. But when it comes to a plant actually growing before one's eyes, not even a three-year-old today would be likely to believe that its root was a tiny man with a tiny dog leashed to his neck.

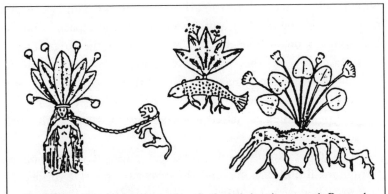

From the left: Mandrake root, pike weed, and the viper weed. Beneath these illustrations, the habitat, harvesttime, uses in compounds, and medical efficacies of each plant were recorded.

Source: Details from a thirteenth-century *Illustrated Botanical Guide.* Reprinted from Yūji Aida, *History of the World: The Renaissance, Volume 12* (Tokyo: Kawade Shobō Publishers, 1969)

Yet these illustrated botanical guidebooks were published and widely consulted at the close of the thirteenth century in Europe, at a time when the medieval era was already coming to an end. The Middle Ages produced countless comparable phenomena.

One of the authoritative documents that long held sway in medieval Europe was a sort of compendium on the devil and all his works. Not surprisingly, as it was a research document that savants and seers from academia and the Church had spent decades compiling, this exhaustive tome went into minute detail concerning the nature, behavior, form, and influences of its subject. Considered especially worthy of attention was the devil's sexual behavior, with such facts as his penis being narrow, hard, and as cold as ice explained at great length.

The investigation of Satan's sexual organs and behavior was a serious matter, since it was believed that women who had sexual intercourse with the devil would be transformed into witches who would then spread poisonous harm and mischief and visit misfortune on any who crossed their path. One of the statutes most venerated in Europe over the next several hundred years was that which dictated that "witches must be burned at the stake." Bassewitz has estimated that at least a million lives were sacrificed under this statute. The practice of burning witches persisted to as recently as the seventeenth century.

These two examples—the botanical guides with their phantasmagorical illustrations, and the obsessive devil "studies"—epitomize medieval culture in that neither even attempts to comprehend things in terms of the sight of one's eyes or the touch of one's hands upon the things of this world. Their explorations belong to another realm entirely.

This orientation may have reached its most striking form in the Christian civilizations of Europe, but it was not unique to that continent. In differing degrees the same tendency was at work in China, India, and the Islamic Middle East during this period.

In ancient art—whether from Greece, Rome, China, or India during the age of Gandhara art—fastidiously realistic depictions are the rule. With the onset of the medieval age, realism vanished, to be replaced by a symbolism that strikes one as almost childish, so artless is its execution.

In the portraits of the Virgin Mary one sees in medieval European churches, the proportions of torsos and faces are often terribly out of balance, while the figures of Christ and the saints that appear in Byzantine mosaics are elongated to the extent that they would seem to be incapable of maintaining an upright stance. The rule in portraiture was to make the bodies nine times as tall as the heads; artists who drew more realistically were rejected as incompetents.

In China, a comparable trend toward formalization commenced during the Tartar Partition (especially from the fifth century through the end of the sixth) when all emperors began to be drawn with virtually the same face. Perhaps the most prominent trait in portraits from this period is the constant tendency to exaggerate the size of the main figure, so that the face of the emperor is shown to be twice as large as those of his retainers. It is hardly as if every emperor of this era was a giant who happened to possess the same features as his predecessors. The artists of this period were compelled to draw their ideal figures on the scale on which they saw them, rather than objectively as the eye perceived.

It was probably Islamic art that carried this tendency to the furthest extreme. It rejected realistic modeling; only complicated abstract patterns were welcomed. The gorgeously complex patterns to be seen in Islamic shrines and palaces throughout the Middle East more than amply demonstrate that these artists possessed technical mastery of the first order. At the same time, they lacked the inclination accurately to observe and depict worldly things as they were. The medieval Islamic portraiture that has been passed down to us is so crude in its execution it hardly seems possible that it could belong to the same time and place that produced those elaborate abstract patterns. Once again we find outsize imperial figures drawn dead center in the composition.

So it would seem that with the onset of the Middle Ages, people turned their attention from the things of this world to allow the revelations and fancies that floated up from their hearts and imaginations to predominate in ways that were guided by the types of esoteric speculations in which their society had faith. The spirit of the medieval culture was one that possessed an abundance not of materialistic objectivity but of social subjectivity, which it held dear.

Medieval man, having small regard for material things, felt no imperative to be precise in acknowledging or recording their quantities. Whether in the West, the Orient, or India, medieval numerical records are almost always exaggerated or inaccurate to the most striking extremes. The numbers cited in the hyperbolic exchanges that appear in the *Song of the Nibelungen* or the *Song of Roland,* or those that allegedly record how many infidels were slain by victorious medieval armies in the histories written at the time, or the license to exaggerate that is a feature of Tang poetry ("until my white hairs grew to 30,000 feet in length"), all point to a penchant for deliberately unrealistic numerical expressions. Likewise, the numbers cited to describe military forces in Japanese classics of medieval thought like the *Hōjōki (An Account of My Hut)* or in the records of the Onin War are implausibly high. It would seem that in the Middle Ages, the stress in communicating information fell more on subjectively describing one's feelings than on accuracy or concreteness.

Such an orientation naturally did not spawn the kind of scientific spirit that closely observes the things of this world and seeks the principles that govern their forms and movements. Scientific technology stagnated completely—nay, even regressed—in the medieval era, particularly during its early phase (the era of the Tartar Partition in China or the fifth to tenth centuries in Europe). Fair progress can be seen in the latter medieval phase—the Tang period in China and the eleventh through thirteenth centuries in Europe—but certainly not at a very rapid pace and certainly not in every discipline; many fields of science needed a good deal of time simply to recover the level of understanding that had been achieved by the ancients.

Why the Religions of Less Developed Regions Were Adopted

Most commentators describe religion as a force that takes hold and thereafter effectively fetters all attempts to resist it. Certainly the Middle Ages were an era in which religion flourished throughout much of the world, at least in the seminal regions of civilization. But what led it to be accepted and to hold sway so powerfully for so long?

During the medieval era Christianity came to dominate Europe, while the hegemony of Islam reached over a vast area from the Iberian Peninsula to India (and subsequently grew to incorporate Malaysia and Indonesia). These two great religions were rooted in the same type of monotheism, which meant that they possessed strict precepts and holy scriptures that followers were forbidden to question or criticize.

In this respect, they could hardly be more different from the religions of the Greek or Japanese traditions, each based on sets of myths that depict the exploits of a pantheon of all-too-human (and numerous) gods; in the universe of Mount

Olympus or that of Japan's 8 million deities, contradictions abound. In monotheistic faiths that do not tolerate criticism, nothing that contradicts the precepts or the holy scriptures can be accommodated, no matter how trivial—even if it is a fact visible to the eyes and audible to the ears. Given that even in this half of the twentieth century trials have been held in some regions of the United States over whether the theory of evolution can be taught in public schools, it should not be hard for us to imagine how powerful the restraints imposed by religion must have been during the medieval era. And if we examine the types of strict rules imposed by modern Islamic fundamentalism, we get an even better idea of how intense must have been their grip in the past.

Yet how did it happen that religions whose origins lay either with conquered and impoverished tribes from Palestine (in the case of Christianity), or with nomads running small caravans through the Arabian desert (in the case of Islam), came to be embraced with fervor by the inhabitants of what were then the most technologically and scientifically advanced, and materially affluent civilizations in the world—those in Rome, Greece, the Middle East, and India? This seems very strange when viewed against the backdrop of our contemporary world in which what passes for culture almost always flows from regions with more advanced technology and concepts to what are seen as underdeveloped regions.

We must bear in mind that religions, while they may retain their original precepts and scriptures, characteristically fuse and blend with the customs and thought of the regions and eras through which they pass as they spread. The forms and content of Christianity, for example, underwent striking mutations in the process of diffusing throughout Europe. A church organization was created that operated within the separation of spiritual and temporal realms (church and state); Christ (born a Jew) became blond; and rites once observed in summer were somehow joined with the German celebration of the winter solstice to create one holiday. The hegemony of the feudal system was accepted and groups like the Donatists, a North African Christian group that insisted on strict adherence to the egalitarian principle, were discarded as heretics along the way. Islam also underwent similar transformations as it spread from Mesopotamia through Persia and into India.

Things did not go so differently in China. The Chinese are seen as being so devoid of religious spirit they have earned such labels as "the faithless invincibles who recognize neither gods nor foes." The indigenous schools of thought—those associated with Confucius, Zhuang Zi (Chuang-tzu), and Lao Zi (Lao-tzu)—were not religions in the original sense of that word but philosophies that present precepts on how to live and how to administer and regulate society. True, Confucianism is linked to ancestor worship and Zhuang Zi and Lao Zi are affiliated with the teachings of the Taoist wizards, but if these schools of thought have acquired a tincture of religious coloration, it is only by association with these early and simple native beliefs. Nonetheless, even among a people with as faint a predisposition for it as the Chinese, religion—particularly Buddhism—became a powerful force during the medieval era bounded by the dynasties of the Three Kingdoms (221–265) and the Tang (618–906).

There are differences of opinion on when Buddhism entered China, but it is generally believed that an emissary to the provincial court of an emperor's half brother on the southern part of the Great Plains orally transmitted portions of its doctrines at the end of the Former Han dynasty, around 2 B.C. Thus it first entered through the Tarim Basin in Central Asia, and the forms of Buddhism practiced in the Xi Yu region formed the model that China adopted for roughly the next six centuries. By the Chinese, therefore, Buddhism was seen less as a product of an advanced Indian civilization than as a religion belonging to a feeble backward region along its western borders. In this respect, like the Christian faith conveyed to Rome and Greece by the subjugated peoples of Palestine among whom it first flourished, and the Islamic faith that originated among nomads running caravans through the Arabian desert but spread to Persia and India, Buddhism was a kind of reverse import of the process whereby advanced civilizations disseminated their influence into outlying regions.

Buddhism, this faith that reached China through peoples whom the Chinese thought of as primitive tribes, was to gain enormous power in China during and after the Tartar Partition. The construction of the great Buddhist cave-temples at Yun Gang and Long Men, hewn with tremendous vigor out of solid rock in the style characteristic of the Xi Yu region through which Buddhism reached China, occurred during this early medieval phase.

What were the forces that created this predisposition to embrace strict orthodoxies from the underdeveloped countries? How did such a state of mind take hold among the peoples of the advanced nations? First, we must not overlook the changes in the composition of the populations of the advanced civilizations. From the second century onward, whether in the Roman empire, northern China, or northwest India, the numbers of indigenous heirs to the civilized traditions of these regions declined while the numbers of barbarians from the north and elsewhere grew enormously. It is hardly remarkable that the missionaries of religious traditions from the underdeveloped peripheries should seek converts from among those having trouble assimilating into the ancient civilizations. However, the readiness to embrace strict orthodoxies cannot be adequately accounted for if we think only in terms of the discontentment of poorly assimilated recent arrivals. The fact is that whether the era is the ancient one or the modern, aliens from underdeveloped countries who move to advanced nations and work as unskilled laborers generally try to assimilate into the advanced culture and do not go out of their way to learn about cultures from underdeveloped countries other than those in which their origins lie. Above and beyond that, we must remember that in every case, whether it was Christianity entering the Roman sphere, Buddhism coming into China, or Islam spreading into Mesopotamia or Persia, very considerable numbers of people with impeccable origins in the advanced cultures showed an inclination to convert. The tendency existed among them as well to want to abandon the ancient civilizations that had produced such brilliant scientific technology and material abundance.

What made such people ready to convert was probably a growing conviction on their part that with the frontiers gone and critical energy shortages looming, it was futile to dream of increasing material production; at the same time, such individuals, finding themselves with more and more time on their hands, developed an increasingly meditative bent. What emerged from this, if I may be so bold as to cite the language of today's new religions, was "the soul that seeks spiritual salvation, not material riches."

Cultures with Too Few Things and Much Time

The societies that together made up ancient civilization ran out of territory into which to expand (and thereby satisfy their craving for more things) around the first century in the West and somewhat earlier in China. At the same time, the gradual depletion of forestry resources led to a growing energy shortage, making it more and more difficult to keep the supply of material things growing. Since this drive to keep making "more" available was ruining the land and aggravating the energy shortage, it was not without reason that people of conscience began to speak out against the materialistic civilization. Under these circumstances, the empathetic impulse induced people to realize that the circumstances had changed; and they moved toward repudiating everything that derived from the guiding principle that happiness comes from consuming more things.

This meant that working oneself into the ground simply to produce and consume more things was not the thing to do. The idea caught on that the truly high-class life-style was one that allowed ample free time in which to enrich one's heart and soul—and this led to a groundswell of interest in the religions of the less advanced regions that had not been contaminated by the evils of ancient civilization.

It seems likely that what the Greeks and Romans found appealing about both the Christian faith that came out of Palestine and the simple beliefs of the tribes of north Germany was their antimaterialistic spirit. In China, where foreign religions did not make their inroads until somewhat later, there was an interlude during which the otherworldly and antimaterialistic Taoism of Lao Zi (Lao-tzu) and Zhuang Zi (Chuang-tzu) and high-flying esoteric discourses and speculations were all the vogue, after which the Buddhism practiced in the regions west of China began to take their place. In the Middle East and India as well, Zoroastrianism and strict Hindu teachings became powerful influences during the interlude prior to the ascendancy of Islam. Thus, while religion itself may not have created the Middle Ages in China and the Middle East in the sense that it did elsewhere, a kind of protomedieval spirit that arrived in advance of religion was busily laying the groundwork that would eventually make it possible for religion to become enormously powerful in those civilizations.

Were I to attempt to describe what makes the Middle Ages unique in a single phrase, it would be "a lack of goods, a surfeit of time." Because the economic level of the medieval civilization was low, many people take it for granted that "being poor men, they had no time to themselves," but all such presumption reveals is the vulgarity of the materialistic bias of our industrial society. The fact is that in both Europe and China as the ancient era ended and the medieval character emerged, the number of holidays increased and working hours were shortened.

Indro Montanelli writes that by the late stages of the Roman Empire (after the fourth century), the number of festival days that had been made into official holidays amounted to an astounding 184 days out of the year. This averages out to three and a half days off per week! Since the hours worked each day also tended to be short, we can surmise that the annual number of hours worked was actually less than 1,500 hours. That figure is some 300 hours less than the figures for today's most advanced industrial nations.

The figure shrinks even further once the authentic medieval era is under way. During the Middle Ages (even in France), most peasants hardly worked at all during the three months of winter and various pretexts were found to establish holidays in the summers as well, according to Geneviève De-Cour. Besides the numerous days on which religious rites or festivals were celebrated, every occupation and region and individual had its designated saint whose day also had to be set aside. Sundays were, of course, a day of absolute rest in which not only jobs but cleaning or study of any kind were absolutely forbidden. In addition, village cooperatives and craft guilds very strictly stipulated the hours in which one was to carry out one's job and forbade work that would allow one to steal a march on one's peers. In the Middle Ages, working when one was not supposed to was considered a far greater sin than not working when one was supposed to.

If this was true in France, situated to the south, one would have to imagine that in Germany and England (with their longer winters) it was only more so. People who lived in homes consisting of a single room where the only sources of light were either small windows covered with parchment or flax, or the glow from the fireplace, had four or more months every winter during which they pursued no productive activities. And despite the fact that winter's enforced idleness lasted so long, these people also refrained from all toil on Sabbath and festival days throughout the summer.

Moreover, there were large numbers of individuals whose work had little or nothing to do with economic production. The families of kings and members of the nobility seldom engaged in farming; the swelling ranks of priests and monks also performed little labor. The monasteries were engaged in farming, cattle breeding, and weaving, but those that reached the point of self-sufficiency were exceptions. According to David Knowles, the daily routine at the Benedictine Monastery of Monte Cassino around the year 540 involved 6 hours and 15 minutes of work (from 8:15 A.M. to 2:30 P.M.); there were, moreover, three prayer breaks during those hours. The Benedictine order established during the first half of the Middle Ages—when medievalism was in its most archetypal phase—consisted of people who Otto Borst describes as having "typically spent their days in unfettered contemplation, as if each was the lord of a domain." The production of butter and wine in which many monasteries now engage did not begin until the modern age.

In environments with limited land and resources, anyone who works too assiduously provokes the fear that his efforts will eat into the land and resources allocated for others. For any party to enter the communal lands and forests that held such a special meaning for medieval people and start hacking trees down right and left was considered a very grave matter. Working diligently while others were at rest was not thought of merely as an act of vulgar meanness; it could even be considered a crime.

Those who won wide respect in the Middle Ages were figures like "Peter the Hermit" and St. Francis of Assisi, "so gentle he could converse with the birds." Each cultivated the spiritual purity of honest poverty and abstinence, living a life unsullied by economic productivity.

This is not to say that the Middle Ages were inhabited only by saints. Most people desired a life of greater material wealth and treasures of gold and silver. However, they lacked the diligence in labor and the logical reasoning or scientific observations and concepts that would have enabled them to attain these things. Much more, they would have found it preposterous to drastically reduce their free time and change their values simply to acquire wealth. We may find this easier to understand if we think of the psychology of today's middle-aged Japanese who, in direct contrast, protests that he wishes for more leisure hours, but is loath to increase his time off in exchange for reduced pay (i.e., reduced potential for consuming material goods).

Since to refrain from seeking material things was thought virtuous in the Middle Ages, people of noble rank who were sensitive to public opinion not only refrained from productive activities to avoid being accused of the onerous crime of diligence, but even went so far as to flaunt their lack of worldly desires by showing off just how extreme was their refined poverty.

Johan Huizinga cites numerous instances of the almost barbaric extremes to which the medieval aristocracy of Europe carried their antimaterialism. Certain aristocratic youths in France vowed to wear the same garment (a single layer of rough cloth) throughout the year, and as a result many froze to death. The beautiful noblewoman Sepia vowed never to take off her underwear until her husband returned from the

Crusades, with the consequence that her underwear became brown with perspiration and soil. People at the time unstintingly praised this act: sepia became a respected color and not changing one's underwear for years became a fad. For the ancients who had so loved their Roman baths, the thought of such an unclean practice would have been unbearable.

But if his contempt for material things drove medieval man to extremes of restraint in their expenditure, he was absolutely lavish in devoting his abundant spare time to groping metaphysical speculations (and to keeping records of them). Out of this came not only idle fancies and daydreams far removed from objective reality, but the establishment of a kind of communal subjective fantasy in which the entire society participated. The illustrated guides to botany and the compendium concerning the devil mentioned earlier were products of such speculations. Weirdly proportioned portraits of saints and of the Virgin Mary were the product of long musings over an ideal form. Medieval men perceived an inner beauty in the very aspects of these figures that to our eyes might appear crude and infantile, and were willing to spend endless hours on efforts to express these visions. It is not at all unusual to find examples of cathedrals that took more than a century to complete.

The situation was similar in China. The Chinese have always enjoyed a reputation as a hardworking and ambitious people, but there was little evidence of this during the Tartar Partition. Throughout the period that began with the Qin dynasty and lasted into the Tang, the high-ranking bureaucrats who constituted China's aristocracy were intoxicated with wine and poetry and not only neglected to have any direct involvement in matters of production, as might have been expected, but even largely disdained their administrative duties. In fact many went so far as to abandon completely any pretense of carrying on their official lives and retreated to bamboo groves where they contented themselves with a life-style of coarse clothing, poor food, and total engrossment in esoteric speculation. Because of this, the paddies and the irrigation systems fell into disrepair and productive output plummeted.

At the end of the fourth century the poet Tao Yuan Ming abandoned his position in the government, declaring, "I shall spend the rest of my life in the fields eating turnips," whereupon he returned to his birthplace—not to become a committed farmer or to provide agricultural leadership, but to live in the old estate he remembered from his youth, strolling down its narrow, weed-choked paths swigging draughts of wine while gazing on wild chrysanthemums and towering trees. Tao Yuan Ming speaks of "being able to feel my life ever so gently coming to its rest" and declares, "Now I know that this is the way to live and that my past life as an official was all a mistake."

What the poet found to lament was not the economic impoverishment of the farming villages but that greedy men were working the land too hard. The spirit in which he returned to his birthplace could hardly provide a more telling contrast to that of the late President Park of South Korea, who went home to push for a movement in which "every village would have its own unique product" to sell to the world. What the poet found to rejoice in was the fact that the trees and grasses of his birthplace had not been cut or disturbed but still grew wild; he deemed a life of long and uninterrupted idleness to be one of unexcelled rectitude.

This outlook on existence has much in common with that of Wang Yen, another poet who lurked among the bamboo groves struggling to forget the passing hours in flights of esoteric conversation. In this sense he, too, symbolizes the spirit of China's early medieval phase, which may help to explain why his highly praised poems have been passed down to us through the generations.

Beginning with the Three Kingdoms dynasty (221–265) and continuing through the Tartar Partition (317–589) and Sui (589–618) and Tang (618–906) dynasties, China produced many "wise and enlightened men" who spent their lives in pastoral idleness, for which they have earned nothing but respect in the eyes of the world. In writing the dynastic chronicle of the Later Han, author Han Yao made a point of noting the exploits of such figures in separate sections on men who "acted alone" or were "outstanding citizens"; he was careful to add that "while they stood apart from history, these were figures whom it would be a pity to see forgotten." The compilation of economic success stories which Sima Qian earnestly penned were less enduring; the category was dropped from later dynastic histories. (Perhaps it should be mentioned that the *Record of the Later Han* was, like all other such histories, written considerably after the fact—in this case, in the early fifth century—and thus belongs to the early medieval era, the spirit of which its emphasis reflects.)

Medieval China was also the site for a great deal of stone and wooden temple construction; such projects required enormous outlays of time to complete. Some, like Long Men and Dunhuang, required literally centuries. And this was at a time when economic production stagnated and many farms were abandoned and went to seed. Both the aristocrats who managed the great estates and the commoners who worked them brought more enthusiasm to entertaining passing flights of fancy than to productive labor on the farms.

The Middle Ages Reject Intellectualism

"The Middle Ages were another world entirely," says Otto Borst. People had scant interest in material things, and preferred to indulge in speculation. There was plenty of time available for that. "Time," as medieval men understood it, was not something to be divided into segments as we do today; it was a continuous flow leading toward the day of final judgment. That is why the heroes in the tales of the medieval knights never grew old. Even the year as such did not have clear divisions; it concluded, more or less, with the winter and began again with the spring. When the "noble minds" who had rejected the materialistic ancient civilization let "time" enter their minds at all, it was only as a topic for metaphysical meditations, or in the vague contexts I have just described.

What sort of societies, possessing what sort of social paradigms evolved under these circumstances? The first thing we can say is that the society as a whole lacked interest in material things, and as a consequence, the value put on material assets was not a decisive factor in determining either the social structure or how people behaved.

In medieval societies with few goods and much time, to economize was considered a morally positive and proper act. Accordingly the production, processing, or distribution of material goods was not held to be important. Of course, medieval man may have individually possessed the "base worldly desire" to own and consume more material goods, but he would hesitate to reveal this overtly, and a social consensus in favor of such consumption never developed. The drive to increase material plenty simply never meant enough to the society at large to become a governing paradigm.

When medieval man, indifferent as he may have been to material things, devoted his ample time to contemplation, many idle fancies and abstract concepts were spawned. What most distinctly compelled his attention was the sense men then had of how strange and unfathomable this world is and how numerous the mysteries life presents are. For people in the Middle Ages, which lagged far behind our own age in terms of scientific knowledge and information, this profusion

of incomprehensible riddles and mysteries proved highly con-
ducive to belief in the existence of a god that presided over
the world and a devil who opposed him. There is little doubt
that the world after death and images of a future life proved
endlessly fascinating to people then.

Under such conditions men's minds turn to religion, especially to varieties in which powerful strains of mysticism and
world-weariness abound, as was the case with the religions
originated by the conquered peoples of Palestine, the impoverished Arabian caravan merchants, and the nomads from
Xi Yu.

Religions are by nature essentially subjective, at least at
their inception. However, as their devotees increase in number, religions become more social in nature, and as they become more organized, they gain the power to enforce and suppress. In the process it is quite natural for religious
subjectivity to mutate into social subjectivity. This in turn
spawns enforcement of their subjectivities or dogma, while
views opposed to these are either ejected or suppressed. This
is the reason why nearly all religions carry with them the dark
specter of severe repression and resistance against heresy and
heterodoxy. The especially feared "foes" of religion are op-
ponents who counter with objective facts. Because these enemies are reinforced by the weapons that facts become in this
context, there is the danger—from the point of view of that
religion—that once any ground is given up, there will only be
continuous deterioration in the subjective point of view that
had been dominant within the society.

It is for this reason that in the medieval era, with its powerful religious spirit, intellectual systems that tried to observe
and acknowledge the material world on its own terms—and
deployed reason to do so—were attacked as the most evil form
of thought. Evidence of this can be found in the reverbera-
tions that shook the Catholic Church during the twelfth and

thirteenth centuries over the reintroduction of Aristotelian intellectualism, which the Church finally deemed a heresy.

In medieval China, the thought of Lao Zi and Zhuang Zi flourished, while the ideas espoused by the legalistic school—which were based on material values—came to be repudiated. However, in Japan, ancient systems of thought that revolved around political and moral concepts or codes rather than religious ones—such as Confucianism—were able to coexist more or less harmoniously with religion and thus continued to be tolerated. To the extent that this harmonious coexistence meant that religious repression never gained the tight grip on Japanese society that it did elsewhere during the medieval era, it may well have contributed to the formation of a protomodern era in Japan from roughly the tenth century. However, I must also add that as Confucianism hardened into a rigid status-quo form of social subjectivity, it probably impeded the protomodern age in Japan from growing into a genuine modern era. It can likewise be said that the misfortune of China lay in the fact that the Confucian spirit, which originally embodied the rationalism of ancient times, eventually ossified into a sterile and ritualized system as it merged with the conservative tendencies of China's bureaucracy.

Priority Is Given to Social Subjectivity over Material Values

The tendency to attribute scant importance to material things and to emphasize instead subjective perceptions was a major determinant of medieval social paradigms. Ancient man, who felt happiness derived from material abundance, had evaluated his fellow beings in terms of their productive capabilities and their possessions, but this ceased to be the case in medieval times.

A system that evaluates a man's efforts on the basis of materially based measurements is undermined when matter is no
longer perceived on its own terms. During the medieval era,
men were seldom quantitatively evaluated in terms of "productive capability" or how much could be produced by X in Y
hours. The last thing that would have occurred to people in
the Middle Ages was to compensate in direct proportion to
volume of output. After all, results obtained through work
came via the grace of God, not a man's abilities or efforts. The
fruits of such labors should be dedicated to God, not paid to
man. What a man received should not be a consequence of
his accomplishments but what he deserved in terms of "respect" or "honor."

But how was the degree of respect determined or conferred?
In medieval Europe, *ordre* ("rank" or "station") corresponded
to the degree of respect an individual commanded. An "ordered society" was one which preserved these ranks or sta-
tions. According to Alcuin's letters, a man's position in the
ordre was a divinely conferred gift (literally, "charisma," in its
original sense). On a more concrete level, it was the reputation
one garnered in men's eyes—again, a matter of social subjectivity. One element that played an important role in how society subjectively beheld a person was that individual's blood-
line—a criterion easy to comprehend and cleave to.

This is how the hereditary class society came into being.
Modern historians have ordained that the medieval world consisted of feudal societies. However, it would seem that the
modern tendency to interpret everything in accordance with
our own obsession with material goods has led such observers
to perceive the word *feudal* as applying only to the hereditary
transmission of the privilege to govern land.

Even in Europe (especially prior to the thirteenth century)
the system by which rank was to be passed down and domains
were to be maintained was not that clear-cut in its operation,

and what commanded respect or conferred honor was the blood relationship to glorious forebears rather than the fief one governed. Thus a prince of illustrious lineage could expect to be treated as a "lofty personage" even if he had not been bequeathed a domain, and a noble who had lost his lands could expect the same. Nor was holding or not holding dominions the main criterion for establishing a person's nobility in the Middle East, India, or China.

Medieval China was also a class society with strong aristocratic rule, but in truth there is no firm basis that proves aristocratic stature was conferred through the inheritance of domains. This notion remains mere conjecture on the part of modern historians under the influence of Western historical scholarship, who leap to the conclusion that "this would have to have been the case."

For example, Esquire Wang of Shandung province is famous for having been "the noblest of noblemen" in early medieval China, but we have no idea how large a domain his clan commanded. One thing we can be sure of is that after the collapse of the Western Jin dynasty, Shandung province came under the rule of conquering forces from the north, meaning that Esquire Wang must have lost his domain. Despite this, his clan flourished even more under the Eastern Jin dynasty; of the 355 men who rose to the three princely ranks during the Eastern Jin years, those from the Wang clan numbered 69. The fame and financial power of Esquire Wang as an aristocrat had to have been sustained through personal connections with other clan members and through his salary as an official, rather than through inheritance of a vast domain. In fact, despite its losses, the fame of the Wang clan as a noble family persisted even through the end of the Tang dynasty (618–906) and into the early part of the Five Dynasties (907–960). It seems fair to conclude that inherited rank among the Chinese aristocracy was preserved through "succession in esteem" rather than domainal succession.

Linear descent was not, of course, the only basis by which respect could be attained. Such traits as a sterling character, devout faith, demonstrable courage, or fervid commitment to a life of honest poverty could also play a part. One in whom the attainment of many such virtues was manifest might be anointed a saint in the West or welcomed to the position of a high official in China. And yet these criteria have little or nothing to do with economic production or political achievements. Rather, the acts that earned respect involved transcendent virtues such as courage, chastity, abstinence, and detachment from worldly pursuits.

Variable Pricing and Barter

If people were being evaluated on a subjective basis, the same was bound to apply to the valuation of goods and services. The prices of goods and the charges for services in the Middle Ages were in many instances determined without relationship to cither their actual worth or the costs involved in making them. What mattered instead were such variables as the mood or atmosphere that prevailed—or the ability of the buyer to pay—at that time and place. It was a generally accepted practice, and not an exception, for the same item to fetch thousands when the purchasers were kings and aristocrats but mere hundreds if they were merchants. The principle could even be reversed, so that at times the same item might be sold for less to a prince. Barter, the common form of conducting business at the time, pushed this tendency to the extreme. When it came to services, standards were totally lacking. Some parties, simply because of their high rank or notoriety, commanded exorbitant fees for doing virtually nothing; the reverse was also seen. Charges for the same service could vary by multiples of ten, depending on the customer. Charges to the same customer might also vary according to the occasion. Few complained and the world was at peace.

In short, the concept of one set price for an item and what we call the pricing mechanism were not operant, whether for labor, materials, or services. Variable pricing and nonparity exchange were the rule. As members of industrial societies caught up in what medieval man would deem the evil practice of seeing life in economic terms, we believe the pricing mechanism is an eternal and immutable concept; but it is not. The prevalence of the pricing mechanism is particular to the ancient and modern eras.

The differences between modern and medieval do not end there. Both giving without any expectation of a return, and plundering with no quarter given, were common in the medieval world. Offerings to God or Buddha and donations to churches and temples seem to have absorbed a very major portion of what was produced in the medieval era; and alms giving to the poor was common practice. Rural cooperatives and crafts guilds made it a practice to support invalids and orphans, even if they were not blood relations of their members. Moreover, it was common to offer extravagant treats of wine and food and clothes, for no particular reason, at festivities and banquets. Generosity was among the virtues taken most seriously during this era; what it meant in concrete terms was not to be stingy, and to treat others to feasts frequently.

However, this does not mean that all medieval men were men of goodwill who were god-fearing and charitable. The facts point to the contrary, and there has never been an era with so many instances of terrible cruelty or savage plunder.

"Even if the party behind something is a barbarian or Scythian who does not know the law, it has become almost automatic with us to take for granted that the perpetrator was an

infidel deliberately breaching the faith and sacred trust."
Thus laments Guibert de Nogent, who was the abbot of a
monastery near Laon in Northern France, in his memoirs.
Murderous fights frequently broke out between sellers and
buyers in the marketplace there, and for merchants to entice
farmers into their homes, lock them in a trunk, and demand
ransom was not uncommon. For knights or their followers to
steal brazenly in broad daylight or commit armed robbery was
not a rare event.

In fact, many murders were committed. The Bishop of
Worms, Burchard, lamented as follows: "The subjects of St.
Peter's Cathedral are murdering each other like wild beasts.
They will suddenly arise and attack people for no reason, simply because they happen to be drunk or want to show off . . .
Moreover, the murderers are not only unrepentant but they
go about, boasting of their deeds." Yet the majority of people,
including those in holy orders, did not take these things seriously enough even to lament them.

Gangs of knights were forever plundering towns; marauding
bands of drifters attacked villages; fights erupted between different neighborhoods within towns. For this reason, churches,
the mansions of the nobility, and towns as well as villages all
had to have tight security. All medieval churches and castles
that remain today are solidly fortified military facilities; and
every medieval town was surrounded by its castle walls. It is
said that when the alarm was sounded by the watch in the
Middle Ages, even domestic animals had acquired the habit
of scurrying inside the castle walls. Furthermore, such cau-
tions were not exercised only against outsiders; there could be
no relaxation of vigilance even against the residents within.
Both the churches and castles in which aristocrats lived had
gun emplacements facing not only toward the world beyond,
but also fronting the streets of the town. These were aptly
referred to as "murder windows."

Circumstances were similar in China. From the era of the Tartar Partition until the Tang dynasty, not only were towns and villages surrounded by castle walls and fences but strict defensive systems were established within. Buildings were linked together in a rigid hierarchy around a central courtyard that could only be entered through the single corridor that opened onto the street. Such measures meant that even Chang'an, the capital of the great Tang dynasty, presented a solemn aspect on every front except in its designated market district. It goes without saying that after sunset, when the gates of the castles and the lodgings of priests were shut for the night, not a single soul could pass through.

Under these circumstances, travel was a risky undertaking and distributing goods extremely difficult. Self-sufficiency among the isolated villages and small territories was the rule in the Middle Ages and commerce of any kind the rare exception. Since what commerce did take place was carried out not on the basis of parity exchange but for whatever price the buyer might agree to, huge profits were sometimes generated, but merchants were always accompanied by danger, and had to move in armed groups.

The decline of autonomous economic forces and most forms of commerce also meant that the monetary economy as such virtually ceased to exist. In medieval Europe there was no monetary economy in the strict sense; and that which existed in China was initially inconsequential in scale. The explosive growth in the quantity of copper coins minted in China did not come until the end of the Five Dynasties (907–960) and in particular after the Song dynasty (960–1279) came into power. The episode in which Ssu Yang, the heir to the last of the Later Zhou emperors under the Five Dynasties, personally smashed the figure of the great Buddha with a hammer so that coins could be minted from its copper is an indication of how the demand for currency surged as China rapidly moved into its protomodern era.

A World of "Total Media"

Another prominent feature of the Middle Ages is that when it came to information, people were less concerned with accurate and specific expressions in words and numbers than they were in the kind of abstract and impressionistic communication that created the atmosphere they wished to impart.

I said earlier that medieval men failed to accurately denote the forms and motions of matter and tended to greatly exaggerate numerical quantities. Under such conditions, it is not surprising that they felt something of an aversion toward having to communicate information in words and numbers. Even on the occasions when words were deployed in long sentences and many numbers marshalled, the powerfully subjective orientation of the society robbed these of clear meaning, while the recipients were neither inclined nor endowed with the ability to make much sense of them. As a result, there were often absurd misinterpretations.

The form in which medieval man preferred to receive the type of information he held dear involved either the exchange of or shared commitment to abstract ambiences or atmospheres. The proper trappings were required to propitiate the sharing of these subjective states. For example, religious sentiments were often communicated in a very special atmosphere suitable to their being perceived as divine revelation, while evaluations of human character depended upon—were in part the result of—the prevailing mood or atmosphere. *Information*, in the special subjective sense that medieval man thought of it, was thus communicated through all five senses working together. Today we refer to this method as *total media*.

All medieval religions relied on this mode of communication. The Christians of Europe prayed in Latin, a language largely incomprehensible not only to the average parishioner, but also to a fair number of those in holy orders. Chinese Buddhists chanted their sutras in tones that rendered them very difficult to follow. And in both cases sound effects were taken seriously, with musical instruments being brought in to enhance the impact of the performance, which was further reinforced by special lighting and the use of costumes that were very different from the ordinary clothes people normally wore.

The architectural settings used for religious purposes also conformed to the needs of these events. Those who built the shrines, theaters, and plazas of ancient Greece and Rome had taken pains with the acoustics so that words could be easily heard and understood, but the medieval church tended rather to step up resonance and echoes so as to produce chords. The interior plan was unsuited to many-sided debates, for the ceilings were far too high. Such features were designed to create a sacred atmosphere through lighting effects, such as beams from heaven overhead, or the creation of a field of vision that faded into the dark. Nor was this all. Sculptures suggestive of heaven and hell were wrought upon the walls and doors of the cathedrals, as part of the effort to impart a sense of yearning and awe.

Similar features are to be found in the structures associated with Chinese Buddhism and Indian Hinduism. The Chinese temples and shrines of the ancient Qin and Han dynasties had been designed to accommodate large gatherings, but from The Three Kingdoms era on (221–265) many Buddhist pagodas began to go up and artists started painting both mandalas depicting paradise and portraits of hell. When we come to the Hindu temples with their formidable arrays of monsters, we find entire structures in which "information as atmosphere"

takes the form of relief carvings that seem to cover every surface. This imaginative pictorial imagery creates worlds of fantasy on a par with those seen in today's animated and science
fiction films.

Even the Islamic mosques in which all icons and idols are
banned achieve comparable success in their deployment of total media. Adorning both the exterior and interior surfaces
with complex geometric patterns creates a world of surreal and
supernatural intensity; in concert with high-pitched voices re-
citing the Koran from the balconies of soaring minarets, it generates a truly heavenly atmosphere. The unique feature of
this religion, which never created a comprehensively structured hierarchy of clerics to act as intermediaries, is its frequent communal worship in which all rub shoulders as they
pray, a practice that heightens the sense of community and
direct participation.

When it comes to literature, prose yields to verse: The extended prose traditions that had prevailed in the ancient civilizations of Greece and Rome, and of China from the Spring
and Autumn period through the Qin and Han dynasties, began to yield to poetry as the medieval era got underway. For
the most part, the writing of this era was more likely to be
composed in a meter that lent itself to lyrical recitation, while
atmospherics were emphasized over literal accuracy.

Since the kind of atmospherics I have been describing were
felt to be the most essential form of information in the medieval era, relatively little emphasis was put on words and language as such, and recourse to written statutes was not perceived as a necessity. Thus, despite the fact that at the time
Europe, India, and China had to cope with much more linguistic diversity within their borders than is the case today,
language never loomed as an overwhelming impediment. It
seems reasonable to suggest that this flexibility was one of the
contributing factors that made possible the uniquely medieval

phenomenon whereby a large number of separate areas with distinct regional identities could coexist as parts of the same vast ideological zone.

The preference for information that was atmospheric and provided an overall sense or impression—the preference for total media—is important in suggesting the shift in interest from the concrete to the impressionistic and from material things to forms of subjectivity (faith, respect, honor) to which the society as a whole subscribed. Atmospheric information always leaves room for the recipient's subjectivity. For this shift to occur, there has to be a social consensus that accuracy can be sacrificed so long as universality of the specific subjectivity is respected.

Medieval Organizations and the Nation-State

The features of medieval culture discussed above also affected organizations and politics. Since interest in material goods was weak and maximizing the supplies of them did not loom large as a priority, efficient organization was not something medieval men strove to achieve. And since people were evaluated not on the basis of ability or achievement at work, but on the basis of some kind of generalized respect for their bloodlines or character, the ranking systems within organizations reflected this. Accordingly, the concept of organizations compartmentalized according to function died out and medieval organizations came to consist simply of a chief and groups of loyalists who consented to enact his will. The position and authority of the chief might be as amorphous as it was in the case of the Knights of the Round Table.

We know that in the ancient era, organizations compartmentalized according to function had developed by the time the "Valley of the Pharaohs" was constructed in Egypt. Dur-

ing the eighth century, when the Japanese, still in their ancient phase, constructed the enormous image of the Buddha
at Nara, the parties in charge of the project put together a
splendidly compartmentalized and function-specific organization for the purpose. But medieval man, who felt he had all
the time in the world, and who preferred to devote himself to
the subjective vision that the atmospherics of total media had
persuaded his entire society had universal relevance, was hap-
pier with organizations centered on charismatic figures.

Another point worth mentioning is that during the medieval
era there were virtually no organizations whose raison d'être
revolved around material goods or assets. In modern societies,
what we call corporations are created as organizations in which
all rights pertaining to certain material goods or assets are embodied. In this sense it is the material assets that form the
basis for the organization, and so long as those continue to
exist, the organization continues unchanged whether or not
the personnel move in or out. This is also true for states, enterprises, and foundations.

In fact, similar conceptions operated in the ancient era,
though not perhaps in as clear-cut a manner. The *polis* of
Greece and of the empire of Rome were bona fide entities that
continued to exist with or without unbroken lineal descent
from one ruler to the next. The ancient Chinese state existed
as a composite of counties and prefectures and the federation-
of-states systems used by Persia and Rome maintained their
organizational personalities and continuity regardless of
changes in the personnel who ruled their subdivisions.

With the onset of the medieval era, however, organizations
conceptualized as being based on material assets became extraordinarily rare. The sovereignty of governing bodies came
to be established only on the personal authority or privilege
to rule of an individual (or family), and if the party possessing
that authority ceased to exist, the governing body lost its very

basis for existing. Should a line of princes become extinct, the principality would also dissolve, to be taken over or usurped by or divided among a blood relative or relatives or another king or prince whose claim might be supported by lineage, force, or both.

On the other hand, this authority to rule was not always based on the assertion of a blood relationship or physical force. Sometimes it was bestowed by the emperor (in the case of China) or the caliph (in the case of Arabia). This type of system was adhered to more or less rigidly in the early phase of the Tang dynasty, when the post of standard-bearer was established on a more or less permanent basis: upon the death (or dismissal by the emperor) of one standard-bearer, the new one would also be assigned by the emperor. Since most of the standard-bearer's retainers were also replaced, we can see that this arrangement not only differed completely from the modern concept of bureaucratic machinery (in which all the interchangeable parts can be replaced), but also from China's ancient system of provincial and prefectural governance. In any case, this situation existed only during the first century of Tang rule when the dynasty was extremely powerful; in the aftermath of the rebellion by An Lu-shan, standard-bearers became independent and the office reverted to being identified with the man who held it. The situation in early Tang should also be clearly distinguished from that which existed during the protomodern era of weakened central government after the Sung dynasty, when the empty shell of the appointive office (which would theoretically outlive its occupant) persisted, but only as a matter of form.

Another exception to the medieval pattern of organizations, in which the chief himself is the sole binding force, are organizations in which ideology forms the nucleus that provides continuity. Religious bodies such as the Church are typical examples. There were many such organizations in the Middle

Ages—Christian churches and monastic orders, Islamic brotherhoods, Buddhist temples, orders of knights, and so on. These organizations kept going even when the personnel changed.

In that respect, they would seem at a glance to resemble the imperial states of the ancient era, as well as modern corporations. But once again we must recognize these ideological groups as distinct from corporations whose function is to embody and legitimize the rights to certain material assets, for these medieval groups were the product of the common ideological assumptions of their participants; they were gatherings of people who shared a social viewpoint. Temples would be rebuilt even if they burned down, the church would continue even after the chief abbot died or was transferred. The group of Johannes knights (the Order of St. John) rose again in Cyprus and later Malta, even after they had forfeited their dominions in Palestine. For churches and temples, bankruptcy did not exist. What existed was a greater or lesser likelihood that its constituents would be succeeded by other constituents.

Medieval man tended to give priority to the collective subjective beliefs of his community over other things, and to repudiate organizations based on material assets. Accordingly, there were no nations in the modern sense—a legal entity defined by its laws and by the territory it possesses—during the medieval era. Instead, there were broad ideological zones—Christian zones, Islamic zones, and Buddhist zones—united by the same collective subjective beliefs, and distinct territories within these zones whose rulers were themselves the ruling principle. This explains why the knights of France, Italy, Germany, and England could so easily unite as a group to organize the Crusades. What we refer to as the Abbasid empire of Islam or the Tang dynasty of China may have been grand empires, but they were not federations of territorial states in the modern sense; they could be more realistically described as ideological zones, each sharing a common religion and culture. That is why one's place of birth or race counted for little or was ignored during this period; it also explains how a Sogdian like An Lu-shan could so rapidly achieve real power in China.

Concern with borders and races is a feature of modern nations. Also modern is the tendency to develop an interest in material goods that accompanies an emerging sensitivity toward differences in human forms and languages. Medieval man, who cared little for material things, did not consider difference due to bodily features and languages to be very important.

What Brought the Middle Ages to an End?

Ancient and modern industrial societies see material abundance as the source of human happiness and find it just and proper to work to achieve such abundance for the entire society. Accordingly, the people of those eras established systems, organizations, and social paradigms appropriate to achieving those ends.

The medieval situation was very different. Material goods were scant but there was scant interest in them; men did not subscribe to the notions that material abundance was the source of joy, beauty, and happiness, or that making such abundance available to the society at large was a just and moral goal. The people of the medieval era, Oriental and Occidental alike, stressed the importance of loyalty to and faith in a communally held vision whose assumptions emerged from considerations of and speculations about metaphysical questions that I daresay sometimes bordered on the fantastical. The most important facets of these communal visions were established and organized in the form of religion.

It would be a great mistake to think that the communal religious visions of the medieval era were completely settled and rigid, since dramatic changes could come with considerable abruptness. Even the Christianity that dominated European society presents numerous examples of precipitous change: in the fifth century when St. Augustine wrote the *City of God*, or the great reforms under Pope Gregory VII in the eleventh century. The Chinese cultural sphere saw even bolder forms of change: the switch from the Taoist mysticism that dominated the second and third centuries to Buddhism after the fourth, or the radical changes within Buddhism itself that occurred thereafter. Hinduism in India also underwent major transformations. Most striking of all was the introduction of a powerful new religion called Islam and the numerous conflicts and consolidations with indigenous religions that it spawned.

But however many changes in doctrine and structure medieval religions may have undergone, the ongoing subjective communal visions underlying those religions maintained their preeminence; there was no return to the tastes and ethics that stressed the objective abundance or scarcity of goods. As these irrational, antiintellectual religious organizations were more and more empowered, the conditions that made it next to impossible to expand production became increasingly entrenched. Just as ancient and modern societies embraced systems and organizations to further material plenty, medieval societies, by establishing systems and rules that worked to undermine material plenty succeeded in alienating the people more and more from material things, even as they created a structure that reinforced the speculative and metaphysical bent of the subjective communal vision. Any form of society that becomes fully established and passed down through generations has self-perpetuating cycles to reinforce the conditions it requires to exist.

That being the case, what caused the breakup of medieval society? An increase in the supply of material things that the society itself had not actively sought.

That even medieval economies underwent substantial fluctuations in productive capacity is well known. Rondo Cameron maintains that three giant waves—which in their totality he refers to as the "logistic curve"—can be witnessed through around 1945: (1) a wave that starts climbing around the mid-fifth century, reaching its peak in the twelfth century, and hitting bottom in the mid-fifteenth century; (2) a second that starts from the mid-fifteenth century, peaking in the late sixteenth century before ending its descent in the mid-eighteenth century; and (3) a third that begins from that point and lasts through the mid-twentieth century.

His chronological breakdown of the wave patterns, and particularly his assertion that the third wave ended in 1945 (which would mean that the fourth wave entered its ascendant phase at that point) have provoked profound skepticism. There are further problems: Cameron never suggests when this fourth wave is to peak. According to Taijirō Ichikawa, some European historians advocate a three-hundred-year-cycle theory with the cut-off at around 2080. One point on which most parties agree, however, is that as the medieval era was ending and the modern era got under way, there were rising movements that peaked around the twelfth century and the latter part of the sixteenth. And these two peaks turn out to have been the very moments when crises occurred within the medieval societies.

The twelfth century was the period when medieval culture as such blossomed forth in repeated expeditions by the Crusaders and construction of one massive cathedral after another. Papal power also reached its zenith toward the end of this century, under Innocent III. Historians today are therefore in the habit of thinking of the twelfth century as the apotheosis of the medieval. Yet the very phenomena that signify this also indicate the emergence of tendencies toward intellectualism accompanied by a strong interest in material things and worldly power. In that respect, these twelfth-century blossomings signified a crisis in the medieval spirit, usually opposed to intellectualism and worldly trappings. The Cathars and the Waldensians emerged, severely criticizing that propensity in the clergy to seek power and material goods and their concomitant penchant for constructing enormous cathedrals. In the end, the Church condemned these critics as heretics and mobilized the Albigensian crusades to vanquish the Cathars and their kind; yet at the same time, ideologies such as Averroism, which incorporated Aristotelian philosophy, were being sanctioned or at least condoned.

Had this twelfth-century trend in fact been sustained for another century, the decline of the medieval era and the onset of the modern one might have been underway much sooner. References to a "twelfth-century renaissance" by recent European historians imply that this period represented a revival of ancient intellectualism. But those who were truly medieval in their outlook lamented the surge in productivity that occurred as their economies entered the ascendant phase of the so-called logistic curve. The sentiment expressed by the author of the eleventh-century "Song of Alexis"—that the world of the past was a better world, one in which men were more faithful, just, and loving—was a refrain taken up by a number of his contemporaries who wrote history (Orderic Vital) or poetry (Guiot de Provins and Walter van der Vogelvaide). Each was highly conscious of living in "the end of an era."

For better or worse, the capacity of the society to produce more goods then began to go down even as the saints Francis and Dominicus professed the piety of poverty; thus was the tide turned. The ideas espoused by the Franciscan monasteries that received official recognition in 1209 were, in substance, identical to those of the early Cathars.

The University of Paris, on the other hand, having taken up the Averroism that had spread in the previous century, was attacked by the Holy See, and those of its professors who were perceived as the chief conspirators were expelled by the Lord Benedict Gaetani, later Pope Boniface VIII. It could be said that between the twelfth and thirteenth centuries, saints and heretics had switched places. As a result, the European middle ages persisted for another three hundred years.

Far more dramatic events, however, accompanied the next ascendant phase of the logistic curve: both the revival of ancient culture that we know as the Renaissance, and the move away from anti-intellectual social subjectivity that culminated in the Protestant Reformation.

When productive capacity slumped once again in the seventeenth century, religious persecutions like those led by the Jesuits in the Counter-Reformation were accompanied by vigorous witch-hunting. The seventeenth century came close to reviving the medieval era.

When medieval societies founded on the guiding assumption that material goods are of little importance suddenly found their supply of these growing, the new situation created a kind of crisis: The empathetic impulse urged man to use up what was plentiful, and the stage was set for a change in values.

What was it that caused the productivity of these medieval societies to increase from the eleventh to the twelfth centuries? A number of theories have been advanced. One stresses climatic factors, pointing out that from roughly 950 to 1300, Europe went through a sustained arid spell that interacted with the especially cold weather during the years 1100–1175 to restrain the growth of vegetation, making it easier to reclaim forests and thereby expand the amount of arable land. The argument seems logical when one considers that the development of Europe, with its persistent cold and its cloudy skies, was mainly a battle against the forests; this was a very different situation from that faced by the seminal regions of ancient civilization—the Mediterranean rim, the Middle East, and the Yalu river region—where much more arid climates meant that depletion of forests was a critical issue from the beginning.

The theory that climatic changes provoked the expansion of development and productivity has not, however, been established as irrefutable. The more generally held view is that the popularization of iron axes and saws made deforestation much easier to carry out. It seems certain that here Europe was influenced by China, where the medieval era wound down much earlier.

The Protomodern Era in Tenth-Century China

Studies that would show what sort of fluctuations occurred in Chinese productivity (a Chinese version of the logistic curve) have yet to be conducted, but we can surmise that conditions over the period from the Sui unification just before the seventh century through the reign of Xuan Zong (712–756) of the Tang dynasty palpably resemble the ascendant phase of eleventh- and twelfth-century Europe. This was the era that saw the intellectual spirit of a materialistic civilization emerge, evidenced in the digging of the Grand Canal (606–610) that joined Jiang Nan and the Yalu River by Emperor Yang Di of the Sui dynasty, and by the quest for the major Buddhist texts in their original Sanskrit on the part of a priest during the early Tang era. The spirit that rejected the versions of these texts that had reached China through the regions on its western borders and arranged instead to have them translated directly from the original into Chinese is akin to the thinking of those in the Reformation who sought out the biblical texts in the original Hebrew and then translated them into their own languages. China also witnessed the types of ideological struggles that occurred in eleventh-century Europe. Empress Wu's policy of imposed conversion to her own mystical beliefs can be seen as a kind of Chinese anticipation of the spirit of the Counter-Reformation.

The fact that the intermediate peak of the logistic curve in China came almost five centuries earlier than it did in Europe was probably due to the persistence in India of an ancient form of civilization that influenced China, as well as to the progress in developing Jiang Nan, which was rich in resources. In any case, at this moment we cannot jump to any absolute conclusion as to its cause; what we can be certain of is that it did not last for very long. China's productive capacities began to trace a downward curve from the mid-eighth century, and this was accompanied by a return to the medieval mode.

In China, the medieval spirit declined decisively around the time of the great suppression of Buddhism (845) by Wu Zong in the late Tang era. The policy of religious persecution was revived four times in the course of 110 years, from this initial incident (known as "Hui Cheng's abolition of Buddhism") through the great suppression of Buddhism (955) by Hsu Tsung of the late Zhou dynasty; collectively, these events are referred to as the "Three Armies—One Faith Disasters" and resemble the Reformation of sixteenth-century Europe in both scale and spirit. In Europe, it was Protestants who more readily permitted the modern rational spirit that emerged as a result of the Reformation, but it was the Confucians who did so in China. The fact that Confucianism—an ideology of the real world that emphasizes administrative skills and human relationships—replaced Buddhism, with its ever-deepening pessimism, meant that the modern rationalist spirit was already flourishing. In fact, the suppressions of Buddhism that followed Hui Cheng's abolition of it were intended to laicize the surplus of nuns and engage them in farming.

It was the expansion in the supply of material goods and advancements in technology that propitiated the rebirth of the rational spirit in China.

Tang China was the scene for a wide range of technological breakthroughs: gunpowder, the compass, and printing are representative. Especially important is how the use of coal spread throughout China in this period.

Rich veins of coal that were discovered in the Jin (now Shanxi province) of China began to be used more and more from around the middle of the Tang era. The increasing reliance on coal surged late in the era with the discovery of techniques for making coke. By the end of the tenth century, coke had become such a popular commodity that it was used to cook rice in homes everywhere from Jin where it was produced to the capital in Pingcheng (now Datong).

Since coal generates more intense heat than does firewood or charcoal, it favors the production of steel and copper, and in fact production of both rose rapidly; annual production levels of 6,000 tons for steel and 9,000 tons for copper were recorded at the peak of the Northern Song (aka Northern Sung) era.

The increase in steel production led to the development of farming implements and tools with blades, making possible the cultivation of rugged mountain terrain that could not have been exploited before. For the first time since the ancient era, man was able to expand his frontiers. The reason nuns were forcibly laicized under the late Tang and the Five Dynasties was that vast tracts were suddenly available for exploitation, and there was a profound shortage of manpower.

Species of plants and vegetables that had not been cultivated previously, such as tea and cotton (and other varieties of plants from whose seeds oils could be extracted), were sown in the just-reclaimed lands.

The production of new agricultural items particular to these regions had the natural effect of stimulating the distribution of goods and commerce in general. This commerce was supported by an increase in the quantity of minted coins made possible by the increased volume of refined copper. From early in their history the Chinese have placed little faith in gold, so most of the coins in use were copper. Massive quantities of Song coins were minted; they circulated not only throughout the Orient but even reached the distant shores of Tanzania in Africa. The Japanese ceased their own minting operations and relied chiefly on the Song coins. Even today, old coins from before the Tang dynasty are considered extreme rarities and command high prices, but Song coins are rated commonplace items.

The development of commerce and the spread of a monetary economy also led to the division of labor in China. The key centers of production for Song porcelain were engaged in mass production involving seventeen completely distinct steps in the labor processes. Farming had also become specialized; there are records of farmers buying vegetables in the town markets, rather than growing their own. This further expanded production capacity and in turn stimulated the development of commerce and the monetary economy.

The development of division of labor also signified the establishment of function-specific organizational structures. The Tang dynasty adopted a system of statutes, but political administration was carried out by officials "to whom the laws did not apply." In other words, the actual state was not as systematically and consistently organized as it might appear to be at first glance. To organize a systematic political organization was not possible until the Song dynasty. In it, upper-grade bureaucrats were selected through rigorously enforced testing in which family status or lineage played no role; it was also possible for individuals to apply for and receive transfers to different positions within the bureaucracy. During this period the army was maintained entirely at the expense of the state and not only was its commander appointed by the emperor, but the headquarters staff that served the empire was required to submit to military authority. This truly can be said to mark the emergence both of the modern political state and of the modern army. To be sure, this modern army soon became too much like the prototypical national bureaucracy. It turned into an instrument for irresponsible rotation of personnel and produced a succession of unsuitable commanders who proved to be poorly qualified on the battlefield. And as it became customary to appoint officials such as the vice minister of finance to two-year stints as commander of the army, we should hardly be surprised that it was completely ineffectual in carrying out its duties.

Notable advances in scientific technology during this period include developments in botany, medicine, and astronomy, among others. Instruments for the observation of the heavenly bodies developed in the Yuan period on the basis of instruments inherited from the Song period eventually became so complicated and refined under the Ming that nobody could figure out how to use them. Representational art also developed at this time, and it became obligatory for artists to make detailed observations of nature. This approach forms a powerful contrast with the Tang painters of literati who interested themselves only in fashionable stylized depictions of the character of the figure, and left no room for painterly technique or innovation.

This period under the northern Song dynasty—from the tenth century to the latter part of the eleventh—so anticipated the modern era in its high economic growth and fiercely rational spirit that to label it merely "an Oriental version of the

Renaissance" is to understate the case—this was truly a pro-tomodern age.

Asia's Moribund Protomodern Age and Europe's Renaissance

There is little in the way of specific historical documents or hard evidence to confirm the extent to which the protomodern age that China experienced in the tenth and eleventh centuries influenced the expansion in productivity that began somewhat later in the West. What is well known, however, is that papermaking technology, the compass, and gunpowder found their way to Europe via the Middle East. That Europe began to make use of coal in the eleventh century is another fact not unrelated to Chinese influence.

It took much longer for the full basis of the "modern" orientation to be passed along to the West. The first arena to receive this kind of stimulus was the Middle East.

In the eleventh century, the Seljuk Turks were at the height of their affluence and regional dominance, which meant that the products of Song civilization flowed into the Middle East both along the Silk Route that traversed the continent and overland via India from sea routes along the south of Asia. The recipients of the prosperity brought by this flow of goods were, however, only the upper crust of the Middle East. The ones who were really able to do something with the fruits of Song civilization that came into their hands were the Europeans who acquired these products from Crusaders returning from the Middle East.

Many historians point out that the Crusaders—whose religious and military activities would seem quintessentially medieval—ultimately brought on the collapse of the religious societies of the Middle Ages, but to proclaim a direct link between the technologies and organizational concepts they brought back from the Middle East and the Renaissance would be to overstate the case. The process was more attenuated. All in all, some three hundred years were required for the infusion of technologies, organizational modes, and exotic items from foreign lands to reawaken Europe's interest in material things.

In truth, the Crusaders of the eleventh century were so utterly detached from material values that they flung themselves heart and soul into collecting holy relics (and nothing else) during their time in Palestine. So single-minded were they that manufacture of counterfeit relics became a virtual industry in Palestine. Yet even the influx of massive quantities of fake relics worked to stimulate man's powers of observation. This attentiveness was then extended to a wide range of material things and became habitual, fostering the development of representational art and the scientific spirit.

By contrast China, where the budding of the modern spirit had begun, sank once again into a stagnant phase after the thirteenth century. Many reasons can be cited to explain this, but first and foremost would have to be the precursor phenomenon: the fact that when a single civilization is the solitary forerunner of a new wave of development, the pace of technological innovation is inevitably slower; at the same time, population in China began to climb so rapidly that increases in productivity could not keep up with it. As a result, the latter half of the Northern Song era (around the time that Wang An Shi emerged in 1069) could hardly be described as a period of material affluence. There were, moreover, enormous pressures from the barbarians to the North who forced the Song to pay out vast sums of money—later, gold—in ransom. This created a financial crisis for the dynasty that not only forced a delay in the reclamation of land but caused a direct outflow of resources, which had further repercussions.

In the end these problems became the decisive factors that ended the protomodern era in China, in the form of the Mongol conquest of the entire country.

Compared with China, Europe, where the move to modernize was delayed by five centuries, was far more fortunate. As I mentioned earlier, productive capacity in Europe also followed the pattern of an initial peak (in the late sixteenth century) followed by a period of stagnation. In the seventeenth century, the forces of modernism faced a crisis on both the spiritual and practical levels that raised the distinct possibility of a revival of medieval values. But for Europe, the discovery of a new continent brought in new resources and allowed excess population to move elsewhere. Also, European relations with the outside world were the complete reverse of China's in the Song era, when enormous quantities of goods had to be expended to appease the Northern barbarians even as large numbers of them entering China had to be accommodated by its economy.

These facts would seem to explain why Europe was able to sustain its material affluence (and fend off a medieval resurgence) that much longer, until the point where the industrial revolution occurred in the eighteenth century.

WHAT CHANGES ARE OCCURRING NOW?

What Does "Postmodern" Mean?

Although I have undertaken a lengthy discussion of medieval culture and its features here, my purpose, as you know, has not been to explain the Middle Ages. What I wished to draw attention to, rather, was the fact that cultures based on assumptions very different from those that have guided modern civilizations have at times held sway, not simply over a few people living in particular regions or at certain points in time, but over the entire world during epochs lasting many centuries.

Moreover, the epochs in question were not necessarily ones in which man, having never known the blessings of material wealth and scientific technology, embraced opposing beliefs out of ignorance or an unregenerate primitivism. The values of material culture were created by men of ancient cultures supported by the means of production we call slavery, which, by restricting some human beings within set confines, attained for those cultures a relative abundance of material things. That these men chose to embrace a different set of values was not the result of coercion or suppression by a few fanatics or governors. Rather, the majority of men then living, perceiving these new values as not simply superior to those of the ancient civilization but as a form of progress that promised a greater level of satisfaction and happiness, embraced and perpetuated them through forms of diligence and devotion intended to vigilantly maintain this superior state of being.

This suggests that modern man could yet progress to a stage in which a different set of tastes and ethics leads him to a society with new paradigms. Indeed, such an outcome does not appear to lie in some distant future, but seems to be waiting just around the corner, for inklings of such a transformation can be sensed from the sorts of changes taking place today, in the 1980s and 1990s. For the "disruptive elements" that signal an imminent social transformation—changes in population, the resource picture, and technology—are beginning to behave in a manner very reminiscent of the way they behaved at the end of the ancient era.

In the previous chapter I mentioned that changes in men's tastes and ethics first make themselves apparent in the realm of art, where individual skills are all that is required for execution. This phenomenon is not unique to the West. The precursor to the protomodern Tang and Song dynasties was a revival of realistic representation in the fine arts. Indications of this trend can be seen in such realistic depictions as the tricolor likenesses of Buddha's disciples or the wooden sculptures of Kannon (the goddess of mercy) which are said to date from the late Tang era or the Five Dynasties that followed. Guo Xi, an artist of the Song era, repeatedly argued the need for an artist to observe and study nature from every angle, in his book, *Teachings of the Mountains and Waters*.

Turning to the more contemporary realm of recent fine arts, we see that realistic representation became obsolete by the late nineteenth century and that since then, artists working in impressionistic or abstract modes have formed the new mainstream. Although one can point to a school of artists who call themselves superrealists and paint pictures that look like gigantic photographs, the overwhelming proportion of art now being produced emphasizes the artist's subjective convictions in its modeling or composition. Furthermore, as paintings by these artists have gained social recognition, what one could fairly describe as a form of social subjectivity has formed among the denizens of the art scene—a kind of communal intuition or sets of shared perceptions about reality.

As far as the artists are concerned, materialistic rationalism that seeks to express things as they objectively are by observing matter on its own terms has been treated a dead issue for almost a century now.

For a long time this rejection of materialistic rationalism was confined to the world of fine arts. In other domains of artistic activity, particularly those more intertwined with the industrial economy such as architecture or design, rationalism, with its quest for greater sensual comfort and dynamic convenience, continued to hold sway and even gain ground. Architects pursued the comforts of year-round "climate control" in buildings that avoided all ornamental flourishes in favor of "form is function," while the trends in clothing and accessories tended to emphasize ease of movement and wash-and-wear convenience and durability. In the area of industrial design, so-called human engineering emphasized functionality, while the theme of lighting and display was to make it easy to see things clearly. Even hairstyles got shorter and simpler to maintain, with the crew cut or short hair worn by GIs and athletes enjoying a symbolic vogue, but even women's styles were sportier, neater, and easier to keep up. In all these fields, one could see the rationalism of the industrial society with its emphasis on functionality and efficiency.

But by the late 1960s there was a major reversal in direction of which the "cultural revolution" triggered by Mary Quant and the Beatles was an embodiment. In almost no time at all, clothing and accessories began to be determined by a form of social subjectivity that, though it might still be described as trendiness or fashion, was no longer controlled by the industrial criteria of ease or comfort; and many men began to wear their hair quite long, heedless of whether it might get in their way or look scraggly or dirty, for being neat meant less to them than looking good in the subjective consensus of their peers.

Trends move at an incredibly rapid pace, so much so that Beatles tunes and miniskirts by Mary Quant have now attained something akin to classical status. The tendency they triggered—to ignore functionality and efficiency in favor of social subjectivity—only seems to reinforce itself with the passing of time. The parade of baggy designer outfits and bizarre haircuts that have gained acceptance at different times in the years since match the clothing and half-shaved heads of medieval priests for sheer indifference to bodily comfort and ease of movement. These outlandish fashions may not last forever; but this trend against functionality and efficiency has continued for over twenty years and gives every indication that it will be a persistent feature for a long time.

The architectural sphere, being far more interlocked with and answerable to industry, was more resistant to the trend against functionality and efficiency. After all, making an architectural statement requires the investment of an enormous sum of money; and buildings are, moreover, almost always constructed on the premise that ordinary people will be making constant use of them over an extended period. Furthermore, the decision to build is influenced by older investors and strict legal constraints; so it is almost inevitable that conservatism will prevail. Architecture in the early medieval era and at the onset of the modern era, while acutely responsible to technological changes in its engineering facets, continued to maintain a conservative external form.

But even architecture has seen the emergence of important changes, with 1980 as the demarcation point. There has been a precipitous decline of the modernism that stressed comfort and convenience, and architects have begun to model the exteriors of buildings to express their convictions. The glass-box style that took the unadorned functionalism of the Bauhaus movement of the 1920s to its extreme limits is now passé; styles that emphasize wall features—small windows, linings of brick tiles or stone—are seen much more. It is not unusual now to hear of supplemental ornamentation being added to a building or of efforts being made to incorporate outdoor temperature changes into the interior environment. The worldwide recognition accorded to architects like Michael Graves, Hans Hollein, Tadao Ando, and Arata Isozaki may be seen as manifestations of this trend.

The cultural trends I have described are in general referred to as postmodern. The fact that the nature of the movement can only be described in negative terms—as the next culture, the one that comes after the culture that belonged to the modern industrial society—suggests its immature state, its inability to settle on firm grounds. Postmodernism is, in other words, still groping in the dark. However, one thing is certain, there is a movement away from the single-minded pursuit of functionality and efficiency that characterized modern industrial society; whatever Postmodernism is, it will not be a direct extension of the aesthetics of the modern industrial society.

More significantly, this secession from the rationalist spirit that began in the fine arts toward the end of the nineteenth century has taken only a century to be adopted by popular culture, design, and architecture. The changes resulting from this appropriation will have profound effects on the industrial economy. The market for fine arts in Japan may account for 4 or 5 billion dollars at most, but industrial activities related to popular culture, design, and architecture are big business, accounting for a respectable proportion of the GNP.

That very fact means, of course, that not everything in these fields is going to change all at once. I cannot find survey data on the number of people wearing bizarre designer suits or off-the-wall haircuts, and taken together their numbers might only add up to a few percentage points of society as a whole. The proportion of precursors who catch on to emerging fashion trends is always small.

Accordingly, there may well be a backlash in fashion in the not-too-distant future that will lead to a revival of the functionalism and the push for efficiency typical of the industrial society. These values are still particularly strong among older people and the administrators still deeply entrenched in the industrial society. In Japan, those Ministry of Education bureaucrats and teachers who have together implemented the nonindividualized, uniform mode of education that exemplifies industrial society are even now carrying on their efforts to isolate students with a postmodern perspective.

The reality within the culture, however, is only moving farther away from functionality and efficiency, as many a cultural manifestation that seemed ultra-advanced a decade ago has become perfectly commonplace. Also, changes in the industrial world will reinforce these trends.

Further evidence to support my point may be seen in the recent revival of religion. The United States, Europe, the USSR, and China are witnessing a deepening interest in religion among their youth. Worth noting are the activities of TV evangelists in the United States, which are suggestive in many ways of how religion will operate in a society advancing rapidly into the information age.

And perhaps even more notable is the spread of religious sects that originated in nations like India and Korea. This phenomenon bears a close resemblance to that witnessed toward the end of the ancient era, when religions of the peripheral and less advanced regions spread to Rome and the Chinese mainland. Further, the rising tide of Islamic fundamentalism can be seen as a cultural challenge by developing nations to the standards of the modern industrial societies. We cannot pass immediate judgment on whether such religious ferment is linked to postmodern tastes and ethics, but each instance can certainly be described as an expression of skepticism toward the modern rationalist spirit.

The Impact of Changes in Population and the Recognition of Resource Limits

What underlies the movement away from rationalism that began in the fine arts and moved from there to affect popular culture, design, and architecture under the name of Postmodernism? What role may have been played by the disrupters of civilization?

The first disrupter to affect mankind probably has been the resource picture, or to place the issue in a broader context, the environment. What is important to us here is not so much actual conditions, but how they are perceived, and what effect they have on the empathetic impulse. The Europeans who are the most sensitive—that is to say, those most prone to pessimism—first began to imagine the limits to global resource supplies at the point when there were no longer any blank spots on the world's map, a state of affairs reached late in the nineteenth century. In those days, when notions of territorial domination were still defined in spatial terms, the fact that there were no longer "uncivilized" lands to be annexed and occupied suggested the limitations to imperialistic expansion—the frontier had vanished. This provoked an intensified scramble for colonies among the Western powers and may even be said to have led to World War I. It was at just this moment that the fine arts forsook strict realistic representation for impressionism, expressionism, and abstract forms of art.

In reality, however, there were still plenty of frontiers remaining and the supply of resources continued to grow. More important, global population growth was still greatest in the areas where there was enough to eat. This pattern boded well for the health of industrial society. It was the worldwide depression of the 1930s that dealt a second and far more severe blow to the setup.

There are still no universally accepted theories as to the causes of this depression but the supply imbalances precipitated by the ravaging of farmland in the American Midwest by climatic forces and the rise in the cost of resources in Europe probably had a good deal to do with it. One thing that seems clear is that many felt that the "heavenly new world" with its promise of freedom had disappeared. Steinbeck allows the farmers driven off their land by dust storms in *The Grapes of Wrath* to declare that America is no longer a land of wide open spaces. And in most other artistic spheres around the same time—literature, drama, films, design—the reaction against rationalism and industrialism became an increasingly powerful force. Both Hitler and the bureaucrats who held sway in Japan during the 1930s condemned such expressions as decadent art; it seems that these members of the Japanese elite thought of themselves as champions of the industrial society, although the contradictions in their outlook were manifold.

Widespread and intense recognition that resources are limited did not really take place, however, until the 1970s were under way, after the global phase of high growth subsequent to World War II. The issues that awakened this sense of limits on growth were environmental rather than resource-related, with the emergence of smog and pollution playing an important role. The 1960s–1970s "cultural revolution" belongs to roughly the same period.

The first report by the Club of Rome, *The Limits to Growth*, issued in 1970, insisted that the harm caused by pollution (which was finally being recognized as a major problem) would not be limited to certain confined areas but would have serious consequences worldwide; and when the oil shock occurred shortly afterward, it lent great credibility to the report's contentions.

Even so, the gravity of the situation was still not appreciated by the general public. That was because the oil shock, seeming to come out of nowhere, created the impression in many minds that it was simply the product of conscious manipulations by politicians and oil barons, and that the situation had been further aggravated by incompetent handling. It was the second oil shock of 1979 that psychologically dissipated such optimism concerning resources.

If the impact of two oil crises drove home the idea that resources are limited, the refugee problems that simultaneously sprang up on an enormous scale in both Asia and Africa impressed the general public with the severe ramifications of demographic changes.

Until then, the concept of an imminent "population explosion" had been a matter of concern only to the intelligentsia. When large numbers of "boat people" began pouring out of Southeast Asia after the Vietnamese invaded Cambodia in 1979, however, many drew the lesson that national borders are in no way absolute lines of demarcation, and that they cannot form lines of defense against an outflow of refugees who deserve our sympathy.

The Vietnam scenario was then put to the test by a number of dictators and poor peoples around the world. Cuba had suppressed the exit of refugees since its Communist revolution, but as it entered the 1980s that nation openly launched a great number of them to the United States. Over the last few years, the number of illegal immigrants who have entered the United States from Mexico is estimated at 12 million, of which 8 million are supposed to have settled in without being discovered. As for the victims of famine and drought from Ethiopia and

the Saharan nations, no resistance was offered to their movement into other countries.

These massive population movements seem to suggest that
there has been a breakdown in the concept of the nationalist
state that has prevailed since the end of World War I. Countries that were supposed to represent a union of individuals
united on the basis of common ethnic or cultural links no
longer hesitate to eject and exile their own brethren to foreign
shores on the basis of ideological differences. If the modern
nation-state or racial state sprang from an industrial society
that categorizes humanity in functional terms—physical features, or languages—the collapse of the nation-state as a concept is apt to be a decisive element in the demise of the industrial society that conceived it.

Satiation with Material Goods
and the Demand for
Nonquantifiable Values

As environmental and refugee issues drew strong attention,
changes also appeared in the thought processes of the inhabitants of the advanced countries. One such change was a growing satiation with material goods that brought with it a yearning for "spiritual riches" as well as greater "quality of life."

"I've already got enough things. What I need is to be able
to give more free play to my heart." "It isn't more quantity I
need in my life, it's more quality." The rapid spread of this
kind of outlook began in the late 1970s and continued through
the 1980s in the United States, Europe, and Japan.

It must be admitted that criticism of this sort has been continuously voiced in one form or another ever since the medieval era and has been the hue and cry of environmental activ-
ists from the moment that movement began. The question,

What's better—steak or clear blue skies? suggests that those crying out against pollution are in a sense merely demanding "goods" in the form of clean air, clear streams, and quiet residential space. In other words, "things" in the sense of goals that can be quantified in units such as PPM (parts per million) or phons (units of loudness). To that extent, no matter how much an antipollution activist might emphasize principles opposed to those of conventional economics, the issue still ultimately concerns a brand of resource distribution. Atmospheric pollution and contamination of water are not problems that must inevitably worsen due to production of material goods or a higher volume of consumption, since these problems can be prevented by equipping plants with appropriate antipollution devices. For instance, despite the considerable expansion in the volume of production and consumption in the 1970s, Japan has been successful in greatly reducing atmospheric pollution and contamination that affects the quality of its water.

However, certain ideas that have spread since the late 1970s and especially since 1980 concern our satiation with material goods and are not simply movements to encourage conservation or restraint in order to prevent pollution. What is now being sought cannot be measured in PPMs or phons; these concerns, such as amenity, stylishness, or feelings of psychological contentment, are unquantifiable.

Many say such reactions are simply the result of people having all they need. I have my doubts. The law of diminishing utility (that consumers attach less value to an item as the overall supply of that item grows) has long been recognized. But it is inconceivable to me that so many people in so many different countries, all with discrete levels of economic development and diverse quantities of assets, would between the late 1970s and early 1980s arrive simultaneously at a level of such utter fulfillment. The fact is, this was not a period of rapid increase in material consumption, but of lack of growth in consumption due to a recession.

Such changes in people's desires cannot be considered the consequence of an increase in the supply and consumption of material goods; they must be seen in the context of a change in people's tastes and ethics. Behind these changes in tastes and ethics is the impact of information people are receiving about the environment, and refugees—information that underscores the point that our planet is not so enormous, that supplies of resources are finite—perceptions that are certain to affect the emerging new values.

As I was working on this book in the mid-1980s, the global outlook actually seemed to point to a virtual glut of resources and agricultural products. Restricting our perspective only to the short-term balance between supply and demand, we might see the present as an era of unprecedented excess. Yet the sense that resources are finite has taken root in people's minds and will not go away. What is important in considering transformations of civilizations from the viewpoint of world history is not the reality that exists at single points in time, but how the overall resource picture and environmental situation compel man's empathetic impulse to influence the formation of new concepts.

How Technological Innovation Creates Surplus Time

Now, what of that other "disrupter," technology? What will society gain from the products that are created out of the new technological progress in the effort to diversify, conserve resources, and integrate knowledge?

The three technological fields that will develop most strikingly, according to the popular view, are electronics, synthetics (the development of new materials), and biotechnology.

However, forecasts of technological progress are seldom accurate, and large-scale surveys of experts and the Delphi methods that have been employed repeatedly in the past—probing and cross-checking, through a playback of expert opinions—have proved to be off the mark when examined after twenty or thirty years. The strong possibility exists, therefore, that phenomenal new technologies could be born in areas other than those we currently expect, while the three areas mentioned may not grow nearly as much as we currently anticipate. There are many inscrutable technological variables, especially in synthetics and biotechnology, and it is still difficult to discuss the economics of pursuing these or the potential demand for the products that would result. What can be discussed with some conviction of certitude are developments in electronics, which are likely to be oriented toward computer communications. So let us ask, what will be the likely impact on society of technological developments related to electronics?

As a matter of fact, there are surprisingly few books or scholars who offer firm answers on this point. There are mountains of books elucidating specific technology or technological possibilities. These possibilities, when explored, are only explored as far as their applications to business—how to improve efficiency or energy savings—and only from a supply-side perspective. That some of these supply-side applications include forecasts of product uses in the context of daily life—such as working in or shopping from home—goes without saying, but they are only presented as "potential applications," and the assertions that they will be popularized (or socially realized) are not very convincing. Moreover, if developments in electronics were to go no further than is being projected by these presentations, it is unlikely they would bring about any general transformation of society.

Take banking, for example: it is said that after computers

were introduced into daily operations, the number of service personnel was cut by between one-quarter to one-seventh, though the number of computer technicians and key punchers rose simultaneously. This may represent an enormous change for banking management, but for the average depositor, the change meant no more than gaining the ability to deposit or withdraw money from any branch or having to spend a little less time in line. Another example, from electronics, is the change in telephone lines from copper to optic fibers—what came over the line, as far as the consumer was concerned, was still a voice. This sort of thing has led one popular science magazine to cynically observe that the impact of computers has been nowhere near that of convenience foods.

So far, progress in computer communication has been limited to changes in the processes whereby companies supply goods or services. This has led to broad-based changes in three areas: energy has been saved; resources have been conserved; and the costs of diversification have been lowered.

A great deal is known about how computer electronics have led to energy savings. What worked well for the banks is also proving effective in distribution services. Automatic vending machines and computerized inventory control are two examples. Progress of this kind has led the service industry to replace many personnel who supplied information or "software" aspects of its operations with electronic hardware, a move that some see as helping to alleviate the sudden tilt within the employment structure toward the service industries. The fact that the service industry, due to its decision to have computers carry out numerous functions previously handled by people, is not growing as fast at the expense of industry as it was before has led some to draw the erroneous conclusion that the fanfare about the impact of the software revolution on industry has been exaggerated.

The savings in labor ("energy" in the broad sense) from

computer-operated equipment used on industrial sites, such as industrial robots, is proving to be even greater than that enjoyed by the service sector. Many researchers feel that if management did not have to concern itself with the thorny complications of labor relations and personnel issues and were simply to proceed to delegate processes to computers wherever practical, many corporations would instantly be able to achieve 20 to 30 percent reductions in personnel. Yet at the same time, the introduction of computers, industrial robots, and on-line services has had the beneficial effect of increasing employment levels in other fields, so its cumulative impact cannot be described in simple terms of reducing employment levels in society as a whole. When automatic switching systems for telephones were introduced, the number of telephone operators went down, but subsequent developments in virtually every other kind of industry meant that overall employment figures actually rose a great deal. The effects of technological development on employment levels is extraordinarily complex and multifaceted.

Energy (labor) savings that can be directly attributed to the development of computer-related technologies are showing up clearly in the statistics. Although the Japanese economy was growing very rapidly in late 1983, not only was there no drop in unemployment, there was actually an increase, until by 1985 the numbers were higher than at any point since the compiling of unemployment statistics began in Japan—although the figure, I hasten to add, was only 3.0 percent.

In the West, where there is no tradition of lifetime employment and where changing the nature or category of one's duties while holding a job is more problematical than it is in Japan, the social impact of energy saving (in the broad sense of the word) through the introduction of computers was even more pronounced through the mid-1980s. The number of unemployed rose rapidly during the recession of the early 1980s, and even in the various European nations where an economic recovery was supposed to have been under way, double-digit unemployment rates were seen in 1985. This despite the fact that each country was pushing hard for shorter working hours.

As might be expected, the unemployment rate declined rapidly in the United States, where an economic growth rate of 6.8 percent was recorded in 1984, but even so, at 7.4 percent unemployment was considerably higher than it had been in the late 1970s.

Technological advances in computer communications and other aspects of electronics lead to the establishment of more and more places to work, each set up differently from those associated with manufacturing, yet the overall effect even of such proliferation is to conserve energy (in this context, labor). That is why higher global unemployment rates were being established throughout the 1980s even though working hours were being cut in countries all over the world. The effort to shorten the work week may not have gotten very far in the United States and Japan during the 1980s, but the rising education levels of youth and the earlier retirement ages in both countries tend to reduce the number of hours worked.

In short, computer communications technology is creating a world in which there will be plenty of time to spare. This is certain to exert a major influence, not only on the conditions of people's daily lives, but also on certain aspects of consumer demand.

How Computers Help to Save Resources and to Diversify

Society also feels the impact of computer technology in the conservation of resources. Not only does computerization eliminate waste through the more precise calculations of the amount of material used in structural components; more thorough control of parts and products also helps to reduce the "unseen inventories" during both the production and distribution processes. The resulting savings in warehouse space and transportation mileage are considerable, not to mention the savings in energy (labor) and resources achieved by eliminating the need for people to prepare invoices and documentation.

As I indicated in the first chapter, an important feature of the business recovery of the 1980s was that demand for basic materials did not grow and that international price levels continued to stagnate. Changes in consumer tastes are certainly a major factor, but another is these energy and labor savings.

Henceforth, as people grow accustomed to the ongoing miniaturization of and price reductions in computers and to advances in software, the savings in resources and energy will only accelerate.

The third way in which society will feel the impact of computer technology—the lowering of the costs involved in diversifying product offerings—is even more significant and pronounced. Diversification reverses the trend toward enlargement, mass production, and standardization, the entire "merit of scale" that modern industrial societies had pursued since the industrial revolution. Fifteen years ago in Japan there were eight standard varieties of beer containers, including both bottles and cans. Now, amazingly, the number has grown to 136. The number of designs and models of cars and electric appliances has also greatly increased; today there are literally hundreds of kinds of telephone receivers one can buy. When it comes to fashionable clothing, cosmetics, or magazines, countless new varieties are being added every year.

This diversification phenomenon has been sustained by the development of the computer, which makes it relatively easy to process a multitude of products on the same production line.

This doesn't mean the cost of diversification has been reduced to the point where it's negligible. The merits of scale have not disappeared. According to one researcher, the proliferation of beer container varieties cited earlier raised the costs of manufacture and distribution for Japanese beer breweries by 25 percent. When it comes to food and clothing, the cost of diversification to offer more varieties must be notably greater due to the necessity for disposing of expired and out-of-fashion items.

Almost every industry is diversifying its offerings for one reason: the consumer's increasing propensity to choose products suited to his individual taste, even if the products in question are somewhat more expensive. Selecting a more expensive item means giving up the opportunity to buy something additional with the money that would have been saved by purchasing the cheaper item. This tendency to individualize decision making about product purchases might also be described as a tendency to choose a single item that fits one's own tastes over the buying of a multitude of cheap generic items. Computers are being used to lower the cost of diversification because of this consumer predilection. Consumer demand and technological advances are reinforcing and aggrandizing one another.

The Meaning and Impact of Diversification

The diversification phenomenon is important because it signifies a reversal of the merit-of-scale concept that was considered economic common sense and eternal truth until little more than a decade ago.

From the beginning of the industrial society until the recent oil shocks, the idea that there were inherent advantages to being large was taken for granted and was applied to everything from ships and airplanes to stores. The management strategies of corporations were aimed at mass production and mass distribution; those who administer government sought comparable efficiencies. In Japan, the government's pursuit of the "merits of scale" accounted for everything from policies that encouraged standardization to the system that granted approval to "quality mark" labeling, to the decision to foster cooperation between medium- and smaller-scale enterprises by creating "horizontal department stores" with arcades spanning commercial streets linking up the various shops.

Given this history, it is only natural that both technocrats, corporate management, and administration bureaucrats are being thrown into confusion by the tendency to diversification that is now the wellspring of huge profits. Because of this confusion, an atmosphere persists in which some parties like to claim that diversification is a temporary phenomenon or an unhealthy tendency.

But the tendency to place priority on selectivity and quality over quantity is a deep-seated current that society at large seems to want to affirm. In the past, radical economists criticized the stimulation of consumption as "waste creation," but now, when such consumption is being practiced on an even larger scale, with more and more alternatives to choose from, such criticism has largely vanished from both Japan and the West. Such viewpoints now gain little support from the average consumer.

In other words, the ethical outlook of the industrial society that spurred men to "make more and more" through standardization and mass production is losing its hold.

Just what is this trend really about in the final analysis? It is about subjective values, an emphasis expressing one's personal preferences over objective values that can be seen in terms of quantifiable material assets. Whether or not each individual consumer is aware of it, such subjectivity is now undeniably part of the social consciousness formed in each member of society by the information they receive on fashion and "what everybody is doing." Thus, progress toward diversification is a marketplace manifestation of the popularization of a system of taste that emphasizes social subjectivity (fashion, what everybody is doing) over quantitative objectivity. In that sense, such consumer behavior is a phenomenon rooted in concepts similar to those that led to the emergence of Postmodernism in the arts.

The diversification phenomenon has had a decisive influence on industry and corporate management. It undermines the predominance of large corporations, the inevitability of whose domination had been treated as an article of faith since the industrial revolution. In economies that aspired to enlargement and mass production, giant corporations, with their superior capital resources and organizational scale constantly benefited from the merit of scale. The competition between these large enterprises and smaller ones always takes the form of a lopsided battle between "those who can produce a million units versus those who can only make ten thousand."

Yet in today's societies, even a large corporation cannot profitably mass-produce one kind of product to the extent that was once possible. In other words, the productive scale for any kind of product is limited, not by capital resources or organizational scale, but by the size of the market, which is determined by consumers' ever more particularized choices. From now on, the difference between larger and smaller corporations will be a difference between making thousands of varieties and making ten or twenty or thirty. Even smaller enterprises can produce results surpassing those of the larger ones if they produce a hit from their ten or so offerings. It is this transformation of the social environment that lies at the root of today's so-called venture-business boom.

However, there's no guarantee that a smaller company that produces only ten or so varieties will always be able to come up with a hit product. The possibility always exists that a company that has grown rapidly through the development of a hugely successful hit product will later go bankrupt, striking out the next ten times at bat. To that extent, a smaller enterprise that has grown rapidly remains a venture business.

On the other hand, for a large corporation that produces thousands of varieties, one or two hits do not make that substantial a contribution to its growth. In a diversified market, even a hit product does not sell on as enormous a scale, and changes in technology and fashions occur very rapidly. For this reason, giant corporations will find it difficult to realize rapid growth in the future.

On the other hand, the probability of one of a thousand varieties becoming a hit is much higher than one of ten, so that companies operating on this scale will always have some hit products, which makes it easier for them to maintain a certain level of performance. It is clear that in terms of stability, large enterprises have an advantage over smaller ones.

In an industrial society that pursued the merits of scale through enlargement and mass production, large corporations possessed both higher profitability and stability. They possessed, in other words, the means to achieve stable growth. From now on, large corporations will possess stability but lack growth potential. Conversely, ambitious smaller companies will possess enormous (but episodic) growth potential but will lack stability. It will be difficult for companies of all sizes to possess both high growth potential and stability. Unquestionably, this will become a important issue for the young as they make decisions about future careers.

The "Information Society": Problems and Prospects

The impact of advances in electronic computer communications technology, which I have just described, will not be confined only to the supply-side issues already alluded to. Another implication of such technology, "information basing," will acquire increased importance in the near future.

There is no expression more abused today than *information basing*. The increasing emphasis on diversification and fashionability discussed above is often made out to be a particular instance of information basing, as are on-line operations of banks or computerization of invoicing. However, I'd like to limit the context of our considerations to information basing in the strictest sense, i.e., the technological advances within and diffusion of information media.

At the moment, the Japanese general public does not seem very interested in the so-called new media that utilize computerized communications. In fact, many Japanese cynics sarcastically describe the new-media fuss as "preparations by the caterer and restaurant for a party without guests."

We shouldn't allow such voices to summarily write off the future of new media for us. The current lack of involvement by the man on the street can be attributed largely to inadequacies in the software developed so far, and not to a fault in the computer technologies behind the new media.

Almost all technological progress begins with a breakthrough in some form of basic hardware, followed by a period of not a few months or years before software appropriate to the hardware is invented. At that point progress takes form in the development and perfection of products in which both the software and hardware are applied, while the "humanware" (more user-friendly systems and more individuals ready and able to make use of them) is still being cultivated. There are many stages in this process: the period it takes for a new basic technology to be popularized among general consumers may last fifteen and as many as thirty years. Given this lag, it's common for some of the general applications to be quite different from those anticipated at the time the particular hardware was invented.

For example, the first recording made for a practical purpose after the invention of the gramophone was of a speech by Bismarck. At first it was assumed that a phonograph recording would be used literally as a record of speech. When motion pictures were invented, it was assumed their application would be limited to the documentary photography of moving objects. Early films were newsreels or recordings of actions and processes. Even when dramatic films began to be made, the idea was to record theatrical performances as seen by those in the best seats in the house. It took fifteen years for phonograph records, as a medium for recording music, to take their place as a part of popular entertainment culture, and twenty-some years for the early makers of motion pictures to produce dramatic films using the uniquely cinematographic vocabulary of zoom-ins and short cuts.

Even an item with a function as simple and straightforward as that of the automobile evolved slowly, since it was first thought of as a substitute for a carriage; as such, it was treated mainly as a means for making pleasant excursions to the countryside. For roughly twenty years after Karl Benz and Gottlieb Daimler invented the Mercedes-Benz automobile in 1885, this "carriage led by a steel horse" entered big cities only to participate in organized events. For this reason, the direction taken in early efforts to improve the automobile was not toward perfecting a workable personal vehicle that anybody could drive; the new machines were treated as novelties that would be driven only by specialists on rough country roads.

Man invariably thinks of a new piece of equipment in terms of expanding the range of functions of equipment already in existence. The phonographic disk was thought of as a means of preserving "records for the ear," and film was first seen as a "moving photograph." The automobile was conceived of as a "horseless carriage," the television set as a "movie theater in the living room." Soon, however, the technology itself created new spheres utilizing functions unique to it.

Computerized communications are currently conceived of as extensions of postal services, telephones, or television sets. Home shopping through two-way television is an extension of catalog sales, and computerized ticket reservation systems are simply extensions of telephone reservation systems. That forty channels of cable television are now available is simply an extension of network television. It will not be surprising if the average person's interest is not highly aroused by such applications alone. In ten or twenty years, however, these systems, with appropriate improvements, will give birth to completely new areas of application.

At this point in time, nobody can guess what these new applications will be. But we have a fair idea of the basic functions of the new equipment systems. They are tools for storing, processing, and communicating knowledge. If a fifth-generation computer with analogical inference functions is created in the near future, it may become possible, to some extent, to convert *knowledge* (data) into *wisdom* (informed judgment based on a comparison of situations). This leads to the almost certain conclusion that the future society will be one that provides ever increasing access to knowledge and wisdom in both the workplace and the home. And this will give the consumer an even wider range of choices.

Having more and more free time, moreover, will expand man's capacity to absorb information, further promoting the formation of various forms of "social subjectivity," and inducing the rapid mutation of such subjectivity. The development of computerized communications will make social subjectivity more fluid in all its permutations and enlarge its influence through the quantitative expansion, diffusion, and diversification of information.

Toward a Society with a Shortage of Things and an Abundance of Wisdom

No doubt the empathetic impulse that moves men to use lots of what exists in abundance will respond sharply to the trends I have just described.

Considered in these terms, the outlines of the coming society become clear. It will be a society with a strong taste for consuming large amounts of abundant time and wisdom; there will be less interest in the quantity of material goods. The people of this coming epoch will use their time to imbibe knowledge, a vital necessity in an atmosphere characterized by diversification and constantly mutating social subjectivity, in which they will repeatedly have to make rapid-fire choices.

People of the coming epoch can be expected to pay a high price for items that correspond to the demands set by the social subjectivity of the group to which they believe they belong; they will be swayed by this consideration rather than by the utility of the item per se. Out of such considerations will come a new brand of value—"knowledge" or "intelligence" value—a value that shows the possessor to be on the cutting edge of social subjectivity, to possess, in other words, good intelligence. This knowledge-value will come to loom larger and larger in the scheme of things. When that happens, the industrial world will find that the importance of developing technology, designs, rhythms, and images that match the social subjectivities of the times is a more important component in their success or failure than the literal products they create. Public-relations activities (in the widest sense) will grow more and more important: they foster the formation of social subjectivities that work to promote particular goods and services—that is, to generate corporate and regional images or identities that form the "humanware" factor in the quotient of value.

The significant criteria for people of the next epoch will not be simplistic, reductive measurements of the quantity of goods or efficiency rates of services; they will be subjective criteria that conform to the ethos of the groups to which particular individuals sense they belong. This emphasis on social subjectivity conforms to the recent cultural tendencies represented by the Postmodernism that has now spread to architecture, design, and popular culture.

The kinds of changes I have just described have already occurred in the "precursor" fields; it will not be long before they are embraced by the entire society. Once these trends find their modus operandi in technological terms, changes in the industrial world take place rapidly. Changes during the 1980s should be considered the harbingers of things to come.

In the coming age, people will no longer be driven to consume more resources, energy, and farm products. They will instead turn toward values created through access to time and wisdom, which is to say, "knowledge-value." The products that sell well will be the ones that contain plenty of knowledge-value. The creation of knowledge-value in and of itself will be the main source of economic growth and corporate profits.

Knowledge-Value Permeates Everything

The concept *knowledge-value* means both "the price of wisdom" and "the value created by wisdom." A more strict definition might be, "the worth or price a society gives to that which the society acknowledges to be creative wisdom."

"That's it?" some will no doubt ask. "The trend toward software and services, in other words?" But the temptation to adopt a reductive approach when thinking about knowledge-value—by lumping it together with vaguely linked concepts such as the "information industry" or the "education industry"—should be avoided, for it will cause us to underestimate the full range of knowledge-value's ramifications for the future.

Certainly the various consulting occupations, such as lawyers and accountants, belong to "knowledge industries" that market information in the form of specialized knowledge. And the education industry as represented by schools, tutorial colleges, or classes on cultural topics belongs to a knowledge industry that markets more general knowledge. Such industries do indeed market knowledge-value and can expect to grow in the coming epoch. However, what they are selling to the consumer is literal units of information and if this is the only function they perform, these knowledge industries will continue to occupy a very limited niche in the overall economy.

The truly large-scale production of knowledge-value will take the form of concrete goods and services in which it is embedded, or to which it can be added, and its distribution will be either synonymous with or conducted in concert with those goods and services. What I mean is that the design, the brand image, the high technology, or a product's capacity for generating specific functions will possess more and more weight in the pricing of goods and services.

In the coming epoch, people, rather than buying a lot of goods and replacing them in rapid succession in the disposable mode of material consumption, will purchase high-priced items possessing preferred designs, high-class brand images, high-level technologies, or specific functional capabilities, and will commit themselves to consumption patterns in which the items purchased are possessed for a much longer period. So, whatever we say about the increase in the weight ascribed to knowledge-value in transactions and the decrease ascribed to material goods, this does mean that there will be a simple "renunciation of material goods." As long as a large proportion of knowledge-value is being transmuted into the goods that are produced and distributed, industrial activities related to "things" are not going to decline all that rapidly.

More important than the distinction between goods and services, or between "hard" and "soft," is the change in the ingredients by which the worth of a good or service is arrived at. The change means that, even with conventional products, the weight of raw materials and simple processing costs as components in the pricing process will decrease and that a pricing structure will emerge in which the knowledge-value portion—the design, technology, and image of a product—will be hypervaluated.

Working Conditions Have Changed More Than We Realize

Gradual changes in working conditions and the composition of the labor force had already been under way in the United States for quite some time, but once the 1980s began they came thick and fast.

It's well known that the balance within the industrial structure is rapidly tilting toward the tertiary industries; the same is true, even more so, for the employment structure. According to 1983 statistics, out of the 100,830,000 employed, the number working in primary industries such as agriculture amounted to only 3.5 percent of the total, while the proportion working in secondary industries such as manufacturing and construction had by then dropped to a mere 26.8 percent. More specifically, the share of people working in manufacturing was only 19.8 percent—the first time in U.S. history that it had fallen below the 20 percent mark. By contrast, the concentration in the tertiary industries had reached 69.7 percent, but within that grouping, the growth in transportation and retail/wholesaling lagged behind other categories. The larger portion of those who made up the 20 million or so newly employed during the preceding ten years were working in information, advertising, design, entertainment, and travel; and within this grouping, those working in categories that create knowledge-value predominated.

Similar trends may be observed in Europe and Japan. Japan has become a country with overwhelming competitive strength in the exporting of manufactured products, and is a goods-producing nation to such an extent that it enjoyed a trade surplus of $50 billion in 1984. Yet even Japan has seen secondary industrial employment slip as a share of overall employment slightly from the peak reached in the early 1970s; the level has stayed below 25 percent since 1978. In contrast, there has been a remarkable increase in the share of workers employed in tertiary industries. In terms of employment in Japan as elsewhere, the booming fields within the tertiary industries are those engaged in the creation of knowledge-value.

However, these statistics do not convey the real situation, because the standard industrial classifications currently in general use are inappropriate for observing the types of changes we are seeing.

Current standard industrial classifications were developed from studies that sought to categorize commodities on the basis of the raw materials and production processes involved in their manufacture. Such studies are effective tools for categorizing primary and secondary industries, but are otherwise useless. The "tertiary industry" classification in these studies includes anything from government services and public works to tourism and cabarets. All it really signifies is something other than a primary or secondary industry. For the purpose of our discussion, the standard industrial classifications are even less useful.

That is not the only obstacle to understanding the situation. It is simply not possible to get a firm handle on the value of production or the numbers employed in the categories we wish to discuss. Current statistical work classifies each workplace according to its industrial classification, so anybody attached to an established company that, as an entire entity, is classified as a manufacturing concern, will thereby be classified as a "manufacturing employee" whether his or her actual work is in design or sales or public relations; the usual practice is to compute such efforts in the category of "manufacturing, added value."

Surveys of occupational categories being conducted to remedy such deficiencies are not adequate. However, the Japanese Ministry of Labor's study of Japan's movement toward a service economy and its impact on labor provides some clues.

The study tells us that in manufacturing enterprises with staffs totaling 100 or more employees (with a sample base of four thousand companies), 60.2 percent of employees were engaged in direct production (such as factory work), but among companies with 1,000 or more employees, the number of employees involved in direct production dropped to only 54.9 percent. Furthermore, the 60.2 percent who were engaged in direct production included 11.3 percent in supplementary roles; so those actually engaged directly in manufacturing amounted to 48.9 percent of the total, or less than half. On the other hand, the breakdown of duties of those not directly involved in manufacturing (amounting to about 40 percent of the total) was as follows: office administration (14.4 percent), sales (13.6 percent), research and development (8.6 percent), and distribution and associated activities (3.2 percent).

This means that in Japan, employees employed in manufacturing accounted for slightly less than 25 percent according to the current standard employment statistics; but of that group, the portion of employees in divisions directly engaged in manufacture really accounted for only 60 percent or about 15 percent of total employment, and a really close analysis of the situation shows that in reality only about 12 percent of all Japanese employees were solely engaged in manufacturing activities. This is roughly the same proportion as were working in the primary sector around 1975.

If the same statistical approach is applied to the United States, those employed in direct manufacturing will account for less than 10 percent. It is thus only to be expected that conventional economics, with its assumption that "the factory is the center of value creation," is no longer applicable.

Classifying Industries by Their Contributions

Now that "tertiary industries" that have yet to be defined in clear and positive terms account for close to 70 percent of the work force in the United States and Britain and more than half of all jobs in Japan and West Germany, the conventional "standard industrial classifications," which were created mainly for the purpose of analyzing primary and secondary industries, are markedly out of date and of little practical use as an analytical tool. If we hope to analyze the real state of the current industrial economy, we must not restrict ourselves to considering only entities that create tangible raw materials and products; what is needed are classifications that acknowledge that all industries have certain things in common and that all contribute to human life in terms of goods of whatever description, in one or more of several fields or sectors.

The system of "Industrial Classifications by Contributions" (see Table 6) that I proposed over a decade ago is a tentative

Table 6: Industrial Classifications by Contributions

Sector / Product	LIFE-STYLE (CONSUMER) SECTOR	PRODUCTION (INDUSTRIAL) SECTOR	PUBLIC (GOV'T) SECTOR
HARD GOODS INDUSTRIES (Industries that produce hard goods and commodities)	Agriculture; manufacturing	Industrial assets; capital assets	Construction of public facilities
POSITIONAL INDUSTRIES (Industries that move things around)	Transportation; distribution; finance	Performing these services for/ between other corporations or within a corporation	Public works; military transport
TIME-BASED INDUSTRIES (Industries that process the consumer's time)	Leisure; medical	Security; agencies	Public service; police; public hygiene
KNOWLEDGE INDUSTRIES (Industries that market knowledge, information or expertise)	Education; the press	Advertising, design	Public information and public relations; military consulting and contracting

The entries listed in each category are meant as illustrations or examples. In every industry there are activities carried out that correspond to each of the other categories alluded to. For example, the management of manufacturing companies that have factory operations and are thus generally classified here as Hard Goods Industries will find it necessary to employ sales specialists, research and development teams, designers, and advertising departments—which fall into the Knowledge Industries category.

attempt to develop more appropriate classifications. In this system, we situate industries in one of four categories according to the goods (value) they produce, while the goods themselves are placed into one of three fields of operation (sectors) in human life.

The Hard Goods Industries are engaged in the literal production and processing of tangible material goods. All on-site operations (direct production divisions) such as agriculture, manufacturing, and construction are included.

The Positional Industries increase value by changing the physical (spatial or chronological), legal, or social position of goods and include transportation, warehousing, finance, and distribution. Those who are accustomed to the traditional industrial classifications may find this category puzzling, but it defines the true state of commerce that has been practiced by merchants since ancient times.

The Time-Based Industries literally give consumers a better time—either by alleviating anxiety, stress, or suffering (by providing insurance, public peace, or medical services) or by providing enjoyment (in such forms as entertainment, leisure facilities, or travel)—during the fixed period covered by the transaction. The defining characteristic of these industries is that they tend to concentrate, purely and simply, on the unit of time during which the consumer is in their care, rather than on residual effects, which distinguishes them from those in the next category.

The Knowledge Industries are those that impart knowledge and information in such forms as education, news reporting, design or advertising activities, or technological development. Even if an activity is conducted in the laboratory or research department of a corporation that is engaged in manufacturing, it is classified in this system as a facet of the knowledge industry. It is the Knowledge Industries that are engaged mainly in knowledge-value creation.

I would remind the reader that the knowledge-value produced by these industries can be distributed in the marketplace as units of knowledge-value, as would be the case with the education industry, consultants, lawyers, and so on, but knowledge-value is more likely to appear and be used in the general consumer market as an ingredient in services generated by the Positional and Time-Based Industries. Therefore knowledge-value directly from Knowledge Industries is not necessarily linked to the drift away from material things or the trend toward software.

How we classify industries is vitally important in establishing short-term industrial policies, particularly when addressing the issue of international economic equilibrium. At the moment, the restrictions imposed by the types of statistics now being generated mean that the work of quantifying the production values and the numbers employed in the categories I've described cannot yet be done.

4

The Essence of the Knowledge-
Value Society

The Knowledge-Value Revolution
Will Spawn a New Society

One way of interpreting the change that overtook us with such speed during the 1980s is to see it simply as one more example of a technological revolution, centered in this instance on the innovations and growing popularity of computer communications technology.

With that limited perspective, the change can be explained away as one more example from the endless parade of breakthroughs in technology that have helped to define the industrial society ever since the industrial revolution began. As I explained in the opening chapter, those who see in the future only a more advanced version of the society we presently inhabit—either an ultra-high-tech or ultraindustrial society—subscribe to this interpretation. Such thinking, which can imagine the world of tomorrow only in terms of a more advanced edition of the industrial society, is prevented by its own assumptions from developing any other kind of perspective on the change we are experiencing.

Those who permit themselves to consider only the single aspect of technological innovation fail to see the panoply of other forces underlying the wider process of change of which technological change forms but one part. To imagine that the revolution in popular culture during the 1960s could combine with the perception of a finite resource environment from the 1970s to produce an atmosphere in which the drive to acquire "more" in physical, quantifiable terms would be diminished, while the quest for the value produced by knowledge would be enlivened, might never occur to such observers because their perspective is so self-limiting.

As Marilyn Ferguson points out, changes that first occur as just so many episodic and disparate sputterings in any number of different fields of human activity can cohere at a certain stage to change the overall social paradigm, creating a new stage in society. In that sense, it is very important to situate the technological innovations now under way in relation to the numerous currents of change affecting other facets of the society as a whole.

The development of electronics-based computer communications is not something that abruptly transpired in the 1980s. Rapid strides were being made in these technologies throughout the late 1960s and 1970s, at which time it was anticipated that they would develop much further. However, the degrees of miniaturization, diversification, and energy savings that have been attained, the number of spin-off technologies that have developed, and the massive number of applications to entertainment and the service industries that have been realized, were not anticipated at the time. The pictures of a "future computer society" painted in profusion during the 1970s focused on the idea of a central point: the time-sharing of supercomputers via a network of terminals throughout the country. Given the path that innovation actually took, it is not surprising that the company that first developed a high-powered small computer—the personal computer—was not a giant corporation like IBM but a new, small company relying on venture capital.

In essence, the developments in and popularization of computer communication technology that all at once burst forth during the 1980s were the result of a steady progression in technology that, as it began to change its course in response to people's desires, spread explosively into a number of un-expected areas. What provoked this development was the change in people's desires—in their tastes and ethics—that resulted from the growing sense that material resources were finite and limited.

The impact upon society of current computer communica-tion technology is entirely different in nature from that in-duced earlier by other technologies such as the internal com-bustion engine, electricity, or the chemical industry. Earlier technological innovations conformed with the then prevalent desire for quantitative increases in material assets. Most tech-nological innovations in progress now aim to increase the knowledge-value variable in products and in society while re-ducing dependence on material assets by deploying greater diversification and information-basing. These are the kind of innovations whose real contribution is to foster increases in the supply of creative knowledge-value.

This is a vital and profound change in emphasis. Since the industrial revolution, the impact of all technological innova-tions—the internal-combustion engine, electricity, the chem-ical industry, and the supply of material assets that their util-ization increased—could be quantified. It is theoretically possible to sum up in unit values (exclusively in price terms) not only raw materials such as rice and steel but manufactured goods such as the automobile, television sets, and buildings. Therefore, concepts such as the gross national product (GNP) can be defined and compared over time or between nations.

However, the creation of knowledge-value is by its very na-ture next to impossible to quantify on either a theoretical or practical basis. Variables like the quality of a design, the greater or lesser value of an "image," whether an item is high-tech or low-tech, whether a life-style is fulfilling or not, or whether an urban space has all the amenities, are inherently variables that can only be assessed in subjective and relative terms. These values can be presented as economic statistics only by tabulating the prices that people have subjectively decided are appropriate to pay for them. Thus there is absolutely no guarantee that such prices will correspond to the amount invested in producing the product, even if one looks at things over the long term.

While there are cases in which a single designer can create a hit product, there are also cases in which a large office employing a thousand people cannot produce a single hit. An eighteen-year-old boy can make a killing on a piece of computer software while a veteran of thirty years may be more or less useless in pursuing such a goal. A store can capture the "hottest" image through word-of-mouth while others can make enormous outlays for advertising and get nowhere. Values that depend on subjectivity, no matter how much they are taken for granted as part of the social landscape, are impossible to quantify, and the prices charged for products and services that contain such values exist independently of the costs involved in generating those values.

The increasing tilt toward forms of knowledge-value determined by variables involving societal subjectivity is anathema to industrial society rationalists who think that objectively derived numerical statistics are all that really counts. The result has been resistance to and resentment of the change. Voices from such quarters will continue to insist that, for better or worse, the prices of products overall should more or less match the costs of producing them, both in the macro view and as an average.

However, even if we were, for example, to assume that for all of Japan, the averages derived from a large data base amassed over many years did show that prices correlated with costs (not that there is evidence that this is the case), such averages would not be the product of movements in which prices repeatedly approximated costs, but the result of the sheer coincidence that prices, in deviating widely above and below costs, ended up by roughly approximating them.

This means that a theory for explaining the pricing of knowledge-value cannot be derived on the basis of the industrial experience; the types of appeals that activate the desire for this kind of value and the attitudes that make consumers unblinkingly pay the corresponding price, derive from principles that by their nature are opposed to the rationalist spirit of the industrial society.

The changes that have been under way in the advanced nations of the world, and particularly in the United States, since 1980 cannot be pigeonholed simply as mere technological innovations or temporary fads. They mark a fundamental transformation that follows the industrial revolution by two centuries, one that could be described as the knowledge-value revolution.

FROM OBJECTIVE TO SUBJECTIVE, FROM SYMBIOTIC TO INDEPENDENT

The Essence of Knowledge-Value:
Transitory Value Based on Social Subjectivity

What sort of society will the knowledge-value society turn out to be? Before answering that question, it seems necessary to consider the essential nature of knowledge-value that I expect to prove increasingly important.

I want to reiterate that knowledge-value is generated by *subjective* perceptions (of a group of people or the society at large) that have established a certain currency throughout the society. This kind of social subjectivity is subject to rapid and fickle changes. This is especially true in societies that allow free expression and possess gigantic information systems. The pattern of such changes is not restricted simply to a series of up-and-down fluctuations, but is by nature far more volatile; they can reduce a prevailing value to zero overnight.

Of course, even if the product in question is a typical material asset or service (those produced by either hard goods or positional industries, to use the classification system introduced in the previous chapter), prices can fluctuate violently up or down depending on supply and demand factors. It is not unusual for steel prices to shoot up from 50,000 yen to 150,000 (or vice versa) in a single year. However, even if the price of steel rises or falls in response to supply and demand, it is still not impossible to imagine its basic price as stable within a certain range determined by the social conditions of the time. Thus, if steel prices plummet too drastically, it's reasonable to expect them to rise again, and when steel prices rise to astronomical levels, it's safe to assume they will drop before long. In other words, the conventional economic wisdom of supply and demand can be applied to steel.

The same is not true of knowledge-value. Take the previously cited case of a necktie of a certain design that was in fashion last year and sold well at 20,000 yen. We often see cases where, a year later, such products have fallen out of fashion and are selling for 4,000 yen. When that occurs, nobody is going to assume that the value will soon rise again. If it did, it would be more like a miracle.

This phenomenon can be described only in terms of the item losing virtually its entire value; to describe it simply as a "price reduction" is to miss the point. The fact that it still sells for 4,000 yen is because of the value of the material used in the necktie—but the knowledge-value of the design has been reduced to nil. This becomes immediately apparent if we consider design as an independent entity.

The same principle can be stated ever more clearly for technology and information. Something that has attained a high value because it represents a splendid new technology will immediately lose its value when another technology supersedes it. As integrated circuits won virtually universal acceptance, the worth of vacuum tubes as such was for the most part forfeited; the emergence of jet engines rendered large-scale propeller engines almost valueless. With advances in word processing, the value of typewriter manufacturing technology in Japan is rapidly approaching zero. It is not unusual for computer software to become valueless in one or two years. Barring an extraordinary happenstance, these items will never regain their viability.

In short, knowledge-value is like a shooting star that burns brightly only for the instant it passes through the particular "field" or atmosphere of social circumstances and subjectivities that make it catch fire in the first place. Recognizing that it is created out of such a combustible set of variables is vital to understanding why knowledge-value has no necessary or absolute relationship to the cost of creating it.

Not only is it impossible to devise a universal principle (like the labor-value theory) that works in relation to knowledge-value, it is also difficult to see how a theory of utility like the one formulated by Léon Walras could explain the workings of knowledge-value.

Of course, since the utility theory as propounded by Walras stresses that value exists in something as subjective as utility, its assumptions do correspond with the reality of knowledge-value. But the centerpiece of the Walras theory is his belief that it is possible to amass a multitude of individual "utility" variables into a statistical base that will form a stable "utility curve." Such a curve (based on the utility per item) would, of course, plot a downward course to the right in response to increases in the numerical supply, since the value of the utility created by adding items declines as availability increases. At the same time, as other suppliers enter the market and compete for the materials used to produce the product, supply costs will chart an upward curve to the right. Therefore (runs the argument) the two curves will intersect at a certain point and an equilibrium value will be established. In short, Walras reaches the same conclusion arrived at by the advocates of the labor-value theory: that value will stabilize at a point commensurate with its cost. (See Chart A.)

However, knowledge-value is not stable. To put it in Walras's terms, the social utility curve of knowledge-value appears only temporarily in the form of a sudden drop to the right, mutates very quickly, and at times sinks completely from view. For this reason, even if the price of a certain unit of knowledge-value far exceeds its costs, it does not necessarily mean that a late entry will earn profits. A strong possibility

Chart A: Pricing and Supply Cost Curves According to the Walras Theory

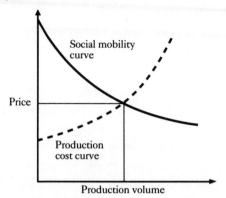

Since it is assumed that the social utility curve will be stable over the long run, the price and production volume are set when they intersect with production costs.

Chart B: Pricing and Production Volume of Items that Contain Knowledge-Value

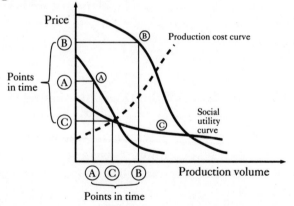

In the first phase, A, a small number of forward-looking types (human "precursors") want the product, while there is no demand from the majority of consumers, so the social-utility curve very quickly falls away to the right.

As a consensus about the knowledge-value of the item builds (in terms of social subjectivity), the social utility curve follows the pattern seen in B. The price goes up, volume increases, and the knowledge-value reaches its maximum level. The item achieves its fashion or trendiness peak.

As more time passes, the utility curve approximates the pattern suggested by Walras's social utility curve, with cost and value falling into line with each other, and the knowledge-value as such disappearing.

exists that by the time production gets going for the new entry, the value may have dropped precipitously or vanished completely. (See Chart B.)

Thus, not only is cost essentially irrelevant to determining the price of knowledge-value, there is no inevitable movement in which pricing approximates cost. This is the crux of the matter—and is what fundamentally differentiates knowledge-value from the material assets and services to which the Walras social utility theory can be applied.

The transitory nature of both knowledge-value and of the process by which it is created make its means of production highly susceptible to instability. Even someone who has displayed superior ability to create knowledge-values that corresponded with a particular field of social subjectivities and technological conditions may lose that capacity when the field mutates. Therefore, sweeping change is an endemic condition of the knowledge-value society, and the society itself is more dynamic than the industrial society that we have seen so far. This is an important aspect for corporations charting a future course.

The Importance of the Decision-Making Cost

How, then, can price be determined without relationship to cost? Simply put, by determining whatever seems "the right price" to consumers, whatever conforms to their sense of an appropriate price.

There are several elements apart from cost that contribute to a consumer's sense that a price is right or appropriate. The price of alternatives is one element that figures in the equation, and certain ideas accepted as common sense within the society also play a part. Advertising, discussions in the mass media, and a product's reputation among opinion leaders can also be significant factors. At times, elements of chance in-trude, since knowledge-value is basically transitory in nature. But the final critical factor will be the decision-making cost.

The discovery of the concept of decision-making cost de-veloped out of such efforts as attempts to forecast the number of people who would attend particular events. The conven-tional way to forecast the distribution of attendees at events, or shoppers at stores, is to use the gravity model. This model postulates that the number of customers generated is in in-verse proportion to the distance. (It should be noted that *dis-tance* in this context is multidimensional and embraces time, economy, etc., as well as physical distance.) However, in re-ality, as we know from the example of the World's Fairs and Science Expositions held in Japan, it doesn't work this way. A notable recent tendency is for more customers to come from farther afield than would be expected from calculations based on this formula. That is why the new forecasting model in-cludes a constant, K, that refers to the decision-making cost.

When a person consumes something, he engages in the act by paying money (financial cost). However, the overwhelming proportion of consumption in a wealthy society does not con-sist of involuntary acts of the kind that are engaged in for the necessity of satisfying a biological need. Rather, the con-sumer, by choosing one form of consumption, is deciding to abandon another form. This decision is always accompanied by a psychological cost. This is the decision-making cost. In times of poverty when there are few alternatives available for consumption, the decision-making cost becomes insignificant compared to the monetary payment (the financial cost). This probably explains why economics did not pay much attention to this point (or did not consider it very important) until fairly recently.

But in a wealthy society, the decision-making cost looms large as a factor in consumer behavior. While there is now enough money around for cost to lose some of its importance as a factor, having to choose from a multiplicity of consumption possibilities has become increasingly difficult, so the importance of the decision-making cost has tended to increase. What we mean when we speak of "abandoning one form of consumption when opting for another" is therefore not necessarily that "buying one thing means not having the money to buy something else" but that factors such as the limitations imposed by the time available for consumption or the social evaluation of the particular form of consuming behavior also come into play. We might even go further and say that time and reputation have become even more important than money for many consumers.

For example, when a consumer is buying a suit, no matter how wealthy he may be, the fact that there are constraints on the time he has in which to wear suits means that the acquisition of this suit is invariably linked to the shedding of another suit. (The point more obviously holds true when it comes to consuming entertainment, meals, housing, and cars.) Furthermore, wearing a certain type of suit also creates an opportunity for self-expression through fashion, so the act is related to the societal evaluation (popular reputation) of that person. The same is true for decisions involving purchases of meals, entertainment, housing, and cars. In other words, no matter how wealthy the consumer may be, selecting one consumption alternative implies abandoning another and bears a decision-making cost.

Those who aspire to increase their sales in the affluent, diversified knowledge-value society of the future will have to pay more attention to the reduction of the decision-making cost than to lowering the financial cost through discounting.

What determines the decision-making cost? Particularities of individual personality and circumstances are of course important, but from the broad perspective, the most important factor may be the perceived resistance or acceptance from the group to which each individual belongs. In other words, the decision-making cost for doing something "everybody is doing" is low; it is high for something "nobody is doing." This is especially true when the "everybody" in the equation is felt to be an overwhelming majority; in such cases, the sense of resistance not only disappears but there's a compulsion to act. In fact, there may be a higher psychological cost in not doing so, which means there is such a thing as a negative decision-making cost.

For example, these days 95 percent of Japanese children advance to senior high school. Therefore, parents whose child says that he or she wants to drop out are placed in a predicament. Tremendous efforts are made at such times to change the child's mind; parents resort to such enticements as declaring that, "If you don't like the public schools, we will look for a private school for you," or, "If you will just go to high school, we will buy you a motorcycle." In this case the financial cost of sending the child to school is outweighed by the psychological cost of the decision "not to send." In this case, the decision-making cost has a minus value. Decision-making costs must play a part in future microeconomic analyses of values and pricing, particularly when it comes to affluent societies.

Disposable Knowledge-Value

What sort of changes will an expansion in knowledge-value produce in the industrial economy?

To begin with, we can state that since knowledge-value is largely a by-product of the insistence that each good or service be distinct from others, an infinite variety of diverse products will be turned out.

In a knowledge-value society, a product's price and sales volume will change greatly if those marketing it can create such perceptions as "It's a product of new technology" or "It has functions not found elsewhere, to match the needs of a specific professional type with highly developed tastes" or "This design represents the latest in fashion." At times, the price differential will be several times the amount invested. It is the perception that will make the difference.

On the other hand, any killing made through the creation of some form of knowledge-value will soon lead others to find a way to create a new "variation with a difference" that will be publicized as even better. Owing to this pattern, there will be more and more product diversification and the size of the run (the production lot) for each product will be further reduced.

I said in the previous chapter that this trend toward diversification will reduce or annihilate the "merit of scale" that predominated in the industrial society; the basis on which corporations compete will be transformed. This has important implications for future corporate structures and corporate leadership.

Another change induced by the switch toward a knowledge-value society has to do with timing. It seems safe to say that the life span for any form of knowledge-value is bound to become shorter and shorter.

In a society in which products are highly variegated and the dissemination of information is increasingly widespread, the speed of change for forms of knowledge-value will be rapid. It follows that the pace of technological change will quicken and the life span for fashion trends will be increasingly finite, while at times the variations will be so minute and short-lived as to seem almost invisible. Rather than being a progressive era with path-breaking inventions and fresh designs appearing in succession, this will be one in which the emphasis on small improvements and the creation of marketable variations based on trivial recombinations of functions and features will likely create cycles of bewildering change. Just as the petroleum culture created a culture in which maximizing the disposability of petroleum and related products became not just an imperative but a virtual fetish, the knowledge-value society is likely to create a world in which "burning up" or "disposing" of knowledge is carried to radical extremes.

It follows naturally that it will become popular to elevate product images by presenting them as embodiments of enormous overdoses of intellect, know-how, and wisdom. In the era of the petroleum culture, the prodigious outlay of energy resources became a goal in itself. Large automobiles were manufactured with unnecessarily huge engines. Material outlays for product packaging vastly exceeded the strict requirements for preserving the product. Heating and cooling were overconsumed with sheer indifference to the impact on health. Producers pandered to the consumer's perception that "class" was to be found in such large-scale, prodigious consumption of energy resources.

Thus, in the future it will probably not be unusual to have products infused with much more knowledge-value than their function requires, simply to create the impression of a great deal of intellectual firepower. Cameras, watches, and personal computers will be produced that have functions a purchaser seldom uses or needs. It is like a retail store owner who buys a calculator that can solve differential calculations, though this is a function he neither understands nor needs. Such excess can also take the form of pretentious designs or overblown image building, a kind of "intellectual trappings overkill."

The desire to buy into a classier knowledge-value image will lead to accelerated demand for output from those fields that create knowledge-value, which society will come to see as playing a much more important, and literally valuable role in the overall process of production. There will be an exponential growth in the number of people employed in such fields. The activities that create knowledge-value will cease to be treated as the special province of a bevy of high-tech technocrats; creating knowledge-value will come to be seen as a normal part of the occupational spectrum. Just as creating manufactured products was at first a process for a mere handful of workers who had the appropriate skills, then came to be a calling an average person could undertake, creating knowledge-value will become a perfectly ordinary occupation carried out by average members of society. A process that makes creating knowledge-value manageable for ordinary individuals will be constructed.

In fact, research has begun that will enable persons only partially skilled in computer use to produce computer software and certain types of designs. We should expect further progress in this direction.

Those who have come to expect a certain "nobility" to be a part of man's intellectual creations may feel a strong resistance toward any scenario in which these take the form of products containing knowledge-value that then not only become the property of "average folks" but are treated as highly disposable. Such a process may fill intellectuals and creative people with a sense that nothing is sacred and everything has become pointless. However, expansion of productive capacity in any industry is inevitably accompanied by an opening up of the ranks. In ancient societies "contaminated" by materialistic values, earnest preaching of religion was the task of a small minority of saints who possessed great nobility of character; but in the Middle Ages, when religion had been popularized, a perfectly ordinary person could become a bishop, a monk, or a nun. In fact, the monasteries and cathedrals of medieval Europe or Tang China became sanctuaries for deadbeats and panhandlers of the time, who swarmed in by the hundreds of thousands to filch a meal. That this signaled a corruption or vulgarization of religion as such is no doubt true. But it was precisely due to such vulgarization that religion became available to the masses.

This does not mean, of course, that every type of knowledge-value creation will be vulgarized. The medieval era produced saints, and the modern era in art has produced masters. There is no reason to expect that fewer creative intellects will emerge from the knowledge-value society than has been the case for the industrial society. However, in all probability most of the knowledge-value mass-produced by industry will consist of products created by people who are not possessed of especially superior intellect.

From Symbiotic Objective Values to Independent Subjective Values

Undoubtedly many will raise doubts and counterarguments in reaction to my forecast. Those who are strongly committed to the values of the industrial society may belittle what I call knowledge-value as just another means of expanding the demand for goods and services, with little significance for society itself. But it is this very distinction between an industrial society in which knowledge-value belongs to the few and a knowledge-value society in which it becomes the property of the general public that is crucial. Let me explain by showing the changes in the process of creating value in one form of "information"—advertising.

In the industrial society, the rationale for advertising was that it allowed manufacturers to sell more goods. The more the industrial producer could sell, the more he could mass-produce and distribute, lowering the per-unit costs of production and distribution. Advertising was a justifiable expenditure because of the part it played in realizing the "benefits of scale" through mass production; advertising increased volume. (See Chart C.) Therefore, the value of advertising was thought of as something objective that was symbiotically linked to the distribution of hard goods, the volume of which it could expand.

The debate thus far over advertising—pro or con—has been based on the perception of the function of advertising I've just described. Even for the socialists who argued that the glory of the planned economy lay in its capacity to produce and distribute goods on a mass scale without resorting to advertising, the underlying assumption was that advertising is a tool that helps drive up the volume of the goods distributed.

In a knowledge-value society, however, the main function of advertising is not to expand the volume of sales for hard goods so much as to make the inhabitants of a certain social setting value more highly (both socially and financially) the product in question. Referring back to the social utility curve and Walras's theory: Advertising of knowledge-value products raises the utility curve, and lowers the decision-making cost. In other words, advertising expands the amount of knowledge-value a particular hard good or service is perceived to contain.

Thus, the value created by advertising in a knowledge-value society has an independent subjective existence. Theoretically, this gives it infinite possibilities for expansion, even in situations where it generates no economies of scale.

We can make more or less the same observations in regard to technology and design. They too are forms of knowledge-value that can be transmuted into hard goods, but to create them does not necessarily involve lowering production costs by expanding volume—the knowledge-value created by creative technology or design is, rather, intrinsic in the product itself. As such, the values of design or technology elements

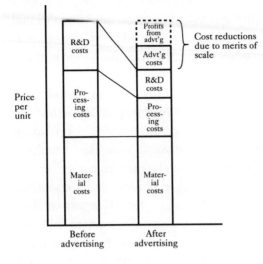

Chart C: How the Industrial Society Regards the Value of Advertising Information

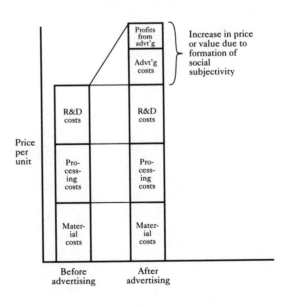

Chart D: How the Knowledge-Value Society Regards the Value of Advertising Information

change from objective values dependent upon (and symbiotically related to) the profits emerging from the conventional production process, to subjective, independent values on their own terms. This fact opens up possibilities for an infinite expansion in knowledge-value.

In a knowledge-value society, not only does the knowledge-value portion of expenditures for research, development, and design grow, but through the enlargement of the independent subjective value these elements possess, increased weight is given to knowledge-value in the pricing structure.

In short, knowledge-value is value poured into a container that can consist of a hard good or a service. The switch from an industrial society to the knowledge-value society will materialize not as a change in these "containers" themselves, but largely as a change in the structure of the value of the overall asset that includes the container. This is why I have repeatedly stressed that we will fail to understand the knowledge-value society if we equate it with a simple trend toward software or against material things as such.

A BIRD'S-EYE VIEW OF THE
KNOWLEDGE-VALUE SOCIETY

Labor and the Means of Production Are Joined

At this early stage, it is very difficult to make firm predictions about a society in which knowledge-value occupies such an important position. Still, by focusing on aspects that seem likely to prove definitive, we can obtain a kind of bird's-eye view of such a society. The first aspect I want to point to is the likely joining of manpower and the means of production in the creation of knowledge-value.

The hard goods of the modern industrial society were produced in mechanized factories, farms, or mines—in other words, through the deployment of gigantic assemblages of machinery. Moreover, the facilities that produced these assets tended to get bigger and bigger, and even the facilities that produced the facilities got bigger and bigger. The economies to be achieved through cost cutting, farming out aspects of production, and driving up productivity and the rate of return on production facilities investments were pursued endlessly.

The modern factory is equipped with and relies upon the power of an array of heavy machinery that is extremely expensive and requires systematically marshaling the efforts of a large number of people. Both the capital and labor needed to set up and operate such a factory lie beyond the capacity of the average person or family. Inevitably, a separation occurs between the owners of productive facilities, here called factories, and "free workers" who in themselves do not possess the means of production.

Marx thought that this separation formed the pivotal difference between the modern industrial society and the preceding medieval one. In the Middle Ages, peasants tended to have certain rights—farming rights—over the lands they plowed; and they owned the seeds and farming implements they required. Merchants owned their stores and merchandise with rights, acknowledged from above, to trade. Craftsmen also possessed their own tools and workshops. The nobility exercised their prerogative to collect tributes and taxes from merchants, artisans, and farmers, but the principle that these parties would not be deprived of their soil, trade, or tools without just reason was taken for granted. From that point of view, labor and the means of production were more or less united during the Middle Ages.

As a consequence, the people of the medieval era, bound in place by both their right to own their own means of production and by their duty to maintain same, could not be free either in their choice of occupation or in terms of the social body to which they belonged. Only vagabonds could freely move about and change jobs in the Middle Ages, and they were dropouts from society. The word *vagabond* was itself virtually a synonym for criminal.

During the transition from the medieval to the modern era, this system was relaxed and the number of people living and working in transitory arrangements increased, but the basic social structure was maintained.

Then modern industry, emerging from the industrial revolution, gave birth to factories that required enormous sums of capital and created a large class of free workers with nothing but their own labor to sell. This is the separation between capital and labor that Marx refers to.

Society was radically transformed as a result. Free workers

in search of a job congregated in the cities, where they formed a group with little consciousness of belonging to a larger polity of fellow citizens. The system of large families whose members were bound one to another by their commonly held rights to a means of production and their commitment to making use of these broke down, and members were dispersed into the smallest family unit (the nuclear family, which happens to be the unit best suited to reproducing manpower in the literal sense), a system that still predominates today.

For all the subsequent progress in technological development, the trend toward separation of capital and labor and toward smaller family units has continued unimpeded, although its progress has been fitful at times. Ownership of the means of production by individuals or the operation of businesses by families has become increasingly problematical.

Most industrial factories and other facilities today are owned either by governmental or other national public bodies or by legal entities such as corporations; few are owned by individuals or families. Of course there are individuals and families who own a percentage of stock in certain enterprises, but although stock ownership may enable one to exercise shareholder's rights or may serve as an income-producing asset, there is a basic difference between this and the ownership of the means of production. At present, in the advanced industrial nations, even the presidents and chairmen of large corporations are in reality no more than management laborers. We would say that capitalists as Marx defined them—those who become fat on the profits that come from the ownership of the means of production—do not exist in sufficient numbers anymore to constitute a class. To that extent, Marx's forecast that society will polarize class-wise into capitalists and workers was wrong. However, the separation of capital and labor he described has occurred.

But what are the means of production or the productive

processes of the knowledge-value that will loom so large in the knowledge-value society to come? Designers will need desks and drafting tools. The cameraman will need a camera. A software house will need small computers. But equipment of this magnitude lies within the reach of individuals. Similarities are substantial and differences only minor in terms of the equipment required by doctors, lawyers, consultants, and researchers. When it comes to research and development, more expensive laboratory and experimentation facilities may be required, but in many cases the costs involved are relatively inconsequential. In many of the technologies that grew the most rapidly during the 1980s, those doing research did not require gigantic research facilities.

What is important for the production of knowledge-value is not so much facilities or equipment in the material sense, but the knowledge, experience, and sensitivity to be found among those engaged in its creation. This is the true direction toward which the production of knowledge-value points; and this kind of production is inseparably bound up with the manpower that produces it. In a knowledge-value society, the trend toward the separation of capital and labor will be reversed; henceforth they will tend to fuse.

In economics, the only technological revolution that was called the "industrial revolution" was the one that started in England in the late eighteenth century with the introduction of the steam engine and the emergence of an industrial system based on factories. It earned that name because, in bringing about the separation of labor and the means of production, it occasioned a true revolution in a sense that the subsequent appearance of the internal combustion engine and other strictly technological breakthroughs did not.

Since the foremost feature of an industrial society is its separation of capital and labor, a society that moves in the opposite direction cannot possibly be considered a continuation of the industrial society. This fusion of labor, capital, and the means of production is the reason we find it possible to distinguish the technological and cultural revolution taking place now from any of the succession of interrelated changes that occurred over the course of the modern era, and why we define the current transformation process as the knowledge-value revolution.

A World Centered
on the Urban Middle Stream

The knowledge, experience, and sensitivity that constitute the means of production by which knowledge-value is created can only be deployed if the owner of the means of production works. Those who engage in knowledge-value creation are thus owners and workers at the same time. In Marxist economics, those who own both a means of production and the manpower to operate it and who do so are called the *petite bourgeoisie*. Were we to cleave to this definition, those engaged in knowledge-value creation might also be described as part of the petite bourgeoisie.

In fact, there are many resemblances between the medium- and smaller-scale proprietors and farmers traditionally thought of as belonging to the petite bourgeoisie and individuals engaged in knowledge-value creation. In terms of income, many are positioned in the middle of society. They are not strongly conscious of themselves as a class and lack the will to combine and organize as workers. On the whole, their involvement in the social economy and cultural change is high, but they are seldom active in politics. Above all, since they own the means of production in terms of specialized knowledge, experience, and sensitivity, and depend on it, they are not "free workers" able to choose any occupation. Although they may change the place they work, it is difficult for them to change the line of work they are engaged in.

Income considerations aside, it would be almost impossible for those who have once been engaged in knowledge-value creation related to design and specialized technology, for example, to become construction or general office workers. I would imagine the same to hold true for doctors and software programmers. That is because such a step would mean abandoning their knowledge, experience, and sensitivity, i.e., the means of production they possess. In that sense, it is almost as unthinkable for them to become free workers as taking the same step proved to be for the so-called petite bourgeoisie.

On the other hand, there is a major point that sets those who engage in knowledge-value creation apart from the petite bourgeoisie. The means of production possessed by this new class—their knowledge, experience, and sensitivity—is not something it is possible to sell intact to others; it is, furthermore, extremely difficult to pass on to one's heirs. (There are cases in which knowledge-value in the form of brand names or personal contacts has been passed on to others, but such assets are difficult to hold together for long and they depreciate severely in value.) In other words, the capacity for creating knowledge-value is not an asset like a factory that is easily transferred into other hands.

The fact that those who are engaged in knowledge-value creation do not own a means of production that can be sold—and thus are obliged to go on working to realize full value of their efforts—puts them closer to the worker than to the petite bourgeoisie. Their work does not shackle them to a particular locale suited to its practice; they are not obliged to be involved in their local community and do not need to have other family members working along with them to carry out their goals. Many who are engaged in knowledge-value creation seem less family-oriented than the average worker. This set of circumstances makes them subject to severe disruptions and changes and they tend to be anxious regarding their own and their children's futures.

In sum, people engaged in knowledge-value creation are a middle layer of society and the economy constituted along lines different from those that have defined the existing petite bourgeoisie; they belong to a segment of society that I will hereafter refer to as the "middle stream."

The knowledge-value creation industry has a tendency to concentrate in cities due to its very low reliance on land and the large benefits it derives from intensive information gathering, but those engaged in it have little interest in the local community and the family as a work unit, so we can expect a heightening of interurban mobility, since there is little to impede this group from hopping around.

The knowledge-value society from now on will be a society in which we should expect a dramatic increase in the numbers of individuals who belong to this highly mobile urban middle stream. This is one facet that will distinguish this world from all preceding societies.

Organizations: From the Corporate to the Personalized

The fact that the means of production of knowledge-value is inseparably bound up with people portends great changes in the organizations that handle production.

Organizations in the industrial society formed around a nucleus of large-scale mechanized facilities and such organizations eventually became characteristic of the economic mainstream. This led to the development of the "corporation," a pseudo-being embodying the entity that owns the means of production. Such a step was taken not only because it was necessary to collect funds from many parties to accumulate the vast capital required for arranging such large-scale productive processes, but also because, in order continuously and effectively to utilize them, it was thought advantageous to have an authoritative main body and management/organizational structure that transcended the mortality and capacities of an individual person.

This concept had originally existed in the ancient era, both in the Roman empire and in the Byzantine empire that followed, where the custom was to consider the nation and the emperor as separate entities. In modern times, the early type of joint stock companies and partnerships emerged and inheritance of property and functional continuance of organizations spread through a system of child adoption. However, carrying this trend to its completion in the shape of a corporation, which became the prevalent form in the industrial society, was the consequence of the move toward huge capital investments and enlargement of organizations for large-scale production.

In a corporation that at its core consists of the means of production, the organization itself remains intact even if the people who staff it change. The "Acme Steel Corporation" remains the "Acme Steel Corporation" even when its president and senior management are relieved or employees are replaced. Its continuity is in no way disrupted.

But when the main components of an organization's means of production are the knowledge, experience, and sensitivity deployed in knowledge-value creation, the existence of the productive process itself depends upon and is bound up with individuals. Therefore, when the individual who provides these components is no longer on board, the means of production of the organization disappears. To state it in extreme terms, the reason for the organization to exist has been extinguished.

Of course, in reality, organizations are rarely entirely dependent on a single individual. Usually a portion of the skills and knowledge have been passed onto (or the seeds of same planted in) others working in the organization in question, so it may be expected that a certain amount of the knowledge, experience, and sensitivity required to function has become common property, which may also be the case for other assets (such as brand names and networks of association—contacts—which are not to be overlooked in considering the question of continuity). So the disappearance of one individual from the scene does not automatically foretell the extinction of an organization. But the retirement from the stage of a key figure can be a considerable blow to an organization and can be expected to at least induce some transformation of its character. This becomes obvious if we imagine such typical purveyors of knowledge-value creation as design, architectural, or law firms, or research labs or R & D firms.

Organizations in the knowledge-value society will be subservient to the people who constitute their means of production and will be far more fluid than those in the industrial society. If the type of organization typical of industrial society could be said to resemble a symphony orchestra, the organizations typical of the knowledge-value society would be more like the line-up of a jazz band.

A symphony orchestra exists as an independent entity and if it happens to be, say, the New York Philharmonic, it will maintain its tradition, capital, and nomenclature as the New York Philharmonic even when the conductor or the concertmaster change, but a jazz lineup such as "The Joe Smith Quintet" changes in substance when Joe Smith is gone.

Another point to keep in mind is that organizations typical of the industrial society—corporations—excelled in a function-specific departmentalized mode of organization. The reason corporations developed along these lines was that it is appropriate for an organization that consistently manages and deploys material assets to appoint specialists to specific functions.

However, in an organization that relies on the ability and character of the personality to which the organization itself is subservient, that central personality will play an enormous role. Numerous types of specialized knowledge and skills will of course be necessary, and the merits of diversification will be great in a knowledge-value society that, in all probability, will have an even more complex social environment than that of the industrial society. However, there will be no need for all of these skills and sources of knowledge to be present in one organization. Design work can be carried out in a design studio, legal matters can be handled by a separate law office, finances by an accounting firm, and industrial technology by a technological institute, all of which can then act jointly. When a designer pivotal to his operation is removed from the scene, an accountant in a design office may face the dire prospect that he no longer has any function to perform.

Recently, trends in management are moving away from the vertical hierarchical organizational structure and toward the holographic type with multidimensional information flow. The computer screen has created significant possibilities for transmitting information multidimensionally, instead of shifting it up and down in an orderly manner along a vertical route according to what positions parties occupy in the hierarchy. This interest in multidimensional information flow indicates a relaxation of the function-specific compartmentalization of the old system, which worked against communication of specific information to divisions whose function was not directly involved. On the other hand, there will be certain limits as to the scale on which a holographically organized organization can operate efficiently, as the work of the persons who form its nucleus becomes more multidimensional and multifaceted.

Bureaucratic Management Ability
Yields to Market Savvy

The changes in the concept of the organization I have just described will wreak changes upon those who work in organizations that create knowledge-value, particularly upon their leadership.

In the industrial society, the drive to lower production costs to achieve "economies of scale" meant large investments and large sales volume. Therefore, a single investment plan or the development of a new product were events of such significance that they could change the destiny of a corporation. Thus it was only natural that for things to run smoothly, it was felt necessary to obtain the consensus and cooperation of all parties involved in the organization.

In such an organizational context, it is essential to have orderly behavior, continuous communication, ongoing adjustments, and tireless lobbying. Bureaucratic management talent was demanded of leaders who hoped to enjoy any certainty of success at executing their functions. Such bureaucratic needs dictate a cautious wait-and-see style and lead to that creative culture of managerial types loaded with "team spirit" which has characterized large corporations from the later stages of the postwar boom years on into the present (especially in Japan). However, radically different talents will be required in a society in which transitory knowledge-value has become the mainspring for economic growth and corporate profits. An organization that aims for the maximization of knowledge-value rather than the lowering of costs through economies of scale must first of all select the *field*—the time and place in which its particular brand of knowledge-value will get maximum play.

It follows that the quality sought above all others in a tribal chief of the future organization is foresight: the ability to forecast what technology is going to grow and what will be fashionable next.

The second requirement is the decision-making ability to execute the forecast. This is essential because the moment for maximizing knowledge-value will be missed if time is spent obtaining social consensus or lobbying. A third requirement will be swift execution of the decision—leaders must be able to get the whole organization moving.

A fourth requirement will be the ability and character to foster the environment necessary for the generation of useful information and ideas that lead to the creation of knowledge-value. This type of ability and character is, if anything, directly opposed to the punctilious and orderly style of management appropriate to the rigidly departmentalized and function-specific industrial style of organization.

Historically, we Japanese have referred to someone who possesses the combination of these traits—foresight, decisiveness, speed in execution, and the ability to amass and assimilate all kinds of information and ideas—as a merchant with "marketplace savvy."

In the industrial society, what mattered most was bureaucratic management ability. In the future knowledge-value society, what will matter most will be the ability to see ahead and think on your feet—being able to demonstrate "marketplace savvy."

The Breakdown of Pricing Mechanisms and Changes in the Criteria for Occupation Selection

By now I hope it is becoming clear that the knowledge-value society will be genuinely different from the industrial society. We are not talking about incremental changes or modifications of the system now in place, but a new social form, another stage in the development of civilization. The most basic parameters that govern social behavior, the so-called social paradigms, will be transformed. Among these paradigms the pricing mechanism is of special importance.

Those of us who have been brought up in the industrial society have regarded its systems as permanent and immutable. Whether we studied economics under the free-enterprise system or economics under socialism, we have always taken the pricing mechanism for granted. This is even more true for those who haven't studied economics: it is part of the set of presumptions that go with the belief in man as *Homo economicus*, an economic creature who acts in his own economic self-interest. Of course, the real world is filled with gifts and inheritances, premiums and bargain sales, and other exceptions to strict observance of the notion that a particular item should have a single fixed price. As can be seen in the sponsorship of sports events or political contributions, money does move around without a specific quid pro quo. As a general rule, however, assets move according to the pricing mechanism, and the assumption that they will do so is thought of as a perfectly sound basis for the operation of the social economy. As a social parameter, the pricing mechanism is the only universally accepted public principle, and the instances I have mentioned that do not accord with its workings are considered exceptions to the rule.

In places where the pricing mechanism is in operation there is constant pressure to push the price for a specific item toward its "true" value. If excess profits are accruing to the sellers, the supply will soon be augmented by new sellers who, in vying for the same market, will lower the price; if, on the other hand, the sellers are losing money, the supply will be reduced and the price will rise. As I mentioned before, both the labor-value theory proposed by Marx and the utility-value theory proposed by Walras ultimately accept this premise about how the pricing mechanism operates.

Yet the pricing mechanism has not been an immutable principle that has persisted undisturbed through the ages, as became clear from the examples of medieval societies we examined in the previous chapter. The knowledge-value society that lies ahead promises to present us with a new divergence from the pricing mechanism.

The social utility curve of knowledge-value drops sharply, and the price itself oscillates wildly, making it impossible to anticipate what price will approach its true value; indeed, it becomes difficult even to establish a single price for a knowledge-value item.

It is no longer surprising for an item that sold in one place at 10,000 yen to sell at 5,000 yen at another, or for a technology that one corporation is trying to bring in at 100 million yen suddenly to have a price tag of one billion yen placed on it by another corporation. Nor is it uncommon any longer for a pair of designs, each of which took a similar number of hours for the same studio to develop, to be valued at one million yen and 2,000 yen respectively. Since the price of knowledge-value bears no direct relationship with manufacturing costs, it fluctuates widely on the basis of subjective feelings and judgments, themselves dependent on the circumstances in which the buyer and the seller find themselves.

The once unchallenged assumption that the pricing mechanism should apply to wages and labor costs is also now breaking down. I am not simply referring to the fact that the Equal Opportunities Act in Employment in the United States or the system of lifetime employment and seniority linked to wages in Japan have come to enforce a distinction between the productivity and wages of one worker and another. One more general indication of the shift away from a literal pricing mechanism for wages is the fact that those who seek work are beginning to be as concerned with the image of a particular job (that is, whether it makes them look good) as with the amount of money they will earn. The reader will remember that in the Middle Ages, people without any talents or skills could sometimes command a lot of money just because they had been born into a good family, while others who lived lives totally divorced from productive activity might be accorded aristocratic status or sainthood for their noble character. What this might mean in a knowledge-value society is that work-places with good images might be able to attract human re-sources at low wages, while other work sites seen as unbecom-ing might not be able to get anybody to work for them, no matter what wages they offer.

In the industrial society, consumer demand was directed toward hard goods such as material resources and energy, so a level of wages that made it possible to satisfy one's desires in this area served as an effective and consistent criteria for job selection. In short, the workplaces that offered high wages attracted the talented workers.

However, in a knowledge-value society, consumer demand will be directed more and more toward forms of knowledge-value. The difference between the consumption standards of the high- and low-income wage earners will be determined by whether one can afford a high-priced brand or has to put up with generic or more commonplace items. In other words, the issue is more one of good image or self-gratification and ego fulfillment.

Wealth Becomes Abstract

None of the above means that everything in a knowledge-value society will revolve around knowledge-value. The prin-ciple of uniform pricing for uniform items will probably continue to hold sway for raw materials, energy, commodities that are more or less indistinguishable from one another, or relatively simple and straightforward services. But even in this area there will be increasing disassociation of pricing from production costs, and wages will no longer be as closely linked to production results. Recent oil and real estate prices might be cited as instances that at least partially exemplify this ongoing shift in pricing behavior.

At the same time, both donations and autocratically or politically imposed redistribution of the "pie" will become even more important economic phenomena. The social burden (taxes plus social insurance costs) already accounts for more than 50 percent of the gross national product in many Western economies, and both redress of income discrepancies and redistribution of income between generations are becoming far-reaching economic phenomena. Since the knowledge-value society is bound to be "a society with time on its hands," it seems safe to assume that redistribution issues presented in terms that have nothing to do with the price mechanism are not going to go away or be easily shrugged off in the future.

Not all attempts to deal with redistribution issues will be effected by national authorities in such forms as public taxation or welfare policy. It seems somewhat more probable that redistribution will be brought about through a breakdown in the principle of parity exchange and uniform pricing.

Even in international or regional redistribution of wealth, mechanisms that are not dependent on parity exchange will become more prevalent. Today, such redistribution takes the primary form of economic cooperation with developing countries, but it is going forward at the same time on an even greater scale in the form of an accumulation of huge loans. Even if such interest-bearing commercial loans are supposed to be paid off at a certain point, there is not even a slight possibility that a large proportion of these loans will be repaid even if extended over extremely long terms. They will in substance disappear, whether through international inflation or political solutions. This will constitute an unintended international redistribution of wealth. The only real difference between the deliberate international redistribution of wealth—which takes the form of economic cooperation or uncompensated assistance—and loans that go unrepaid is whether the sums in question remain on a bank's books as loans.

Underlying this behavior can be glimpsed an important change in the concept of *currency*. From the first, the currencies devised and used by mankind were metals such as gold, silver, and copper, which could be described as a form of hard goods. To be sure, metal coins have been less and less likely to be involved directly in transactions, but our dependence on metals, and especially gold, to back currency continued through the course of many centuries.

This arrangement was more or less maintained until the dollar went off the gold standard in 1972. Up to that point, each country's foreign-exchange policies had been limited by the ability of the dollar to back up payments, while the United States itself was restricted by having to maintain gold reserves to meet the contingency of demands for exchange in gold. Therefore, unless there were capitulations on the part of the system such as currency devaluations, each currency had been governed in a roundabout way through gold.

The "Nixon Shock" of 1972, by suspending the exchange of the dollar for gold, transformed the situation in one stroke. A currency's value came to be subjected to people's political or financial states of mind, or to a kind of social subjectivity. These days the United States is suffering the debilitation of a budget deficit amounting to $150 billion per annum; but there was no way such an enormous deficit could have been sustained before 1972, when the dollar was subject to being exchanged for gold.

The kinds of small change we put into our purses have a tangible existence in that they can be exchanged for goods and services, but the huge capital requirements involved in international finance and national debts can be said to have already entered the realm of abstraction. In the knowledge-value society, the most typical assets with which consumers will surround themselves will consist of "soft goods" whose valuation depends on social subjectivity, while the huge amounts of capital discussed in the international context will become abstractions, since there is no way to realize them in a tangible form.

The End of Racial States and the Establishment of Ideological Zones

In tandem with the tendency for wealth to become an extremely abstract entity flowing freely between nations, another factor likely to transform societies at the international level is the demise of the concept of the racially based nation-state.

Earlier I mentioned that the idea that a state is or ought to be essentially a racially based entity (a nation-state) emerged during the modern era when people started to take note of the physical and functional features of all forms of matter; such a notion of the state was utterly absent in the medieval era and before. The very idea of classifying humans by their forms and functions—in the same manner that material goods were classified—was what led to the conclusion that a state organized on the basis of members of the same race or ethnic group was superior to other forms of political organization.

However, decisive changes regarding even this rather basic

assumption have been under way since 1972. I am not referring simply to the development and expansion of multiracial
societies such as the United States and the Soviet Union. Even
in Europe, which deliberately organized itself into racial
states, great numbers of individuals from different races have
migrated to join the polities there; West Germany and Britain
are in fact becoming multiracial states. These countries have
taken up policies of restraining foreign workers and encouraging their return in reaction to the rise in unemployment during the 1980s, but the multiracial trends in these societies are
not likely to be "resolved" by such measures, in part due to
differences in the birth rates of the original Caucasian inhabitants and the immigrant minorities. On the contrary, the recent trend in the United States, the USSR, and Europe is for
these minorities to emphasize their own cultural roots; and
the direction being taken is toward a strengthening of the
multiracial character of these societies and of their cultures.
However, an even more dramatic change was the surge in the
number of refugees that started toward the end of the 1970s;
particularly significant was the emergence of government-
sanctioned refugee movements. The fact that the governments of Vietnam and Cambodia officially permitted, or at
least tacitly approved, the outflow of hundreds of thousands
of their own nationals without specific destinations was an
amazing occurrence in which can be seen forebodings of decisive change in the concept of the nation-state. Not only does
such action destroy the ideology of the racial state—the concept that man's true state and happiness lies in rule by a government that has been organized by the same race—but it
simultaneously denies the political ethos according to which a
government ought to be ashamed to see a large voluntary outflow of its nationals who share the same racial identity.
Through their attitudes, the governments of Vietnam and
Cambodia sent out the clear message that whether or not

these refugees (or others to come) happen to be of the same race and nationality as the government officials themselves, "if they do not agree with the government's political ideology, they should leave." In the end, ideology proved more important than race or nationality. This was also the case during the medieval era, which emphasized cohesion along lines of social subjectivity.

The ideas and policies set forth by the Communist governments of Vietnam and Cambodia spread to other Communist countries, and Cuba and Ethiopia began to pursue the same course during the 1980s. Countries such as the United States found themselves completely helpless to develop effective countermeasures, other than to help the refugees on humanistic grounds. In effect, what the Vietnamese and Cambodian governments did received ex post facto approval.

Now that it is evident that national borders, law, and military might are helpless against the flow of actual human beings across borders, not only has the ideology of the racial state been exploded conceptually, but it is clear to all who dare look that it can no longer be maintained. How would even Japan, one of the world's most homogeneous nations, and one that appears to possess some determination to remain so, cope with a sudden infusion of hundreds of thousands of boat people from another country? The police and the self-defense forces might be able to restrain these people at their landing points and accommodate them temporarily in special facilities, but if the countries they'd left refused to accept these people back, as did Vietnam and Cambodia, there would ultimately be no alternative but to look after them and place them in jobs.

If this sort of thing is repeated over and over throughout the world, many countries—regardless of whatever statutes or defensive capabilities they may possess—are inevitably going to end up as multiethnic states. For landlocked countries such as those on the American and Asian continents, preventing such an outcome is virtually impossible. We are forced to contemplate a finale like that faced by the Roman empire and the various Chinese empires that found themselves unable to impede the influx of the peoples thought of at the time as "barbarians."

In the world of the knowledge-value society, race is unlikely to be the main organizing principle of a country. The dominant form of political organization will not be the racially based nation-state, but the ideological zone loosely held together by a shared social viewpoint.

To this extent, the possibility seems strong that international societies in the knowledge-value mode will bear a strong resemblance to their predecessors from the medieval era—although the ideological zones in this future world will of course not be divided along the same religious lines as were their medieval predecessors.

5

The Ongoing Knowledge-Value
Revolution

The Knowledge-Value Revolution Has Begun

In the preceding chapters, I outlined my view that certain changes taking place during the 1980s not only represented a break from the cycle of technological innovations and social progress going on within the framework of industrial society, but repudiated industrial society itself and were therefore certain to bring on the birth of a new social framework. I went on to forecast that the society to come out of this would be built around the knowledge-value that can be created through access to mankind's cumulative wisdom, experience, and sensitivity.

Since this forecast hints at social changes more far-reaching and all-embracing than other theories so far presented (by Daniel Bell, Alvin Toffler, and others), it seems likely to be dismissed by many as simply too radical and extreme in its assumptions—or as a kind of daydream about a future far too distant from the world we know to amount to more than a fantasy.

Forecasts of emerging new societies invariably meet with this kind of criticism. When Adam Smith preached the benefits of a function-specific division of labor and insisted that manufacturing was to be the major industry in the generation ahead, the conservative Physiocrats led by François Quesnay leveled the same sort of charges against Smith.

And I must say that I do not think of the advent of the

knowledge-value society as an event taking place in some remote and distant future. Far from it; I am convinced that the myriad changes by which we find ourselves besieged now are part of an ongoing transformation leading to a knowledge-value society.

Transformations of the social economy are not accomplished in an instant. It took several decades for the industrial revolution to be completed in England; in the advanced nations of Europe, it required some thirty years; and in Japan, roughly twenty years. The knowledge-value revolution is also likely to maintain a tentative pattern—one step forward, two steps back—for two to three decades.

But I consider it unlikely that the knowledge-value revolution will grind to a worldwide halt, let alone reverse its direction. And I expect it to be well under way in certain parts of the world's most advanced regions before the end of the century.

Having said that, I concede it will probably be a good, long time before all of the features of the knowledge-value society I've discussed are realized in any particular society. In transitions from primary to ancient civilization, from ancient to medieval, and from medieval to modern, a minimum of a century was required before even those seminal advanced regions that exemplified a particular transformation completely accomplished it. Modern industrial society, for that matter, took over a century to reach its full form in many advanced regions and has yet to reach full maturity in the developing nations.

In other words, the industrial revolution launched the industrial society into being, but this does not mean the evolutionary process was completed simultaneously. The industrial revolution reinforced certain key features of the industrial society and at the same time moved that society as a whole in directions that further consolidated those features. Undergoing such a revolution did not mean that the volume of manufacturing production or the numbers of workers employed in manufacturing exceeded those of agriculture the moment the revolution occurred, but that the revolution set the stage for manufacturing to become the principal wellspring for the growth of the social economy and for the accumulation of capital stock.

My claim that the knowledge-value revolution started in the 1980s is made in the context of the assumptions I've just outlined about how social revolutions occur. I'm not saying that the value of production from knowledge-value creation, a phenomenon initiated in the 1980s, will soon surpass those of hard goods or conventional services, or that the numbers of workers employed in knowledge-value creation will necessarily soon exceed those in the hard-goods industries or other industries in place; but I do contend that knowledge-value creation will soon come to be seen as the principal wellspring for the growth of the social economy and for the accumulation of capital in the form of stock investment.

Free workers who lack their own means of production will not immediately disappear; the pricing mechanism will not vanish from the entire society. Farm communities with vestiges of the medieval environment and family-operated handicraft industries persisted for a long time after the industrial revolution. It is said that these entities did not lose their significance for society until after World War I—or, in certain places like Germany, until the rise of Nazism in the 1930s. In Japan's case, this kind of final break with the medieval did not occur until the mid-1950s ushered in high economic growth.

We should therefore expect that, within the knowledge-value society, free workers will continue to be employed and that industries will continue to turn out raw materials or mass-produced items and market them according to the classical pricing mechanism. It is not as if conventional industries will no longer be needed to sustain man and permit society to function.

However, such industries will cease to play a large role in economic growth and in the accumulation of capital through stock offerings—as was true for small-scale farms and family-run handicraft operations, although they persisted as a minor force in the economy long after the industrial revolution.

Further, we should never assume that because an industry has ceased to be the principal wellspring for the growth of the social economy, it is simply going to be politically and socially ignored or overlooked. If we recall Japan before World War II—indeed, if we think of Japan and America today—it would seem that it is the very spheres that lack potential for growth that tend to exert the greatest political strength and enjoy the highest esteem from society. It seems that in every age, new cultures and industries that are growing rapidly are looked at with suspicion while the older, stagnant ones bask in the solemnity that comes from past glories and traditions.

This glorification of the stagnant will assume significance when future policies are considered. Its importance will become especially evident as we examine the future political course of Japan and the practical issues posed by the Japanese way of life and the speed and scale with which it can accommodate social change.

JAPAN IN TRANSITION

Something Very Like the Ideal State

In the 1980s it was truly splendid to be a citizen of Japan. As far as we Japanese were concerned, Japan was as pleasant and comfortable as any nation could be expected to be, and well worth the labor we put into making it that way.

The public was at ease, the crime rate was low, and we had not been at war for a long, long time. The 1980s must surely rank as the happiest moment in our history, as a time when Japan could be counted among the most livable places in the modern world.

Numerous facts bear this out. For example: per capita income in Japan, while in the middle range among the advanced nations, was distributed far more equitably than in most of them, so that the standard of living enjoyed by the average citizen was higher than the per capita figure might suggest.

The Japanese were also in the forefront not only in consumption of durable goods, but in the richness of their diet and what they spent on clothing.

Even Japanese housing, which had been considered substandard, is now fourth in the world in area (square footage) per home; it is behind the United States, West Germany, and Sweden, but ahead of France, England, and Italy. And if there are inherent limits on available space, the quality of furnishings and the attention lavished on details in these homes go far toward compensating for the lack of space. Since the rate of home ownership is, moreover, the highest on earth, it is certainly fair to conclude that housing conditions are quite satisfactory.

Japan's productivity gives clear evidence of its superb economic position. When per capita production volume is examined, there are many categories—iron and steel, electric machinery and tools, optics and fine instruments—where Japanese have a decisive lead. In terms both of quality and of price, Japanese manufacturing is, if anything, overly competitive in the international arena.

Furthermore, in many categories of cutting-edge technology—machine tools, high-grade office equipment, electronics, etc.—Japan was advancing rapidly and overwhelming its competition as it came into the 1980s.

That is not all. Because of Japan's excellent technological characteristics, its quality control capabilities, and the high standards maintained throughout its labor force, the number of countries trying to learn from Japanese management know-how kept growing throughout this period. These days, the real power of Japanese industry is seen not just in terms of its financial success, but in some appreciation of the cultural factors in which it is rooted.

Thanks to these achievements, Japan has chalked up an enormous trade surplus despite the fact that it imports the bulk of its raw energy and food. In 1984, when this surplus rose to an astounding $45 billion, Japan overtook the great oil-producing nation of Saudi Arabia and became the country with the largest trade surplus on earth. Moreover, this trend is expected to continue for some time to come.

At the same time, the stability of the Japanese economy seems unshakable. Prices and the cost of living are on an even keel, the savings rate is extraordinary; the country has maintained the highest rate of personal savings of any nation in the world for over thirty years. The wonder of it all is that the savings rate has not gone down despite the steady improvement in social welfare over the past twenty years.

Another piece of good fortune in the "Japanese miracle" is that the labor supply has always been in equilibrium. Apart from the period of disruption just after World War II, the Japanese unemployment rate has always been the lowest among the advanced nations; yet despite this, there was never an imperative need to bring in large numbers of migrant workers to fill a serious gap in labor supply.

In other words, postwar Japan not only got its economy to grow, improved its technology, built a gigantic productive machine, and attained a high standard of living; it also succeeded in creating a society with very little unemployment or poverty, with an egalitarian orientation in material matters within that society, all the while creating conditions that predispose it to continue to enjoy both a chronic trade surplus and a high level of savings.

Japan's good fortune is not restricted to the economics sphere. Basic education is universal and the percentage of Japanese who advance to senior high school is the highest in the world. If we were to include tutorial programs, the various types of specialty schools, and the education programs Japanese companies operate on their premises, a case could undoubtedly be made that Japan supplies more education per person than any other country.

Health standards are likewise extraordinarily high. The average life expectancy is 76.2 years for males and 79.8 for females, which marks an increase of almost thirty years over the four postwar decades; these figures are also the world's highest. Japanese hygienic controls and medical facilities have attained standards that make the likelihood of an acute epidemic of fatal infectious disease seem next to nonexistent. Even the physical stature of the Japanese people has improved; they have grown so much larger in such a short time that some have suggested that if future archaeologists were to excavate their bones, they would conclude that at some point a different race had taken over.

Japan is also a remarkably safe place to live. Women and children feel no fear about going out at night, and armed robberies of banks or burglaries of homes are rare. The sociological tenet that "as urbanization proceeds, crime increases" does not apply to Japan. At the same time, accidental deaths are few and work injuries have also declined rapidly. This is true because transportation services, buildings, factories, and work sites observe no limits in their pursuit of safety.

The ultimate good fortune that Japan continues to enjoy is four decades of uninterrupted peace. The Japanese homeland has not been visited by the fires of war since the end of the Pacific conflict and not a single Japanese has been sent to the front. That nobody in Japan need fear involuntary conscription into an army is a blessing its people can truly treasure.

Other sources of happiness that are perhaps of even greater concrete impact are the atmosphere and human relations in the Japanese working environment. Thanks to lifetime employment and the seniority pay system established in the course of the high economic growth of the postwar years, the average Japanese male wage earner can expect to work at the same place until he retires and watch his wages and position improve throughout his career. Most Japanese men do not have to worry about ever losing their jobs.

As a result, peace and harmony reign in the workplace. For the great majority of Japanese employees, the office or the factory at times functions as much as a kind of cultural salon as it does as a workplace. In the same way we designate the various phases of historical European culture, such as the "court culture" of the eighteenth century or the "club or salon culture" of the nineteenth, we might speak of Japan in the late twentieth century as exemplifying the "workplace culture."

If this is what the modern industrial state is all about—the realization of material abundance and its equitable distribution, of safety and stability in living conditions—then Japan today may be said to be the country that most closely approaches the ideal; it is the "star pupil" among modern industrial societies.

Can Today's Star Pupil Become Tomorrow's Success Story?

"As an infant he was a prodigy; as a student he was brilliant; but after twenty he was just another young man." This Japanese saying is meant to admonish parents who have fallen into the habit of seeing only what they want to see about their children to remember that different standards apply as people reach different stages in life, and warns them not to build up great expectations prematurely.

The admonition can also apply to nations and races. It is not necessarily easy for a country that prospered under one set of conditions to maintain its prosperity in the next era.

World history records some instances of civilizations that managed to maintain vast territories and high levels of achievement over centuries, as did ancient Rome or the great Chinese empires of the Han and the Tang dynasties, but these types of successes have proven to be as rare as the types of personages who can perpetrate them—figures like the first Ming emperor or the great shogun, Toyotomi Hideyoshi. The world is filled with nations and races that have achieved a certain amount of prosperity only to see it decline immediately in the era that followed, so that the fact of their short-lived peak is scarcely remembered today.

So Japan's current status as "star pupil" offers no guarantee about its rank in the next era. The blowhards who are trumpeting about the twenty-first century as "the Japanese century" are behaving like a mother who's dead certain that her brilliant eight-year-old will grow up to be a Nobel laureate.

The vexing question we must face is whether the very things that made Japan the "star pupil" as an industrial society will in fact serve it well in the era of the knowledge-value society.

We will know the answer before very long. The postwar petroleum culture that epitomized the industrial society peaked around 1980 and has already begun its descent. For better or worse, despite the fact that Japan is now a "star pupil"—or rather, because of that fact—it will face many inherent problems and liabilities in making this transition to a new society. Japan will have to reform itself on a number of fronts.

Domestically, Japan's financial and governmental institutions need to be rebuilt on different lines, while its tax and education systems promise to be very resistant to reform. Measures to cope with the aging of the Japanese population must be pushed through, and even more extensive industrial and technological reform will be required. Externally, economic frictions have taken a serious turn and this will require fresh thinking and fresh approaches. The star pupil, in the process of earning good grades, has embraced numerous distortions and frictions in its domestic and international relations.

If we are to cope with or even ruminate upon these problems effectively, it will be necessary to have a basic ideology that can serve as a guide to the future direction of Japan. I will assume that the advent of the knowledge-value society is a given, and discuss what sort of reforms Japan must undertake if it is to succeed in the era to come.

The Japanese Cultural Base
That Gave Birth to Groupism

When considering Japan's future, we must clarify at the outset that Japan as a nation was able to attain its current preeminence only in the second half of this century and really only since the late 1960s. Japan accomplished its high growth during the atypical period I described as the postwar petroleum culture—the zenith of the industrial society. This unique period provided advantageous conditions to the unique country that Japan happens to be.

In Chapter 2, I identified three factors—changes in technology, population patterns, and the resource picture (or the environment, in the broadest sense)—as the "disruptive elements" that work to transform civilization.

Of paramount importance when we consider Japanese society are the geographical conditions under which it developed.

While the archipelago that constitutes the Japanese domain is positioned on the eastern edge of the Eurasian continent and is separated from the surrounding nations by fairly wide seas, the four main islands themselves are coherently and contiguously interlocked. Their topography tends to be mountainous with few plains. The climate is generally temperate with ample rainfall, and although there are short, intermittent bursts of typhoons, earthquakes, and other minor calamities, long-term droughts or cold weather are virtually unheard of. Thus, not only has the "lay of the land" worked to establish the resourcce picture, but geographical conditions have historically limited Japan's intercourse with foreign countries and set the conditions for its technology and population patterns. The perceptible effects of the Japanese domain on its inhabitants are multifaceted, as numerous scholars have repeatedly stressed.

A temperate climate with abundant rain and the mountainous terrain works to promote luxuriant vegetation. While the long and irregular coastline has been propitious for fishing, the rugged and uneven topography is ill suited to hunting and nomadic living. For these reasons, the early inhabitants of these islands did not undergo the experiences of hunting and nomadic living, although they did engage in some fishing activities along the coasts; thus, the early Japanese were an almost purely herbivorous tribe, and during the primary stage of their civilization, interaction with animals—either as sources of food or as beasts of labor—was minimal. Lack of such contact fosters a penchant for harmony and egalitarianism among one's own species. If a tribe practices hunting and nomadic living, its fortunes as a group will likely be influenced by the ability and judgment of the leader; if on the other hand, a tribe picks nuts and berries or engages in fishing, group harmony and patience will allow it to achieve the best results.

The climate and topography of the Japanese isles exerted an even greater influence once farming began. A landscape that features tiny plains scattered between small mountain ranges is ideal for rice cultivation and fosters a high concentration of population. Rice cultivation, although it yields high productivity per acre (and permits successive harvesting because the needed nutrients are carried by water), requires intensive labor. To that extent, Japanese farming resembles the primary stage of farming in world history, which started in the fertile lands around riverbanks and oases.

However, since transportation between the patches of arable land—through mountain paths and inland seas—was relatively simple to carry out in these isles, those who sought political power were able to expand their governance of territory promptly; technological developments tended therefore to proceed at a slower pace than territorial consolidation. This

enabled the formation of territorial powers without the formation of an urban state in the strict sense.

The ancestors of today's Japanese, therefore, had virtually
no experience of hunting and nomadic living, and their experience of the primary stage of civilization was, in comparison with that of other cultures around the globe, quite short-
lived.

How Isolation Let Japan Digest
or Reject Foreign Influences

The distance by sea between Japan and the Eurasian mainland has never been inconsequential. Even now, when the trip
requires but one or two hours by plane, both Korea and China
are still geographically a long distance away. When it comes
to moving people and goods or exchanges of information
across this distance, there is no comparison with the exchange
achieved within our own borders. This is not to say that inter-
changes were ever far beyond the realm of possibility. For
those willing to embrace certain risks and expenses, making
the crossing was a possibility even with the technology available in the ancient era.

Thus, Japan was not so far away that continental technology
and ideas were prevented from flowing in, but neither was it
so close that the political systems and ideologies of a powerful
neighbor could be forced upon the nation. The Korean peninsula, by contrast, was connected by land to China, and so
felt constant pressure from the Chinese.

Sporadic contact between Japan and the continent evidently
began before the first century, but regular contact only got
under way from the late fourth century. It was about this time
that Japan began to take on some of the vestiges of an ancient
territorial state. By that time, however, the Chinese version of

ancient civilization that had reached its zenith in the Han dynasty had already gone into an utter decline and China had entered its medieval stage, characterized by the popularity of mysticism and Buddhism.

The disparity in their respective stages of development between Japan and China at this stage left significant marks on Japanese culture. Despite having declined, Chinese technology was then at such a comparably high level as to be perceived as near magic by the Japanese. It is only to be expected that the Japanese, who had but recently developed the ability to cultivate land and enrich themselves with material goods, would jump at the chance to obtain this superior technology.

At the same time the ideologies flowing in from China, which had turned to medievalism, bewildered the Japanese. The men who had formed the ancient territorial state and who had just begun to enjoy material wealth found the Chinese disdain for productive activities and love for esoteric speculation beyond their comprehension.

Eventually they started to reject the concepts and ideas emanating from China, even as they went on pursuing its technological knowledge. Examples of Chinese concepts and customs the Japanese would not incorporate include Taoism, eunuchs as an institution, mysticism, and the practice of forbidding marriage between those with the same family name.

To study certain things and flatly to reject others is a process that involves more than simple selection; to carry out the process requires having a set of one's own criteria. Forced to act by the huge discrepancy between the respective stages of development of their own country and China, the Japanese became truly adept at such study and at reforming their own system to accommodate what they picked up. Since they were only studying the technology and were not being forced to submit to the influence of alien ideology, there was little psychological resistance. This made it possible to have a steady increase in the numbers studying foreign technology, but mitigated against any comprehensive understanding of foreign cultural systems on the part of the Japanese.

The Japanese have long had the ability to extract the practical facets of foreign technology that they wanted and to improve upon them. This holds true not only for the anecdotes everyone has heard about television, automobiles, and electronics in the postwar era or for the modern manufacturing technology that Japan adopted during and after the Meiji period. In every age the Japanese, having mastered a particular foreign technology, carried it within 40 years to a higher level than the original.

For example, it is said that the technology to make large-scale moldings by melding bronze reached Japan from China via Korea during Japan's bronze age of the early eighth century. Yet the construction of the Great Buddha of Nara was begun in 747, only about forty years later, and its casting was completed two years after that. When completed, the Great Buddha of Nara was for some 1,200 years the world's largest bronze statue, until a Japanese industrialist decided to build an even larger one in Fukui prefecture.

In a similar vein, it is said that guns first arrived in Japan in 1543, but by the time forty years had passed and work had begun on Osaka Castle, Japanese guns led the world in both quality and quantity. Since we know that 15 guns were being produced a day in Sakai near Osaka, it seems reasonable to project that annual production of guns approached 5,000. At the time of the battle of Sekigahara in 1600, the total quantity possessed by the combatants was in the range of 60,000. That figure exceeds the quantity of guns in stock on the entire European continent during the corresponding period.

In almost every period during which a basic form of technology reached Japan, the Japanese managed to introduce so many practical improvements to it that their version eventually outshone that of the creators of that technology. It is probably fair to say that it was Japanese pragmatism, which studied things only in terms of the practical uses they might be put to, and was unfettered by any conceptual trappings, that enabled this improvement.

Utilitarianism Without an Absolute Sense of Justice

In the sixth century, as the political situation changed in the Korean peninsula and large numbers of naturalized persons (most of them Buddhists) entered Japan, the question of whether or not to recognize Buddhism became an especially important political issue. Because the status and authority of the Japanese imperial line is based on Shinto mythology, it was feared that if Buddhism, which denies the validity of such mythology, were sanctioned, the imperial institution would lose its raison d'être.

Thus, none of the three emperors of the late sixth century would overtly embrace Buddhism, though they made a point of demonstrating their understanding of it in order to obtain the support of naturalized immigrants with superior technology. Then Crown Prince Shōtoku Taishi emerged from the imperial household. The prince (resorting to sophistries such as, "Our gods must be worshiped. Some capricious gods, however, persist in casting curses upon us even when we worship them. It is Buddha who can dispel such curses.") thought of a way to preserve Shinto while simultaneously sanctioning Buddhism. As regent, he was able to put this idea into practice as official policy. Establishing the Shitennōji and Hōryūji temples, he issued an edict exhorting men to "respect the gods" as part of the seventeen-article constitution promulgated in 604. Such actions must have astonished devout Buddhists.

Crown Prince Shōtoku's arguments for coexistence of the two religions may have verged on sophistry, but in their aftermath, religious issues as such disappeared from the Japanese landscape and wars that stemmed from conflicts over religious ideology never occurred. This has gone far toward fostering peace in Japan, but the greater significance of the Shōtoku doctrine is that it eliminated from the Japanese mind any sense of absolute right based on religious belief.

The Japanese ability simultaneously to worship a multiplicity of gods is due to having no belief in a single, absolute, eternal truth. What the Japanese feel to be right is what is conceived of as being right by everybody in the particular time and place where the issue arises. Carrying this to its extreme, we can say that, as far as the Japanese are concerned, anything everybody will agree to is what is right. When times and social conditions change, the perception of what is right is rapidly transformed. It is characteristic of Japan that once such a consensus has formed, there is little resistance to it.

The Japanese have never been dominated by any single, absolute religious faith. In that sense, not only can it be argued that Japanese history lacks an era corresponding to the primary stage of city-states; the case can also be made that Japan did not pass through a true medieval phase, in the strict sense.

Religious pluralism supported the tendency toward utilitarian pragmatism. Those who do not possess an absolute sense of justice tend to support things that are to their own benefit. It follows that what benefits the majority, or the dominant social force, will naturally be designated "right."

The notion of what benefits the majority is a kind of social subjectivity. In the absence of a sense of absolute right, however, social subjectivity tends to be driven by utilitarian considerations. Japan's process of modernization, beginning with the Meiji era, is a case in point; the way in which economic issues have been prioritized in Japan since World War II presents a particularly vivid example of rational social subjectivity in action, with the Japanese pushing to increase the supply of material goods in the name of both profit and justice.

The Idea That the State and Its People Are One Was Fostered by Peace

Japan's geographical separation from the Eurasian continent by a fairly wide expanse of sea has meant that it was never subjected to large-scale invasions or political domination by foreigners. With the exception of the Pacific War, the only time that Japan underwent systematic military assault by foreigners was when the Mongols attempted to invade, and they never got farther than a short landing in northern Kyushu. The absence of more significant conflict meant that the Japanese never had to equip themselves, either psychologically or physically, for wars against foreigners. On top of that, Japan's civil wars tended to be short-lived affairs, so most Japanese were enabled to lead existences far removed from concerns over war and peace. Even in Japan's bellicose sixteenth century, military conflicts were generally considered to be settled once the defeated lord and several of his senior retainers had committed suicide; there are almost no instances in which the average citizenry were massacred.

For this reason, the Japanese have tended to have only a superficial understanding of military thought and never developed the habit of lavishing funds on military defenses, the single exception being their short flirtation with producing guns. During the 260 years of extended peace under the Tokugawa, Japan became a virtually unarmed nation and its army—in the sense of units prepared to carry out collective battle formations—virtually ceased to exist.

The samurai clans of the Tokugawa era inherited the social duty to act as custodians of such military groups as then existed, but their function and organizational status had disappeared. For a long time after the mid-seventeenth century, there are no records of concerted warlike actions, which had in fact become a practical impossibility in organizational terms. As a result, military expenditures were reduced to almost nothing and the budget for the government and the feudal lords was squandered on maintaining splendid mansions in Edo (old Tokyo), or on pursuits such as upholding public order, collecting taxes, or carrying out public works.

For a state and a society to form itself along such lines is very unusual. In most other countries, the state emerged and developed with its main duty being to establish defenses against external foes, and such an orientation was long retained. Taxes were collected for the very purpose of maintaining soldiers for defensive purposes, and public order was upheld and the citizenry governed so that taxes could be collected. For the citizenry of such nations, the taxes were an onerous burden and the monies, once collected, never returned to the region where they had been paid out. If the rulers were foreign, the situation was even more onerous.

Under such circumstances, local inhabitants develop a custom of keeping their actual income and life-style out of the purview of the government wherever possible, so that the state is obliged to forcibly investigate on its own. Inevitably, the governing and the governed are in conflict.

However, in the case of Japan, since military expenditures were usually small, taxes were relatively light, and some of the funds were returned to the local communities. The ardor with which the Tokugawa era lords pursued regional development dwarfs even that of today's governors.

Since, moreover, the Tokugawa leadership shared racial heritage and customs with their constituents, the court system operated on terms that more or less coincided with what was felt to be fair. At times things actually went so far that the magistrates and the local inhabitants worked together to circumvent the letter of the law.

The citizens could count on government to be there, and developed the penchant for appealing to it at the drop of a hat.

The docile, "easily governed" quality of the Japanese people can be cited as one cause for the economic growth of and beneficent public peace in today's Japan. Aspects of Japan that puzzle foreigners—acceptance by the people of administrative guidance and the system of cooperation between citizens and their officials—are products of this tradition, as is the propensity of popular Japanese opinion to display reliance on those above and to blame the government for everything from fires in buildings to unscrupulous merchandising.

How Limited Resources Made the Japanese Diligent

Not all the geographical conditions that characterize the Japanese domain were propitious. Separation from other nations by a wide expanse of sea meant that Japan could not expand beyond the shores of the archipelago. One might say that the country was deficient in frontiers and in the stimulation they provide to the national spirit. As a result, whenever technological progress stagnated and the population began to increase, the country would immediately be faced with resource shortages. The late eighteenth century under Tokugawa rule presents a typical example.

There have been three periods in Japanese history when both the economy and the culture underwent explosive growth due to technological progress and the concomitant development of land resources. The first was in the ancient era from the sixth to eighth century, when exchanges between Japan and China began to be conducted on a serious scale. The second period involved introduction of new Chinese and Portuguese technology in the fifteenth to seventeenth centuries. The full-scale contact with modern Western civilization, which began during the Meiji era, is the third instance. Between these phases of intense contact, however, came long periods of stagnation. The extended internecine strife during the fifteenth and sixteenth centuries also saw the introduction of land reform and new gold-mining technology, as well as new varieties of crops from China; in response, the Japanese economy surged to great heights and in the course of a single century, Japan's population doubled (from 7 million to 14 million), while its GNP trebled. The subsequent century is said to have produced comparable growth in both categories. In a mere two centuries, then, the population quadrupled and the GNP itself increased ninefold.

As a result, Japan enjoyed relative opulence in the sixteenth century. In the dazzling splendors of this cultural blossoming we can see man's empathetic impulse being stimulated by the condition of "material surplus."

However, acute shortages of resources beset Japan from early in the eighteenth century, by which time the population had substantially increased. The supply of land for potential development had by then declined and the production of gold, silver, and copper plummeted. Depletion of forest resources in parts of Western Japan created an energy crisis.

Fortunately, the energy crisis was somewhat alleviated by the introduction of coal; but the larger resource picture simply grew bleaker and bleaker. As a result, the empathetic impulse in man responded to this material shortage by developing an ethical perspective in which frugality was celebrated as the most important virtue; as this outlook became well established, it became the Japanese habit to see attachment to material goods as demeaning.

However, due to their lack of an absolute sense of right, the Japanese, who had experienced extended periods of growth in the sixteenth and seventeenth centuries, did not revert to a medieval outlook. In the first three decades of the seventeenth century, torn between their penchant for growth and the realities posed by shortages of resources, the Japanese went through agonized contortions. Out of this was born the Japanese philosophy of "diligence" preached by Baigan Ishida and others.

One of the key features in the Japanese philosophy of diligence (of which the Ishida school of practical ethics is representative) was its unusual attempt to reconcile the call for diligence with the need to practice frugality, a proposition it justified by its insistence that in every human calling hard work acts to enhance man's knowledge. Out of this developed what has been called the "culture of contraction" (*chijimi*), in which unlimited amounts of labor were lavished upon limited resources and land in order to perfect products down to the most trivial details. The exquisite detail work and the relative absence of minor defects that have helped make Japanese manufactured products internationally competitive are in all probability manifestations of this tradition.

The other important feature that characterizes the Japanese during this period was the diligence with which they learned to go about acquiring "software" that did not require resources. Training and education in a multitude of disciplines flourished, including: *kenjutsu* (the art of fencing); *jūjitsu* (the precursor to *jūdō*); *saka* (tea ceremony and flower arrangement); *go* and *shōgi* (Japanese "chess"); not to mention reading, writing, and the use of the abacus. As a result, Japan was already a major nation in terms of education by 1868, when the Meiji Restoration began. Forty percent of the males and

25 percent of the females were attending educational institutions such as the *terakoya,* or temple schools; in Britain, then the most advanced manufacturing nation, only 25 percent of the males were attending educational institutions at this time, and there was not a single school for females.

The reason Japan was able to digest Western technology so speedily after the Meiji Restoration was that the ethical outlook was already in place—one that supported diligence and basic education. Today's developing nations lack such a tradition, which means that the Japanese experience in the years following the Meiji Restoration is not analogous to theirs and its "lessons" are inapplicable.

This Japanese notion of diligence also forms a contrast with the industriousness which Max Weber ascribes to the Protestants. It is a fact that the Western and Japanese traditions became the spiritual and material foundations upon which capitalistic, modern industrial societies were built, but there are fundamental differences between those traditions. European Protestantism soon distanced itself from its sixteenth-century roots and began to acknowledge that a comfortable life (the pursuit of happiness) could be achieved as a result of hard work; this philosophy was developed in reaction to the situation of material surplus that occurred as resources flowed in from India and the new continent. Japan, however, remained subject to conditions of material paucity and so persisted with a philosophy that reconciled diligence with honest poverty. The ideas seen in the Ishida school of practical ethics allowed no room for consciously acknowledging productivity, let alone an aesthetics of consumption. This difference in orientation continues to underlie misinterpretations of Japanese diligence (and long working hours) by the West even today.

The Explosive Growth Potential Unleashed
by Enriched Resource Supplies

I hope that the preceding discussion has made it clear that Japanese tradition and culture contained features that ideally suited the nation for the transition to a modern industrial society.

The habit of studying foreign technologies purely for their practical applications, in a context utterly divorced from the ideologies or social characteristics that produced them, helped Japan to introduce, absorb, and transform the world's foremost technologies. A relativism that lacks any absolute sense of right and in which right is synonymous with what "everybody" thinks worked to pigeonhole or confine the impact of minority opinions and sent virtually all of Japan's citizens galloping to carry out the type of development characteristic of the industrial society. In instances where the "everybody" to whom people felt answerable consisted of the mini-society or social group to which they individually belonged, it gave birth to a code of conduct that was specific to the workplace and brought about what we often call Japanese "groupism," resulting in labor/management concord and the bottom-up style of management.

Japan's tradition as a peaceful nation enabled it, in the aftermath of defeat, to abandon easily its dream of becoming a military power and thereby lightened the burden its arms budget posed for the economy at large. Even more important was the trust the Japanese system generated for figures of authority (one's "betters"). This made possible arrangements based on the assumption of cooperation between governing and governed. Such a system also enabled Japan to avoid the breakdown of public peace and order that has almost invariably accompanied urbanization in other industrial societies.

Most important of all, the philosophy of diligence that has

held sway since the Tokugawa era has produced the work ethic and deep attention to detail that have become the foundation for Japan's economic growth. The educational system that was already in place created a superb manpower base and served as the foundation from which a vast number of competent technicians and small- and medium-sized business operators could develop.

In addition to these specifically Japanese conditions, the world situation during the postwar years also worked to Japan's advantage, particularly the worldwide surplus of resources triggered by the successive discoveries of giant oil fields in the Middle East. As I suggested in Chapter 1, the global situation after World War II not only enabled Japan to benefit from its positive strengths; it even made its limitations in terms of resource supplies, nominally the country's greatest weakness, a tremendous advantage.

In addition, the introduction of new postwar technologies was linked to a rise in productivity. The Japanese, ever the "clever students," accepted these new technologies without any ideological resistance and absorbed them in Japanese fashion, successfully fine-tuning them by adding Japanese details to what were largely American designs.

Since the Japanese people had both their national agenda (economic growth) and the general outlines of the technology by which they were to achieve this set for them by others, they were excused from the task of conceptualization, something they are not very good at, and were allowed instead to display fully what they excel at: diligence and detailed execution.

When these things are taken into consideration, the fact that the Japanese economy grew explosively and Japan became the star pupil of the industrial society no longer seems puzzling. It would therefore be reasonable to expect that for as long as the industrial society lasts, the Japanese economy will continue to develop and to maintain its preeminent position in the international community. The tendency for the advanced West to move away from involvement in material things, and for its technological development to be less and less involved with mass production and economies of scale and more and more caught up with considerations of energy conservation and information systems, does not work to the disadvantage of the Japanese. This is because the very characteristics of the Japanese culture that drove it to refine details and gobble up the "software" of civilization will also serve it well in handling conservation and information issues.

However, Japan's success in coming to grips with these variables will in all likelihood serve only to exacerbate the economic frictions between Japan and various other countries. The reason is that in Japan, still under the sway of the practical ethics of the Ishida school that reconciles diligence with frugality, a rise in income does not necessarily produce a comparable rise in consumption. Baigan Ishida seems to have sensed this himself, but in any case, if this mode of conduct is pursued, the macroeconomic balance between supply and demand cannot be achieved without pulling down productivity. In other words, it is inevitable that Japan's trade surplus will continue to grow.

The Limitations of an Economy Guided by an Alliance Between Business Leaders and Government Bureaucrats

The direction taken by events over the five years since publication of the first Japanese edition of this book may be seen by some as bringing Japan ever closer to becoming the ideal industrial society. After all, the rising yen lifted per capita income in Japan until it attained the highest level in the world.

The rising value of land and stock holdings in Japan raised the personal assets figure for individuals in Japan to three times that of their American counterparts. To be sure, the escalation of land and stock prices had gotten so out of hand by 1990 that a drastic readjustment was under way, causing the estimated value of Japan's total assets to drop by almost one-half in a mere eight months. The trend seems likely to continue for some time.

What best expresses the strength of Japan's mass-production, high-volume, industrial sector over the past five years is the enormous trade surplus the country has enjoyed over this period. Despite the fact that the yen nearly doubled in value against the dollar during the period of little more than a year between the fall of 1985 and the beginning of 1987, Japan's trade surpluses actually increased, passing the $90 billion mark in 1987. After that point the government policy of driving up domestic demand to encourage more imports while restraining exports caused a slight contraction of the trade surplus, but it was still over $60 billion for 1989.

What this suggests is how perfectly adapted to the large-scale mass production of standardized products like automobiles and electrical appliances the Japanese social structure has become. Japan today really has turned itself into the "ultimate industrial society."

However, the price in sacrifices the Japanese have paid to achieve such success is also high. To push the nation's companies to pursue standardized mass production, the government bureaucrats have for over a century set quality standards and established a system of collective cooperation among the companies of the industrial sector, with the result that in Japan both the goods and services available to consumers have sorely lacked variety. Elementary schools, hospitals, and clinics are so standardized that there would seem to be but a single prototype for each. Resort development is booming, but the facilities and services available at them seem to have been stamped from a single mold. The tightly run distribution system of small retail outlets, which Americans have found so impenetrable as a market for their goods, is another force that acts to suppress the variety of goods and services made available to Japanese consumers.

Japan's version of the "knowledge-value revolution," in other words, has yet to approach anywhere near the level attained in the United States. Many Japanese are unable to take pleasure in the forms of entertainment or leisure to their liking—if they have even reached the stage where they would know what these are. Trying to find schools that offer individualized programs to meet the particular needs of students, or hospitals that offer the types of services one needs, can be an extremely perplexing exercise in most of Japan. If one happens to be an employee or manager in a corporation, or a teacher or a doctor or a storeowner, dealing with one's fellow man from a position of strength as a "supplier" can be wonderfully gratifying in Japan. But if, alas, one is confined to the perspective of "consumer," one must contend with a paucity of choices and a real dearth of pleasant possibilities.

The Japanese people, having long lived with a system managed by an alliance of government bureaucrats and business leaders, are not nearly as put out by the dearth of what is offered as a foreign observer would be likely to assume. But even in Japan, over the last five years there has been a welling up of discontentment, which expresses itself in such statements as: "Now I've made all this money, but I really don't feel any better off than I was before. Where's the payoff?"

The biggest problem for Japan is not international trade frictions or the high cost of real estate, but the fact that as a society it offers so little that a person can get excited about or take pleasure in. Moreover, the Japanese seem to lack (or are in the process of losing) a conceptual framework for thinking about the dilemma posed by this paucity of alternatives, not to mention the courage to address it. There may well be a nasty showdown in the 1990s between the demands of those in Japan who hope to see more diversity made available, and the rigid stance taken by the bureaucrats and other groups whose occupations predispose them toward preserving the status quo of Japan's standardized mass-production system. What this boils down to is a battle between the powerful current pushing the entire society into the knowledge-value revolution, and the old guard doing its best to resist.

ESTABLISHING A DEMOCRACY OF DEMAND

The 1990s, a Time of Intense Change

No change ever occurs simultaneously in every part of the world. Not only are there large differences in the speed of change among the advanced areas—those "seminal regions" that play a central and formative role in a particular era—but there are often quite substantial differences between territories within the same country. Even in the transition from the primary stage to the ancient era or in that from the ancient to the medieval mode of civilization, the process and timetable by which change was carried out varied considerably from region to region. It was also quite common for a region that had flourished economically and could boast of cultural accomplishments of a high order at one point in time to then be left behind in a state of poverty and ignorance in the next age. An overview of world history suggests, in fact, that the seminal civilizations of a new age are more likely to be perfected in the peripheries or outlying regions than in the culturally dominant center of the epoch that is ending.

The industrial revolution that gave birth to the industrial society in which we lived until recently is no exception. It began in England, which was situated on the periphery of the medieval civilization. It did not spread to the advanced regions of medieval Europe—in the direction of Northern France, West Germany, Holland, and Belgium—until more than a generation later, and reached Italy and the Iberian Pen-

320

insula (the first regions to modernize their polities) even more slowly. In the case of the United States, while major variances between regions can be pointed out, the general consensus is that industrialism reached the Eastern seaboard a century later than it reached Europe and did not spread to the South and the West until after the Civil War. Japan's industrial revolution is generally described as occurring during the final decade of the last century and the first decade of this one. When it comes to the so-called Asian NICs (Newly Industrialized Countries) such as South Korea, Taiwan, and Singapore, most did not begin the serious transition into industrialized societies until after World War II and did not fully attain this status until after 1960. Even in the modern era, with its communication and transportation technologies, the dissemination of the enormous social and economic changes we label the industrial revolution required almost two centuries, and the process has yet to reach even half of the world's population.

Therefore, it is only natural to anticipate huge differences in the process and timing by which the knowledge-value revolution currently under way in the advanced nations is taken up in different areas around the world. The NICs that arrived at an authentic industrial stage after World War II are sure to take a different path from the advanced nations, and it is quite conceivable that most of the Asian and African countries that have yet to reach this stage may bypass the industrial-society phase completely in the course of becoming knowledge-value societies.

However, if we look only at the advanced nations (the United States, Japan, and the countries of Western Europe), the knowledge-value revolution, unlike the industrial revolution before it, seems to be happening everywhere with virtual simultaneity. This should not be explained only in terms of the faster and more intense pace of information, technology, and ideas. More important is the fact that in the multilateral global system of free trade, the "resource picture" has become more of a unified global than a particularized national matter; and even as its ramifications have assumed increasingly universal proportions, the internationalist atmosphere (with more far-reaching political alliances being formed) has also worked to level the playing field, so that those events that act to stimulate the empathetic impulse in men have become common (and simultaneous) experiences for nations throughout the world, particularly the advanced ones.

For example, the two oil crises of 1973 and 1979 were accepted as energy crises in both Japan, the United States, and the various European nations, and had a direct effect on people's tastes and ethics in all those places. Technological developments (in electronics or synthetic materials) also no longer took a decade to reach Japan and Western Europe.

What sets the current knowledge-value revolution apart from the industrial revolution is that, at least among the advanced nations with open economies, conditions for something like spontaneous combustion on both the technological and social levels now exist.

Still, even given all these conditions, in actuality this global transformation may not occur in certain places, or if and when it does, the degree, speed, and the direction taken will not necessarily be the same from place to place. There will be differences due to the economic and social conditions in each country and each district; differences in politics and customs, in birth rates and population composition, will also affect the process.

The Crisis Caused by Increased Longevity in Western Europe

All social changes are accompanied by tangible or intangible battles. In the case of political changes, they are relatively easily understood battles: elections, internecine strife, assassinations, riots and their suppression, revolutions, wars, and the like. Economic changes emerge in such forms as shifts to new technologies, price fluctuations, movements within or away from markets, transfers of capital, and changes in occupational preferences; the outcomes of such "battles" are ultimately read in terms of the prosperity or bankruptcy of the economy as a whole. Rising powers and reformists propel change on the one hand, while on the other, political and labor forces stage countermoves and resist by posing ethical questions or by conferring or removing social honors. The battle associated with any economic change is always accompanied by political struggle; such battles also tend to create a schism in which the terms by which culture is evaluated are pitted against the terms by which social ethics are debated.

How rapidly and thoroughly the industrial economy of a particular country adapts depends not only on how vital the forces propelling the changes are, but on how strong or weak are the powers that try to prevent them.

Taking this into account as we examine the global knowledge-value revolution currently in progress, I would say that the vital forces propelling change in the United States and Japan are strong and those in Western Europe somewhat weaker. Among the reasons for this are differences in respective abilities for technological development and available surplus reserves, but of greatest relevance are differences in the growth and dynamics of the respective populations and especially in the quantity and quality of those entering the work force.

The average age of the population in the Western European countries is very high; citizens over sixty-five make up over fifteen percent of the population in most countries there while birthrates have markedly declined, with the average number of births per woman coming in at well below two. In the case of West Germany, the figure has remained below 1.4 for some time now. As a result, the number of people entering the work force has been on the decline since the 1970s and in the United Kingdom, West Germany, and France in particular, the increases in the working population over the last decade sank beneath 5 percent. This is less than half the figure for Japan and one quarter that of the United States. Such stagnation in population growth—a very substantial decline—and the overall aging of the population is exerting pressure on the Western European economies in many forms.

First and foremost is the increased social burden due to the increase in pension payments to the elderly. Even now, the proportion of the various Western European economies required to assume this public burden—which includes the monies paid out in taxes plus social insurance—exceeds 50 percent of the GNP in every case and is 15 to 20 percent higher than in Japan or the United States. As many point out, this heavy social burden reduces the national incentive to work and is one of the causes for the lowering of industrial vitality.

The second type of pressure the aging population exerts on the Western European economies takes the form of stronger resistance to changes in the industrial structure or to technological innovations accompanied by occupational switching, because of the high proportion of senior workers who find it hard to do the latter. Since Europeans have a tendency to cling to traditional skills to begin with, this constitutes a serious issue.

The resistance of older workers to change also creates rising unemployment among the young. The fact that a substantial portion of youthful workers—the ones capable of flexible thinking and action—are in effect shut out of areas of the Western European economy represents a great loss.

Thus, even when Europeans do engage in activities of the

type that create knowledge-value, problems posed by the aging population make it difficult for them to carry out such activities on an industrial scale. For Western Europe, in short, one of the "disruptive elements" that induce a social transformation—the dynamics of the population—is in a condition that renders Western Europe rather more moribund than Japan and the United States.

The very traditional social environments of Western European countries make it difficult for immigrant labor from the developing countries to participate in great numbers in areas involving knowledge-value creation. There are many foreigners who work as college professors, researchers, or designers in the United States, but relatively few do so in Europe. The "guest workers" who were effective in resolving the labor shortages at production sites during the heights of the postwar petroleum civilization are finding it difficult to play any precipitating role in the Western European version of the knowledge-value revolution.

The Collapse of the Socialist Governments and the Knowledge-Value Revolution

The great political drama that began in the fall of 1989 and continued into 1990—the collapse of the Communist administrations of East Europe—is certain to profoundly influence Europe's knowledge-value revolution.

Over the short term, the infusion of European labor and the increase in investment opportunities in the Eastern Bloc nations, beginning with East Germany, will lead to a resurgence of large-scale mass production, thereby creating an atmosphere in which the industrial society seems to be staging a comeback. However, since the Socialist regimes collapsed because the ideology of socialism was based on the industrial society—it was, in other words, industrial-society thinking as such that was being repudiated, a point I will explore in more detail later—the collapse of the Socialist regimes will prove, over the long run, to be yet another element acting to propitiate the realization of the knowledge-value society.

Another such element and the major movement in Europe in the 1990s is the formation of the European Community and the resurgence of regionalism that will accompany it. As I discussed earlier, the emergence of the modern nation-state was inextricably linked to the development of industrial society, while the formation of such states can also be seen as having contributed to and reinforced the development of the industrial society. The formation of the European Community can be expected to profoundly alter the character of these states over time: the formation of a unified economic marketplace will lead to the formation of a common culture for the community at large.

Given the skepticism about the efficacy of military power, and given the unified European market, the very necessity for maintaining the institution of the modern nation-state, which was after all created to augment military power and protect markets within particular national boundaries, is likely to come in for a surprising amount of questioning. On the other hand, as the consolidation of the European Community leads to the emergence of an homogeneous "common European culture," regional differences and idiosyncrasies are likely to stand out more strikingly by relief. At the same time, within the boundaries of what have been, up to now, particular nations, are various regions with their own clearly defined cultures, and these are likely to draw together to assert their independence and identity more forcibly. The harbingers of such movements may be seen in the drive for independence of Spain's Catalonia, in the economic linkage of Alsace and the Black Forest region on the Upper Rhine, as well as in the cultural linkage formed between the northeastern section of Italy, eastern Austria, and Yugoslavia's Slovenia and Croatia regions.

This tendency is that much more radical and extreme in the Soviet Union and Eastern bloc countries that were consolidated and ruled under the auspices of Socialist ideology and the Communist party. In the Soviet Union, both republics where a single ethnic group predominates, such as Lithuania or Azerbaijan, and other republics such as Russia, within whose borders a number of ethnic groups co-reside, are now seeking their own independent governments and policies. Gorbachev's *perestroika*, in the course of introducing a market economy, has at the same time gradually severed the bonds of ideology and the state system that held the Soviet Union together. Whether the Soviet state, which grew out of Czarist Russia and Stalinism, will even remain as an entity with a shared cultural identity like that of the European Community is an open question at this point.

A not dissimilar scenario is currently unfolding in Yugoslavia. Due to the differences between the northern regions of Slovenia and Croatia, which still preserve the cultural traditions of the Austrian Empire, and districts such as Serbia, which are part of the Slavic cultural tradition, the political unity of Yugoslavia is in a state of crisis. The subjectivity so crucial to a knowledge-value revolution has led to a demand for political institutions that reflect the different customs and tastes of each region.

Europe's knowledge-value revolution will lead to changes both in the economic system and the political institutions of that continent and can be expected to advance significantly during the 1990s.

The United States Is Ahead
in the Knowledge-Value Revolution

The United States is moving faster toward change than is Western Europe. However, when it comes to corporate willingness to invest in research and development and to the individual drive to save, American society cannot compete with Japan. The other side of the coin is that the influx of personnel and foreign capital to the United States dwarfs the influx of these resources to Japan. Reliance on the U.S. dollar as an international currency has resulted in colossal amounts of foreign money flowing into the United States, and despite a low savings rate, the U.S. money supply continues to grow. The average rate of increase between 1975 and 1984 was 15.4 percent, which tops Japan's figure (10.2 percent) by a substantial margin.

Another force aiding America's transformation is the tremendous growth in its labor force. Between 1975 and 1984, the working population in the United States increased by an amazing 20 million, with an increase in the number employed of about 19 million, even in the midst of recession. The increase was, numerically speaking, four times that of Japan; as a rate it was more than double.

In addition to the matriculation of its own youth into the labor force (natural increase), the United States also absorbed vast numbers of immigrants from Asia as well as Central and South America. Of course, the great majority were engaged in physical labor for low pay but in a "melting pot" society like the United States, there is considerable opportunity for immigrants to move into areas of knowledge-value creation. The proportion of foreigners in the United States among college professors, researchers, technicians, specialists, artists, and performers is extremely high.

Such injections of overseas capital and human resources

make it easy to start up new industries in the United States. This fact, together with the vitality of a freely competitive society, is giving birth to the stupendous energy driving the knowledge-value revolution in the United States.

American society has the capacity to attract such capital and labor from overseas. This is not simply a matter of high wages or job opportunities; the comfortable American life-style and the abundant freedom of choice are also potent draws. Having created the most freely competitive society in the world, the United States has the system best able to engender changes in response to the demands of its people. That is why the United States is now pouring such stupendous energy into carrying out the knowledge-value revolution.

The Knowledge-Value Revolution and the "Hollowing of Industries"

The knowledge-value revolution is going forward with great speed in the United States. Its momentum there over the decade following 1975 and especially since 1980 has been extraordinary.

As I stated earlier, employment rolls in the United States swelled by 19 million in the decade after 1975; but of that increase, primary industries such as agriculture accounted for only 10,000 new jobs, and even manufacturing added only 100,000 to the rolls. It is said that in the United States, high-tech industries such as electronics are on the fast track in terms of growth; but in reality, their growth sufficed only to compensate for the number of jobs that disappeared in traditional manufacturing. As a result, the proportion of workers employed in manufacturing plummeted, shrinking to less than 20 percent after 1983, which was surely the lowest figure since the founding of the nation. The grounds for claiming that the United States is no longer an industrial nation are not simply a function of issues that arise from the structure of international trade.

The construction industry, which is classified as a secondary industry, has grown relative to the whole, with an increase of 2 million in employment over the preceding decade. Here too, however, marked increases can be seen in such subdivisions of "construction" as planning and design, jobs involved with legal or financing issues, or real-estate information networks, rather than in literal construction. Were these types of jobs to be repositioned in terms of the industrial classification system I proposed in Chapter 3, most of these new "construction" positions would actually fall into the category of "knowledge industries" rather than "hard goods industries." In the decade after 1975 in the United States, the numbers engaged in hard-goods industries hardly increased at all even in absolute terms; and there has been a precipitous drop in the share of the economy they represent.

Almost 90 percent of the increase in employment during that decade occurred in the so-called tertiary industries, but it is not as if the share represented by the retail and wholesaling industry has expanded to any great extent; nor has that of the transportation industry. Rather, the overwhelming bulk of new jobs has opened up in the service and information industries (defining these in the broadest sense): mass media, advertising, law, accounting and office duties, design, research and development, various education and public utility activities, and so on. Going by my industrial classification system, they belong to "Time-Based" and "Knowledge" industries, or as Gibbon defined them in *The Decline and Fall of the Roman Empire*, the secondary (sedentary) occupations—that is to say, knowledge-value creation in the broadest context.

The issue cannot be understood simply by citing statistics. There is a strong tendency among American youth to seek work in secondary occupation in the cities and to avoid on-site or factory floor work. The job aspirations of college graduates are skewed toward such areas as mass media, law, finance, accounting, the nonprofit or public service sector, and the like. The proportion of science and engineering graduates is far lower than in Japan; and most of those who do such study aspire to work for university laboratories; doing R & D for manufacturers is unpopular, and even those who join the manufacturing firms seem to prefer to work in sales. The aspirations of average youths seem to be directed at work in travel industries, entertainment, sales, or restaurant management.

This does not mean that in the United States, secondary (sedentary) occupations in the service industry pay higher wages than those in the physical (upright) industries; in fact, the reverse is true. The reason why Americans—and especially the young—are oblivious to issues of compensation and seek secondary occupations is that they find such work more becoming and attractive; it has "style." Here we can see that change in basic notions of taste that deems subjective stylishness more important than bulk material consumption.

Because of this, traditional heavy industries such as steel and automobile manufacturing now have to pay wages far above the average in order to marshal workers and this, coupled with the strength of the unions, has been the cause of the weakening of international competitiveness on the part of American manufacturing.

On the other hand, American employers are not actively countering this situation. American manufacturing management, hard-driven as they are by the profit motive, have given up to a great extent on building factories in the United States, where wages were ridiculously high in relation to the quality of labor, and have shifted their productive sites to Asia, the NICs, and Central or South America, where wages are lower.

Manufacturing management is also tending to neglect the floor and to rely more on R & D or financial expertise.

Thus, the United States' ability to supply manufactured goods has leveled out, and any time there is a business recovery with a demand increase, the United States in no time sees its import levels surge. Even if the United States generates new forms of knowledge-value in terms of technological developments and designs, because of the stagnation in the productive capacity on which it must rely to turn out products in which these knowledge-values are embedded, its creation of knowledge-value actually leads in the end to increases in the number of imports and an even more huge trade deficit. This has created the phenomenon that some call the "hollowing out" of American industries.

In countries such as Japan, intimidated by trade frictions with the United States, there are many critical voices raised against the "attitude problem" of American management, which is described as indulging only in the pursuit of profits while neglecting the factory floor. However, we must not overlook the fact that behind this orientation is the growing tendency throughout American society for workers to try to avoid physical (upright) occupations on the floor and to seek instead secondary (sedentary) occupations in the cities.

America, Where the Knowledge-Value Revolution Won't Stop

The reality of America since 1985 attests to the accuracy of the description given above.

Exchange rates for the U.S. dollar fell precipitously in 1986, particularly against the yen and the Deutschemark, where it lost 30 to 40 percent of its value. According to the accepted economic wisdom based on observations of industrial society, America should have seen its exports shoot up and its imports plummet, leading to a restoration of its trade balance. What happened instead was that the trade deficit, already running at $159.6 billion, stayed very high in 1987, at $153 billion. Then it began shrinking at a fairly rapid rate, dropping to $109.4 billion in 1989; but when we compare its drop to the precipitous drop in the exchange rate over the same period, the positive impact that might have been hoped for was not achieved. Despite the Reagan administration's commitment to boosting the extent to which domestic demand is met by domestic suppliers and despite the drop in the dollar, the productivity of American industry did not increase to any considerable extent.

More important, manufacturing during this period failed to capture the imaginations of either the country's younger job applicants or its investors. Rather, it was the firms that performed well in finance, takeovers and acquisitions, retail chains, or research and development—not manufacturing—that were rated as excellent companies.

This suggests that it is impossible to get American industry back on its feet again by resorting to such corrective measures as manipulating exchange rates. To put it another way, manufacturing has an image problem in the United States that exchange rates and trade policy can do little to redress. Drastic manipulation of the exchange rates will not restore the relative status of manufacturing in the United States, because the knowledge-value revolution in America is too far along to be turned back.

In American society as a whole, white collar jobs in offices are considered much more of a draw than blue collar jobs in factories, and the stronger this tendency becomes the less likely it is that American industry will experience a major comeback. In a knowledge-value society, whether an occupation is considered "sexy" or "cool" is a major issue, so that even if occupations that do not command such images in the eyes of job applicants pay high wages, they will have a hard time drawing the most talented workers into their ranks.

There are more than a few voices in America that loudly bemoan the fact that manufacturing has sunk in status in the public imagination. In the book *Manufacturing Matters: The Myth of the Post-Industrial Economy,* by Stephen S. Cohen and John Zysman, the relationship between agricultural operations and crop-dusting helicopter services is cited to make the point that the service industry and information firms can prosper precisely because manufacturing is there to make use of them. Even in Japan, which has developed into the ultimate industrial society, the same sorts of ideas now form a dominant theme.

However, as I noted earlier in pursuing a similar point, the final form of a product and the features that create its special value as a product are interconnected and inseparable. Even if the "software" (some specific programmed function) and "service" functions associated with a product are built right into the product in its final form, the tendency will be for the knowledge-value factor to assume ever greater weight in determining how much value a product possesses. For the knowledge-value to become the final product, it has to be incorporated into a "vessel of knowledge-value," or it will not be marketable as such.

Believers in physiocracy like François Quesnay once argued that manufacturing could not exist without the "fruits of nature" (agricultural products and minerals) and concluded that what gives manufactured products their value derives ultimately from the cultivation of nature (agriculture, in the broadest sense). Certainly it is unarguably true that manufacturing as such could not exist if there were no agricultural or mineral products in the world for it to draw on as raw materials. However, the reality is that production of agricultural and mineral products is hardly likely to cease; while even in a place like Hong Kong, which is almost completely dependent on imports of raw materials from the outside world, manufacturing is able to go on creating economic value.

Those who argue today that only manufacturing matters and that the value and marketability and profitability of a product derives only from the way it is manufactured remind me of the Physiocrats of the eighteenth century. But while the function of manufacturing in the creation of a product is carried out after the agricultural products and minerals are assembled, enabling the producer to sell the end product at a price that reflects the manufacturing stage, the knowledge-value that enters a product usually does so before it is manufactured, so that it becomes much more difficult to sell the knowledge-value at full value as a component in itself. What is unfortunate for America right now is not that manufacturing has lost its allure for the U.S. work force, but that the international marketplace has not yet developed a conceptual framework and a system to market knowledge-value that is not incorporated into a product.

Two Views of the Current U.S. Situation

It should be clear by now that I consider the "hollowing" of industries in the United States and the knowledge-value revolution to be two sides of the same coin. In fact, this is a phenomenon always seen when a preexisting social structure is rapidly abandoned as society embarks on a new phase.

We would do well to think back on the moment when the Italian peninsula, the center of the Roman Empire, in coming to grips with resource shortages, a shrinking population, citizens who were forsaking physical occupations for sedentary occupations, and the ongoing collapse of the family system, started to embrace medievalism. In the final stages of the ancient era, what sustained the fading economy and the civilization of the Roman Empire was neither the Greek tradition that had ushered in ancient civilization nor the traditions of the Italian peninsula that had brought it to full flower; it was, rather, the civilization of Asia Minor, centered in Byzantium, which to the Romans represented a far-flung frontier.

The return to the wealth of a materialistic civilization was not to occur for a long time in Italy, although it functioned as the hub of the Christian world and Christian thought during the early part of the Middle Ages.

England at the end of the eighteenth century is also worth considering. Being the first nation in the world to implement the industrial revolution did not immediately make England a rich country. As a result of the second enclosure in the late eighteenth century, England experienced a widespread agricultural decline accompanied by unemployment on a vast scale; under these conditions, London became a cesspool of thieves, thugs, and the indigent in the years preceding the full-scale development of manufacturing. England in the late eighteenth century ran a huge trade deficit, built up by importing grain from Prussia and Russia; having run through whatever wealth remained from the days of Elizabeth I and whatever proceeds had accumulated from shipping simply to get rid of these debts, and having to catch up on its payments for tea imported from China, England resorted to pushing opium to the Chinese.

Vicomte François-Auguste-René Chateaubriand, the French ambassador to London after the Napoleonic wars, painted a picture of a hellish city on the road to ruin, its heavens covered with an umbrella of smoke while the earth below was covered with the impoverished. The ambassador boasted that France, which had maintained a rich farming society, had won the industrial and financial competition. Since we are all too familiar with the prosperity Victorian England enjoyed after the establishment of its industrial society, we tend to forget the wretched spectacles encountered on the path to that prosperity.

It might be fair to say that, just as the progress of the industrial revolution in late eighteenth-century England led to the collapse of its older agrarian society, the knowledge-value revolution in the United States of the 1980s is precipitating the decline of the old society (the industrial society) and inducing the hollowing of industries. If this is the case, it must be said that in the short term, it would be extremely difficult for either America's manufacturing production to greatly expand, or for its exports to increase markedly. To turn back the clock and force American society to revert to hard-goods production when the entire social structure and the tastes and ethics of the American people have come to embrace knowledge-value creation seems an impossible task.

However, the United States of the late twentieth century is an incomparably more powerful and diversified entity than was England in the late eighteenth century. Even now, great numbers of driven, ambitious foreigners are flowing in and new societies within the society are being formed in regions of the country not previously developed. There is always the possibility that new industrial societies will be formed in such places. The movement toward the "Sun Belt" and the "New South" in recent years, and manufacturing developments in Silicon Valley and other places along the Pacific Coast can be seen as manifestations of such potential.

Given how the formerly mighty Roman Empire, even after its nucleus on the Italian peninsula had been transmuted into a medieval society, was able to keep the afterglow of ancient civilization alive in the outlying Byzantine regions, one cannot rule out the possibility that the Sun Belt and the Pacific Coast regions of the United States will be able to keep America's industrial society alive. However, even if that turns out to be the case for those areas, it will not keep the United States— or the nation as a whole—in a holding pattern as an industrial society.

The situation as it now stands could go either way. What will determine the outcome of the issue will be whether or not, as we enter the twenty-first century, the knowledge-value revolution that America is leading the world toward produces results people consider beneficial, useful, and to the point. I scarcely need add the standards by which they define "beneficial, useful, and to the point" will be other than those applied in the days of the industrial society.

Japan Is Powerfully Equipped to Maintain the Industrial Society

The situation faced by the Japanese is rather different from that faced by their U.S. counterparts. In Japan the forces acting to propel the knowledge-value revolution are no less strong than in the United States. Japan has a high savings rate and mighty capital reserves and continues to build up its working population. The "second generation of baby boomers," born around 1970, will be entering the Japanese work force during the first half of the 1990s. These factors would seem to indicate that for some time to come, Japan has the potential for a dynamic revitalization and reform of its industrial structure. However, there are also powerful reactionary forces that act to defend and maintain the status quo of the industrial society. The belief that the production of hard goods is truly the most important social activity and that creating knowledge-value is a spurious and peripheral way to spend one's career lives on as a dominant principle in Japan. There is a powerfully rooted feeling among Japanese that the types of work knowledge-value creation involves—particularly such archetypal trades as design, fashion, entertainment, and travel—are highly suspect and do not contribute significantly to society.

This way of thinking is not unique to elderly Japanese, who as a group continue to exert a powerful influence in contemporary Japan. Nor is it an attitude confined to an older generation nostalgic for the boom years when hard-goods production grew at such a breathtaking rate. The vast majority of youths who hope to get a job with a large corporation subscribe to this way of thinking as well.

However, even those Japanese who describe themselves as staunch advocates of hard-goods production as "the way" will, when asked to list occupations they would like to see themselves or their child practice, often name categories with powerful "knowledge-value creation" connotations: jobs as officials in government agencies or the private sector, or as professionals in advertising, medicine, or architecture, or as technocrats carrying out R & D. What this tells us is that their hard line on the "nobility" of hard-goods production represents a kind of smoke screen—the answer they think they "should" give—and not their genuine desire. To that extent, it seems that even in Japanese society, substantial advances are being made toward a knowledge-value revolution. Government policy and administration, however, is still being determined by what "should" be, rather than what people want. It must be further recognized that in Japan, these outmoded but persistent notions of what should be form a solid foundation for the policy of preserving the industrial society.

There are two important reasons for this state of affairs. First is the notion that "success comes through expanding the scale of manufacturing production." Men find it difficult to forget a successful experience. Thus they tend to repeat any methods that worked, over and over again. It is not unusual for individuals to become compulsive gamblers and destroy themselves simply because they made a few killings in their first outings at the race track. The army and navy of Japan kept repeating the strategies that had produced their early successes in the Pacific War, an approach that led them to disastrous defeat.

Since the leadership finds it next to impossible to change course even in the face of repeated failure, it is only natural that Japan, currently at the pinnacle of success in manufacturing, may not learn hhow to extricate itself from policies oriented toward hard goods developed during its era of high growth.

A second reason for resistance to the knowledge-value revolution in Japan is the large role the government plays there; I am alluding to the Japanese system in which government bureaucrats lead a cooperative corporate sector in arriving at policies deemed to be of mutual benefit. Since it is the very nature of the government to acknowledge only established authorities, it cannot help but be conservative in what it chooses to recognize or acknowledge about the society. And insofar as governments apply a single system or regulation across the board, their very mode of operation precludes their ever being able to lead the way in approving anything for which the outcome is not yet a foregone conclusion; the government is the least likely party to execute policies based on anything risky or indeterminate.

In short, Japan now faces powerful forces who are doing their best to prevent any transition to a new knowledge-value society. Is this not the reason why Japan, which possesses both the power and the inclination to reform itself as a society, has yet done next to nothing to break away from the framework of the industrial society?

Japan's Alternatives

Up to now Japan's approach, which has been to keep the movement toward a knowledge-value society in check by treating it as an undercurrent while working hard through both its guiding social principles and actual policies to reinforce and maintain the industrial society, has achieved great success.

However, it does not follow that today's successful methods will remain effective tomorrow, and there is no guarantee that what has been accomplished today can be sustained until tomorrow. I think that even in Japan, if the knowledge-value revolution progresses one step farther, opposition to the policy of trying to maintain the industrial society will grow more powerful while the influences from other societies, particularly the United States, will deepen. I anticipate a situation in which certain segments of the society will precede others into the knowledge-value society, even as yet other segments will remain as intact vestiges of the industrial society, and that the two traits will coexist and commingle for some time to come, with rivalries and conflicts breaking out from time to time. Sooner rather than later, however, the overall social paradigm will ultimately have to rest on one or the other and those who execute policy will inevitably be forced to choose between the alternatives. What should Japan do when this happens?

In the final analysis, there are only three alternatives: (1) boldly to promote and propitiate the knowledge-value revolution and to adopt policies that will encourage the switch to a new society; (2) to work toward the maintenance of the industrial society and to suppress the knowledge-value revolution; and (3) to do everything possible to prevent political interference from affecting the outcome.

The first approach, of encouraging the forward march to a new society, has been adopted in the past—albeit largely unconsciously—by countries or regions that formed new societies ahead of the rest of the world. A good example of this would be England at the time of the industrial revolution, from the late eighteenth century into the nineteenth century.

At that time England not only cut farmers loose through the practice of enclosure then being carried out by large estates; once these hapless ex-farmers overflowed into the cities, forced labor was often then imposed on them as a "punishment for laziness"; thus did England foster the creation of factory workers. While this policy worked on the one hand to curtail the power of the army, which drew its ranks from the agricultural sector of the society, the British navy, which relied heavily on manufacturers and their products for its support, was reinforced. At the time of the Napoleonic wars, the British army was so enfeebled that it could not stand up on its own to any of the European armies, but the British navy already possessed the genuine capacity to rule the seven seas. The British policy of opening its gates to exiles from other countries also brought in human resources in large quantities, who possessed both capital and the ability to manage the emergent manufacturing sector. The ancestors of the Rothschilds, Warburgs, and Reuters who contributed so much to British industrial development were German immigrants.

The policies advocated by the Reagan administration during the 1980s bear a certain similarity. Opposing a Congress that sought to protect the manufacturing sector, the Reagan administration was cool both to industrial protectionism and to farm subsidies, but sought to liberalize money markets and to open the doors of the legal profession in foreign nations to non-natives. Policies affecting communications firms, airlines, and the domestic money markets were steadily liberalized and attempts were made to accelerate software development in each of these spheres. Tax reform, which lowered rates for high-income groups and corporations, proved beneficial on the one hand to knowledge-value creation, a field in which profits tend to fluctuate; it worked to the disadvantage, on the other hand, of the highly capital-intensive heavy and chemical industries, since it abolished preferential treatment of depreciation reserves.

On military issues the Reagan administration, rather than replenishing its reserves with conventional weapons that tend to be manufactured products of the mass-produced type, instead plunged into new kinds of strategies dependent on advanced technology and software, like the SDI ("Star Wars") plan. Although the Reagan administration was labeled "conservative," in reality its aspirations were pitched toward the future and the implications of its policies consistently moved in directions that helped expedite the knowledge-value revolution.

For the Japanese government ever to promulgate this kind of bold, forward-thinking policy is a near impossibility. Apart from the particular dynamics of its bureaucrat-guided fusion of government and the corporate sector, which I earlier described, the terrible misgivings aroused in the Japanese mind by the mere thought of sacrificing the interests of any sector within the society to the good of the whole work to inhibit the government from any form of bold action.

Since the alternative of embracing the knowledge-value revolution seems out of the question for Japanese leaders, what about the second potential approach, that of moving actively to restrain the knowledge-value revolution?

History of course offers numerous examples of countries and regions that adopted policies meant to maintain the old social order. Typical of the countries that offer vivid contrast to the case of England cited earlier are Russia and particularly Prussia. At the time the British were vigorously promoting their industrial revolution, exports to England of Prussian farm products rose rapidly, greatly enriching the Prussian national treasury. In response to this, agriculture on an enormous scale was implemented in Prussia under the Junkers, and a policy of actively binding the farmers to the land they worked was developed—the very opposite of what the British were pursuing.

Prussian military goals were also the virtual antithesis of those pursued by the British. The Prussians not only disparaged the navy, they were even averse to artillery, which they saw as too dependent on manufactured components, and instead built up a peasant infantry in the medieval tradition, also under the management of the Junkers. That this policy worked to suppress the creation of free workers and delayed the development of an industrial society goes without saying. Prussia took some steps to modify this policy in response to the shock of its resounding defeat at Napoleon's hands, but the policy's aftereffects lingered on into the 1930s.

There is a strong possibility that Japan will continue to cling to similar policies aimed at maintaining the industrial society. It's easier to maintain an ongoing successful policy, particularly from a political point of view.

That such a route will be easier does not mean that long-term benefits will accrue to Japan as a result of it. If Japan, having built up a society that is all too well suited to the industrial norm, makes it its policy to maintain the industrial society as such, the country could petrify into a state of such rigidity that it would forsake its ability to respond effectively to the changes occurring in the international environment. Worse, the dissonance and contradictions between the knowledge-value revolution that its citizens and youth aspire to, and are moving toward, and the policy of industrialism the government continues to profess, could loom larger and larger as time passes. Persisting in such a policy could in the end drastically exacerbate international trade frictions and cause a serious domestic schism as well.

We must not forget that, just as today's Japan is not blessed with conditions that enable it boldly to adopt the knowledge-value revolution in advance of other nations, it also is not equipped with either the domestic situation or the political will to enable it to withstand either international isolation or a major rending of its domestic harmony.

When Japanese Culture Itself Is in Question

The third alternative available to the Japanese leadership is deliberately to refrain from getting involved—through politics or policy—in pushing for either maintaining its industrial policy or for the knowledge-value revolution. Refraining from intervention is, of course, by no means synonymous with continuing the policies in place. It means acting to get rid of the interventions currently in force, and moving to make government smaller. This also happens to be the route to resolving Japan's most urgent priorities—reducing its economic frictions with other nations and addressing its budget problems.

To reduce political and policy interventions and make government smaller will mean playing down the impact of elective democracy, the political system that nurtured the industrial society, and accentuating what I will call the "democracy of demand," whereby social change is brought about through the actions of people seeking the things they want. In other words, the extent to which a citizen who reaches adulthood is content to limit the expression of his or her will to a vote cast once every few years will be reduced, and the changes that can occur as a result of each citizen acting daily to fulfill his or her desires will be given more leeway.

In the knowledge-value society the desire for values based on social subjectivity increases, which is why I call it a "new medieval era." But in the present we possess highly developed technology and systems to disperse and diffuse information, so our form of social subjectivity will be much more fragmented and fluid than was the case in the medieval era. This will create a constant need for individualized activity aimed at creating new intellectual insights. Insights will be demanded, not ideas hammered out by groups working together; courageous decisions are called for, not organizational consensus.

In the midst of such conditions, the results produced by voter intentions voiced but once every few years via elective democracy will fall short of what is required to carry out the ideals people will embrace.

Naturally, what is voted on tends to be determined by the issues in which the voters show the greatest interest and concern. But the issues the Japanese government addresses under our present system are largely issues that concern suppliers rather than consumers. Our version of elective democracy tends to produce an aggregation of spokespersons for what is advantageous to manufacturers. This will put it on a collision course with the knowledge-value society, in which consumer demand and will is subject to severe and rapid change.

A true "democracy of demand" in which the government did not favor manufacturers would, by contrast, oblige those manufacturers to put all their energy into meeting the demands consumers express. Such responsiveness to consumers would provide a stark contrast to the stance taken by the Japanese government throughout the postwar era, which in the name of the nation's larger economic self-interest attuned itself more to the needs of the manufacturers than to consumers. A system in which government was minimized and citizens were empowered to freely express their will as consumers—and not just as voters providing a rubber stamp every few years—would be better able to constantly respond to changes based on social subjectivity.

Japan in the Grip of Forces of Change

Over the last five years, policies aimed at maintaining Japan's status quo as an industrial society have continued to dominate the nation's agenda, but resistance to this stance has arisen from two directions: foreign countries that have pressed for change, and domestic critics who have sharpened their demands for "real prosperity."

The pressure from other nations had been a fact of life since the early 1970s and has usually taken the form of cries for voluntary restraint on particular export products. By the mid-1980s, however, with Japan's trade surpluses mushrooming to gigantic proportions, the overall trade balance became the issue; it was to redress this that the policy of strengthening the yen was devised.

Still, the Japanese trade surpluses were not driven down to any great extent. The fact that Japan could sustain trade surpluses despite virtually doubling the value of the yen on the exchange market resulted in part from the progress most Japanese companies made in driving down production costs through greater rationalization of production processes. Another source of their success, however, was the policy the Japanese devised of sustaining domestic price levels for their products while lowering their yen-based export prices, making up the differences by maintaining a high volume of exports. Japan's policy, in other words, was to increase the return it enjoyed from lowering production costs by maintaining the domestic prices for its products at their former levels, while at the same time forgoing profits in order to sustain volume on its exports by keeping the export prices low.

The fact that the Japanese economy is so structured as to allow it to maintain domestic prices even when it lowers production costs, thus leaving it the leeway to lower its export prices, led in turn to this structure itself being identified as the source of the Japanese trade surplus problem. It was the negotations between the Japanese and American governments on this issue, the so-called structural-impediments initiatives, that became the major political issue in Japan during the first half of 1990.

The most important themes of these negotiations have been the calls for revising or eliminating the Large-Scale Retail Shop Law, which severely restricts expansion of retail chains, as well as Japan's permissive antimonopoly law, which allows blocs of corporations to buy substantial shares in each other's firms and thus act in concert as an economic force. The result of the negotiations so far is resistance from small- and medium-sized enterprises within Japan that forced substantial concessions, making it likely that a long period will be required before any measures actually get carried out.

What really matters here is not the revision or elimination of particular statutes or laws. The vital point is the fact that the type of society Japan has developed so successfully up to this point—the "ultimate industrial society" that suppresses new approaches and individualized products in every field but is perfect for large-scale mass production—is coming in for severe rebuke and criticism from other countries for its political and economic policies. The important lesson for the Japanese is that the very notion of the ultimate industrial society that they have believed in since 1941, which dictated that "the consumer's freedom of choice and personal pleasure must necessarily be sacrificed" in order to achieve its goals, is not a notion given universal credence throughout the world.

The other form of pressure on the Japanese status quo, domestic criticism, is proving more powerful through its actions than in its words. The last five years have left the Japanese even richer than they were before and they are more and more inclined to demand forms of knowledge-value even if they have to buck government regulations and the framework of the industrial society to achieve this. Consumer demand has diversified and grown more quality-conscious, with Japanese consumers buying up copious amounts of the finest brand-name products from all over the world. Over 50 percent of the total sales of France's finest maker of bags and luggage, Louis Vuitton, were to Japanese customers, with the figures for Hermès and Chanel products running nearly as high.

On top of that, the number of Japanese heading overseas to do their shopping has nearly doubled in the last five years and is expected to pass the ten-million mark this year. This is an enormous figure when one considers that Japan is surrounded by oceans on every side. Grown rich, the Japanese will no longer settle for the narrow limits set on the consumer's freedom of choice by the "ultimate industrial society" they have grown up in, and are willing to travel far from home in search of greater diversity.

Naturally Japanese companies are making an effort to meet the demand for greater diversity by supplying more variety. In that sense, even Japan is giving birth to a form of the new "democracy of demand." But Japan's giant corporations, having long lived with the system of collective cooperation between business and the government bureaucracy, are sorely lacking the imagination needed to develop new concepts. The government is, if anything, actually working to suppress efforts to develop new thinking. But even if it takes foreign pressure to accomplish the task, there is a strong possibility that government regulations will be relaxed and the will of the mass of consumers will lead to a vigorous introduction of the knowledge-value revolution in Japan during the 1990s.

6

Socialism Is Defeated by the Knowledge-Value Revolution

Socialism Was Based on
the Assumptions of the Industrial Society

The great political spectacle that commenced in the fall of 1989—the collapse of the Socialist governments of the Eastern bloc countries—allows me to affirm that as of 1990, the knowledge-value revolution described in this book has been carried one step farther.

Although the first Japanese edition of this book appeared in December 1985, I believe it contained plenty of clear indications that socialism was reaching the end of the road. Not because the Soviet or Eastern European leadership was inept or lazy or negligent. The real issue was that socialist ideology was based entirely on the assumptions of the industrial society and could not survive in a world in which the knowledge-value revolution had become the dominant force.

Socialism as it was originally conceived—that is to say, Marxism—is founded on the assumption that if man has enough information and is in a situation where he can make clear-headed judgments, we can expect him to make objective, rational choices as to what economic step will be the most advantageous. Man (*Homo economicus*, or economic man), as Marx saw him, is capable of acting on the rational basis of materialism. The reason that Socialists believed in and accepted a planned economy and one-party rule is that they accepted the premise that man can make rational, "scientific" decisions about economic matters.

If men were in fact rational versions of *Homo economicus*, there would be no reason to expect that what they might want or demand would be affected by their individual tastes or what sort of tradition they grew up in. From the assumption that they are rational is derived the hypothesis that for every potential good or service (every "product") there ought to be an optimum standard design or format or mode that can be scientifically determined by specialists so as to conform to the needs of every individual as well as to the economic and technological conditions of the society in question. All the specialists require is good will and sufficient information.

An able specialist might be asked, for example, to design the one and only perfect, standard car design that would conform to the needs of a white-collar family of four with an annual income of $50,000. If we accept the premise that the process is fundamentally rational, there should be a single correct and ideal solution to this problem, one that would incorporate the proper size, accessories, and styling to suit the situation.

The same would also hold true for clothing design, housing, forms of leisure, and medical services. This concept was embraced not only in socialist countries, but tended to be accepted in every country where government bureaucrats had a strong hand in running things. In Germany such thinking caught on in the 1930s, while Japan embraced this approach during the 1940s. The principles of modern manufacturing created the imperative to limit the variety of goods to a single standard model. The perceived cost efficiency of this approach accounts for the standard "national uniforms" and the standard car models that were produced in socialist nations.

When such thinking is carried further, a stage is reached where third parties decide how much the society at large can afford to allot for its people as a whole to consume; they then determine, based on that assessment, what the optimum individual allotment should amount to. Things reach the stage where every white-collar worker is allotted the standard white-collar-worker allotment, every farmworker the standard farmworker allotment, and so on, on the assumption that trained experts acting in good conscience are capable of determining objectively the proper standard of living and proper life-style for each person.

It follows that by calculating what will be required to provide all the workers in their various categories with the prescribed allotment for their respective occupations, we should be able to determine a budget based on the collective needs (demand) of the entire national economy, and propose a plan for a wage and distribution system calculated to provide all concerned with their predetermined allotment. The socialist faith that an able and conscientious people's party would be able to provide positive guidance to true happiness for all citizens if it ran a planned economy is based on the assumptions I have just described.

Once one accepts the validity of these assumptions, one must by extension accept the logic of the socialist system of economic planning and recognize furthermore that enlightened dictatorship by an able and conscientious people's party makes sense. And if one accepts that there can be objectively determined "perfect" model designs for products and even life-styles and living conditions, then it ought to make sense to entrust the formulization and promulgation of these to a system of qualified and conscientious experts. And if political forces opposed to this perfect system should arise, they may be suppressed as plotters resisting a plan that has been objectively shown to be the best possible plan.

For a long time the majority of people in the world believed in the socialist philosophy. I refer not only to the overt supporters of socialism, but also to the numerous individuals who, although they were opposed to actual Socialist government, acknowledged that "theoretically speaking," Socialist government represented a means by which the waste and inequality of capitalism could be reduced.

Actually, my impression is that until recently the brunt of the criticism directed at socialist economics, at least in Japan and Europe, has concerned itself less with its alleged flaws as a theory than with the difficulties that seem to arise in carrying out its vision. The essence of this outlook might be stated as follows: "I know it sounds like it ought to work, but some third party who happens to be an expert is bound to have a very hard time putting his finger on what would be the perfect product for each group or individual. And there's just no way for someone to determine what the optimum allotment or perfect life-style for each individual should be. We don't have enough of the kind of information you would have to amass to attempt that, nor do we have enough people to process the information even if we did manage to collect it."

This kind of criticism is not, in other words, a denial of socialist philosophy; it merely argues that the realization of socialism is at too early a stage to be judged. In Japan and Western Europe until the 1970s, we learned to refer to parties seeking to draw closer to socialism as "reform" or "progressive" parties, while those which sought to put a stop to its realization came to be labelled as "conservative" or "old guard." Implicit in such terminology was the assumption that the world at large was gradually moving toward socialism.

It is likely for that very reason that such criticism has at times been used to vindicate socialist doctrine. Compared with the advanced Western nations, the results achieved by the Soviet Union or the Eastern bloc nations that have actually practiced socialism are poor; they failed to amass either the necessary capital or information, and this has been blamed on the incompetence of the organizations and people, rather than on socialism itself. Behind such excuses lurks the assumption

that if the necessary technological progress, capital, and organizational restructuring were brought to bear, socialist societies would achieve results far superior to those possible under
capitalism.

Another group of thinkers contends that the unfortunate
state of things in the Socialist nations is a result of the chaos
brought on by war and foreign pressure, which made it possible for a man like Stalin to seize power. The fault, in other
words, lies not with the doctrine, but with the leadership.
Thus we have a brand of socialist criticism that contends that
once the Communist power structure was contaminated by
the ascendancy of leaders like Stalin, it became virtually impossible to purge it of that lingering and pernicious influence;
but critics who cleave to this position do not mean it as an
attack on the fundamental notion that a Socialist state
founded on socialist principles could work.

When in 1960 Khrushchev, the general secretary of the
Communist Party and a harsh critic of Stalin, declared that
"twenty-five years from now, in 1985, per capita income in
the Soviet Union will overtake that of the United States, the
most advanced of the capitalist nations," many listeners in
Japan and Western Europe took him at his word. They expected that with the repudiation of the bad leader, Stalin,
there would be a return to the "true path" of socialism that
would enable the Soviet Union to develop the technology and
accumulate the capital needed to create an absolutely efficient
and just socialist paradise on earth. But the reality is that by
1985 the Soviet economy, far from outstripping that of the
United States, had been surpassed by even those of Singapore
and Taiwan.

The socialist economies, far from improving themselves
over time, have been in a state of ever-increasing deterioration
since 1970. What this suggests is that the fatal flaw of socialism is not a matter of insufficient capital or information or

incompetent institutions or staff; the flaw must involve something in its conceptual core that renders it incapable of adapting to reality (particularly to the conditions that have existed since 1970). What has kept socialism, which at first glance seems such a well-conceived and comprehensive theory, from working out are two flawed assumptions on which it is based: first, its materialism; second, its hypothesis that man is an economic being capable of objectively determining and seeking what is in his own best interest.

The Great Failing of Socialist Culture

What distinguishes the modern thought that emerged after the Renaissance is its heavy emphasis on objectivity. The standard according to which modern man judges things is not the concept of *God*, which had dominated the Middle Ages, but his newfound faith in scientific objectivity.

Such thinking resulted on the one hand in the spirit of scientific inquiry, which relies upon objective observation of phenomena in order to discern their operating principles and structure; it also led to the development of a value system that defined happiness in terms of an objectively quantifiable abundance of possessions. The modern industrial society created by the industrial revolution credits itself for having actually produced the bounteous fruits of its labor, rather than thanking God for them. This gave industrial society a built-in impetus or rationale for encouraging the further advancement of scientific technique and product manufacture.

Socialism, with its absolute view of and faith in objectivity—the assumption that for every type of product and every individual life-style an optimal prototype exists that can be scientifically and objectively arrived at—becomes the ultimate expression of modern industrial social thought. There are those who praise socialism as the system of the future that has "gone beyond" the values of modern industrial society, but since in fact socialism and capitalism alike define happiness in terms of the volume of goods produced, both are merely variations on the theme of modern industrial values. Far from transcending these values, socialism, by insisting so absolutely on objectivity, is a system defined and delimited to the ultimate degree by industrial society.

Beginning in the late 1960s, however, the advanced nations of the West began to value subjectivity over objectivity, and to attach more importance to the feeling of satisfaction a product could give than to its strict functional convenience. Today this trend, involving life-styles and culture and known as Postmodernism, has spread to a considerable extent.

It is this spread of a postmodern aesthetic that has undermined both theoretically and practically the absolute objectivity and materialism that formed the foundation for socialism. The reason that the Soviets and the leadership of the Eastern bloc were so opposed to letting in any manifestation of postmodern culture must have been their instinctive grasp of the threat it posed.

In the Soviet Union during the years just after the Bolshevik revolution, works of abstract and Expressionist art that trumpeted the subjectivity of the artist on every level were praised as avant-garde art, but the situation had not continued for very long before such works began to be suppressed. Soviet art after the 1930s practiced only the most conservative type of socialist realism.

Socialist society, committed to the assumption that everything from the standardized form of its products to the life-styles of its people could be objectively and scientifically determined, could not very well encourage the creation of powerfully subjective works of art. It is well known that in the Soviet Union under Stalin, transparent fallacies were perpetrated in fields such as biology and history, but even then the perpetrators did not forget to don the mask of objectivity when making their presentations. In such a society it was only to be expected that the postmodern culture, which so unabashedly tears down objective rationality, could not possibly be permitted.

If the impact of the postmodern "cultural revolution" had been limited to such fields as fashion and music, the socialist cultures no doubt could have withstood the assault without great strain. But the two oil crises of the 1970s and the increasing gravity of environmental problems drove home the sense that resources are limited and decisively turned the people away from the notion that "more is better," steering them instead to demand subjective knowledge-value in their products.

As I have detailed in previous passages, man is equipped with an empathetic impulse to hoard or economize on that which is in short supply while using up as much as possible of whatever is plentiful.

By the late 1980s, the phenomenon that most clearly reflected the impact of technological development and the tightening supply of available resources—in other words, the knowledge-value revolution—had reached a stage of such intense development in the West that neither the Soviet Union nor the Eastern bloc nations—nor even, in part, China—could completely block its influence from being felt. With news of the knowledge-value revolution being carried by satellite transmissions and on videocassettes, the Iron Curtain no longer functioned as a barrier.

What the people wanted ceased to be defined in terms of objective rational principles, shifting instead toward a form of demand based on subjective perceptions. This change dealt the planned economy a decisive blow. One may be able to make objective predictions regarding the supply of wheat or steel for the coming year, but when it comes to whether red neckties will be in or whether blue ones will be all the rage, making an objective forecast is simply impossible. That is why Soviet and Eastern European leaders during the 1980s found themselves with stockpiles of certain types of goods accumulating at the same time that angry consumers were waiting in longer and longer lines for other commodities in short supply. Because efforts to address these problems led to endless revisions of the economic plan, the result was even worse bottlenecks and confusion, as people awaited new orders and the required materials lay about in untouched piles. Systems of economic planning created to fulfill the norms and needs of the idealized socialist society lacked the flexibility to respond to the abruptly shifting demands of societies increasingly inclined toward subjective and almost faddish redefinitions of what they wanted.

People who are forced into situations they can't possibly handle inevitably develop a decadent philosophy. The bureaucrats of the socialist nations were no exception. As the demand for knowledge-value mounted and it became ever more impossible to adjust and coordinate the planned economy in order to cope with this, the bureaucratic rationales proffered by the socialist leadership in the Soviet Union as well as that of Eastern Europe and China grew increasingly cynical and evasive; it began to be said that the bureaucracy was degenerate, avoided taking responsibility, and took care only to see that its own needs were met. The *Nomenklatura*, the specially empowered bureaucracy of the Soviet Union, grew increasingly high-handed, while in China cries of "Down with the bureaucrats!" and "Bureaucratic corruption!" grew louder and louder. At the same time, as the balance between supply and demand in the planned economy was lost, attempts to cope with this caused the black market economy to flourish. This is not to say that there is not a great deal of economic activity in the United States and Japan that is "off the books," but the black markets that have sprung up under the free-market systems in these nations are illegal forms of activity, not a force vital to keep the legitimate society going. In the Soviet Union and Eastern Europe, the black-market economy was essential to redress the imbalance between the unvarying nature of what was officially supplied by the planned economy and the constantly fluctuating demand that subjective perceptions created. If the black market had not been on hand to help supplant the official market system, the latter would likely have been unable to stand on its own.

The spread of the notion that the bureaucracy empowered to create plans and standards had become decadent signaled the bankruptcy of the socialist ideology and the collapse of the socialist culture. What ultimately brought down the socialist administrations of the Soviet Union and Eastern Europe was a drastic economic downturn. But what really precipitated the problems was the collapse of the culture founded on the socialist assumption that man is a rational economic being.

Socialism, the most extreme expression of the assumptions that underlay the industrial society, lost its reason for existing as the industrial society began to founder and lose its grip. What is in the process of collapsing is not the Stalinist form of rigidly centralized leadership or the specially empowered bureaucratic system that was carried out under Brezhnev, but socialism (Marxism) itself.

The 1990s as the New Post-Cold-War Era

In February 1989, as the Berlin Wall came down and the East Germans began pouring into West Berlin, the cold war that had been waged for over forty years came to an end. What this meant was that neither the East German nor Soviet governments any longer possessed the will or the ability to defend the wall that had symbolized the opposition of East and West.

The first reaction of those in the West was not even joy so much as sheer surprise. What had brought the long cold war to an end was less a matter of intellectual choice than a consequence of the fact that those in the Eastern camp no longer possessed the ability to go on fighting the battle. As news began to come in about actual conditions within the Soviet Union and the Eastern bloc nations, it became clear that they had reached a dead end not only with regard to economic issues, but were slipping behind in technology even as their environmental problems were growing critical. With the bureaucracy succumbing to decadence and the citizens to apathy while a welter of problems faced them on every side, the notion of mustering the strength to go on fighting the cold war had become unthinkable.

Socialism, which had once been called the "system of the future for mankind" and had developed the technology to launch Sputnik before the West even entered the field, had come to such a pathetic pass because its system, mired deeply in the assumptions of the industrial society, was simply too rigid to cope with the challenge posed by the knowledge-value revolution. In the Soviet Union and the Eastern bloc nations the knowledge-value revolution had barely begun and its impact, where felt at all, was localized; yet the economy and the system of rule it toppled had functioned on an absolutely enormous scale.

In the advanced Western nations, characterized by both a higher economic level and more widespread dissemination of technology and technology in general, the knowledge-value revolution has progressed much further and its impact has been far more multifaceted. If it has not brought the Western nations as near to the brink of destruction as it did those of the East, this is certainly not because the knowledge-value revolution has ushered in fewer changes in the Western countries, for in fact it has ushered in many more; but the free economic systems of the West possessed the flexibility to cope with these changes.

What proved the decisive factor in determining the outcome of the cold war was one side's greater ability to cope with fundamental changes. One is reminded of how the French, with their more rigid and inflexible system, were unable to absorb the impact of the industrial revolution and thus were doomed to repeat several cycles of revolution and reform, while the more flexible and pragmatic English cleverly managed to encourage the industrial revolution while maintaining their political system in a more or less intact state. That the English system was not rent by full-scale bloodshed and revolutionary uproar does not mean that the English social structure underwent less change than did the French; in fact, the rapidity of the English transition to a modern industrial state meant that English society experienced a far more radical transformation.

Now that the cold war that persisted for over forty years is behind us, we must come to grips with its immediate aftermath. There is no escaping the fact that in the 1990s the world will have to cope with the trauma and chaos that always follow a major conflict. Labor surpluses and shortages of capital and resources are givens in the aftermath of major hostilities. Inevitably some of the economic and philosophical desolation that has attended the socialist nations will arise to haunt their former adversaries in the cold war as well. The West will also have to contend with major and unavoidable changes in its industrial and employment structures.

We should also gird ourselves to cope with the regional conflicts and shake-ups that always seem to be the sequel to a major war. There are sure to be any number of examples of the type of regional crisis that Iraq's invasion of Kuwait has brought about. That such conflicts will furthermore exacerbate the shortages of capital and resources is also a distinct possibility. This is the case because amid the changed conditions that result from the termination of a great conflict, the world needs a good deal of time to create the groundwork for a stable international environment.

Yet all these changes will do little to impede the movement toward a knowledge-value revolution, which is the dominant social trend. The shortages of capital and resources will likely activate and bring into play man's empathetic impulse, even as the grand defeat of that ultimate industrial philosophy called socialism will work to free people's minds of the assumptions and credos that the industrial society had held dear for so long, thereby liberating their imaginations to create new types of solutions and concepts from here on in.

The 1990s may not be as pleasant a decade as the one that preceded it. But I believe it will be remembered throughout history as the decade in which a new society was created.

Editor's Notes

Chapter 1

p. 7   *Annales School*: leading French school of social and economic history, which takes its name from the journal *Annales d'histoire économique et social* founded in 1929 by Lucien Febvre and Marc Bloch. (The journal is now known as *Annales: Économie, Société, Civilization*.) Annales historians emphasize the study of seemingly evanescent social phenomena gauged over long-term periods of structural change (*longue durée*); in contrast to more traditionally minded institutional and political historians, Annalistes eschew the chronicles of kings and other "great men," focusing instead on the daily lives and thought structures (*mentalités*) of common folk, often employing statistical analyses of their subject matter to construct "totalizing" histories of whole societies, regions or cultural epochs.

p. 7   *Braudel Center*: located at the State University of New York in Binghamton, this research institute was established by Immanuel Wallerstein, noted proponent of the "world-systems" theory, which incorporates many of the premises of Annales historiography. The center is named after Fernand Braudel, author of *The Mediterranean and the Mediterranean World in the Age of Philip II* and a former student of Bloch and Febvre.

p. 7   *Rondo Cameron*: economic historian of Europe; his books include: *A Concise Economic History of the World: from Paleolithic Times to the Present* (London: Oxford University Press, 1989); *Banking & Economic Development: Some Lessons of History* (London: Oxford University Press, 1972); with Olga Crisp, Hugh T. Patrick & Richard Tilly, *Banking in the Early Stages of Industrialization* (London: Oxford University Press, 1967).

p. 10   *Simon Kuznets*: U.S. trained economist, author of numerous works including: *Growth, Population & Income Distribution* (New York: W. W. Norton, 1979); *Economic Growth of Nations: Total Output & Production Structures* (Cambridge, Mass.: Harvard University Press, 1971); *Postwar Economic Growth: Selected Essays* (Cambridge, Mass.: Harvard University Press, 1964).

Chapter 2

p. 86   *Georges Duby*: noted French historian of medieval Europe; Duby's research extends over a wide range of topics such as marriage in "the age of chivalry," medieval architecture and town planning, as well as studies on the agrarian economy. His book, *Rural Economy & Country Life in the Medieval West* is still the standard survey text for agrarian history in the Middle Ages; his research on grain yields for the Carolingian Period, such as the one based on the *Wolfenbüttel* archive, may be found in: *The Early Growth of the European Economy: Warriors & Peasants from the Seventh to the Twelfth Century* (Ithaca, N.Y.: Cornell University Press, 1974). Other recent works translated into English include: *The Chivalrous Society* (Berkeley: University of California Press, 1977) and *The Three Orders* (Chicago: University of Chicago Press, 1980).

p. 91   *Four Powers' Period*: refers to the establishment of four ancient Indian states, Magadha, Kosala, Kashi and Vrijis; between the eighth and seventh centuries B.C., a battle for political control of the Ganges plain was waged between these states. By 600 B.C. Magadha (modern southern Bihar) emerged victorious and remained the political center of northern India for several centuries thereafter.

p. 100   *Elagabalus*: Roman emperor (218–222) also known as Heliogabalus; famous as a religious fanatic who introduced customs of Syrian theocracy, indulging in lavish displays and festivals to honor the Sun-god, as well as acts of debauchery; murdered by the Praetorian guards.

p. 101   *Indro Montanelli*: popular Italian historian whose studies on ancient Roman festivals, customs, and slavery have been published in the following: *Romans Without Laurels* (New York: Pantheon, 1962); *Giorno di festa & Storia di Roma* (Milan, 1988). Montanelli has also authored several books on modern Italian history, among them: *Storia d'Italia* (1974), *Garibaldi* (1982), and *Figure Figuri del Risorgimento* (1987).

p. 104   *slavery as an "energy source"*: this reference to a study by Takemochi Ishii, professor at Tokyo University, may find parallels in books such as Alfred H. Conrad, *The Economics of Slavery and Other Studies in Econometric History* (Chicago: University of Chicago Press, 1964); or perhaps, in period studies such as Herman Jeremias Nieboer, *Slavery as an Industrial System* (The Hague, 1910).

p. 107   *Āndhra Dynasty*: ancient Indian kingdom of the Satavahanas which arose in first century B.C. out of the breakup of the Mauryan dynasty in Northwest Deccan.

p. 110   *Jean-Noel Biraben and John D. Durand*: demographers renowned for innovative methods of calculating world population figures over millenia; Biraben's estimates have been published in *Le devenir de la population mondiale* (Paris, 1974) & *Spatial Structures of the Population & Historical Demography* (1974); Durand's work has been published in *Population* (1969, 1977), *Novos Umbrias* 17 (1977), and *Population & Development Review* (1977).

p. 120   *The Seven Sages of the Bamboo Grove*: refers to Ruan Ji (210–263), Shi Kang (223–262) and other third-century Chinese thinkers who indulged in "light conversation" (*qing tan*), a philosophical movement that favored discussions of poetry, the arts or sex over political or economic issues. These neo-Taoists would often meet in bamboo groves to drink and discourse in unconventional ways and were ultimately seen as being subversive to the state.

p. 124   *advocates of the Great Peace*: peasant rebels in ancient China, followers of a Taoist millenarian sect that foretold the coming of the "great peace" (*tai ping*) while organizing themselves into phalansteries or rural communities as well as military units. In A.D. 184, they overran large territories in northern China, precipitating the overthrow of the Later Han dynasty.

p. 137   *Allen J. Wilcox, Timothy J. Carr & Susan Saunders*: contemporary demographers who have published extensively on perinatal mortality, fertility, and contraceptive methods respectively. Their papers have been published in *Math-*

ematical Policy Research, International Journal of Epidemiology, Population Reports and other journals.

Chapter 3

p. 162 *Wang Yen and Shi Lo*: Wang Yen (A.D. 256–311), known as a libertine and practitioner of *qing tan*, was also the last military Constable of China's Western Jin dynasty. He met his defeat at the hands of Shi Lo, the leader of the invading Huns. Wang Yen's "lamentation," in which he expresses remorse for having ignored matters of state in favor of metaphysical speculations into the "mysterious void" (*xuan-xu*) and for having lost the dynasty, is recorded in the Chronicles of the Western Jin (Jin-Shu 43.7a–b; Jin-shu jiao-ju 43.25 a–b).

p. 163 *Yong-jia Uprising* (A.D. 311–316): this "uprising" refers to a series of internal fights between members of the ruling Sima clan at the end of the Western Jin dynasty, following what is often referred to as "the War of the Eight Princes" (A.D. 290–306). The Hun invasions from the North finally forced the court to flee south and establish a new capital in Nanjing, thereby beginning the dynastic split between Northern and Southern China.

p. 176 *David Knowles*: author of *The Monastic Order in England: 943–1216* and renowned expert on Benedictine monasticism; also translated *Lanfranc's Monastic Customs* (in series *Medieval Classics*) in which the daily routines of a monastery are described.

p. 177 *Johan Huizinga*: Dutch expert on the intellectual and artistic trends of France and the Netherlands in the fourteenth and fifteenth centuries. His most famous work, *The Waning of the Middle Ages*, is also a social history of the late medieval period in those two countries. Huizinga's other works include a biography of *Erasmus* and *Homo Ludens*.

p. 180 *Sima Qian* (145–90 A.D.): preeminent historian of ancient China who established the practice of writing dynastic histories; his *Historical Records*, covering the history of China to his own times, are noteworthy for their meticu-

lous attention to sourcing and literary flair. In addition to
the basic "annals," the *Records* contain a large biograph-
ical section, essays on government, rituals, the calendar,
and economic affairs.

p. 180   *Otto Borst*: German historian of medieval towns and cities, particularly of Esslingen and Württemberg; published books include: *Die Esslingen Altstadt: Materialien zu
ihren Erneuerung* (Stuttgart, 1972); *Alte Stadt in Württemberg* (Munchen, 1968); *Schule des Schwabenlands; Geschichte
d. Univ. Stuttgart* (Deutsche Verlags Anstalt, 1979).

p. 184   *Alcuin*: eighth-century British reformer of the Frankish
Church who was also a master-teacher (*magistri*) to Char-
lemagne.

p. 188   *Guibert, Abbot of Nogent*: born c. 1065 of a noble family in
Beauvais, later became abbot in diocese of Laon. Wrote
Deeds of God through the Franks in 1108 and his *Memoirs* in
1115; preached a conservative doctrine of social order
and fealty against the communal uprisings of his day, and
a strict code of conduct aiming at maximizing sexual purity.

p. 188   *Burchard, Bishop of Worms*: eleventh-century ecclesiastic
noted for his attempts to develop a code of laws based on
ancient judgments (c. 1023).

Index

ABOUT THE AUTHOR

Taichi Sakaiya was born in 1935 in Osaka, Japan. After receiving an economics degree from Tokyo University, he joined Japan's Ministry of International Trade and Industry (MITI), where he was responsible for planning and presenting the 1970 Osaka Expo and the 1975 Okinawa Marine Expo. Since leaving MITI, he has worked as producer of the Japan Pavilion at the 1982 Barcelona Expo, and served as president of the Asia Club in Japan. An economist, essayist, translator, and novelist of great influence in Japan, Mr. Sakaiya is the author of more than thirty books. *The Knowledge-Value Revolution* is his first book to be translated into English.